WRITING
LIFE STORIES

BILL ROORBACH

STORY PRESS
CINCINNATI, OHIO

Writing Life Stories. Copyright © 1998 by Bill Roorbach. Printed and bound in the United States of America. All rights reserved. No part of this book may be reproduced in any form or by any electronic or mechanical means including information storage and retrieval systems without permission in writing from the publisher, except by a reviewer, who may quote brief passages in a review. Published by Story Press, an imprint of F&W Publications, Inc., 1507 Dana Avenue, Cincinnati, Ohio 45207. (800) 289-0963. First edition.

Story Press Books are available from your local bookstore or direct from the publisher.

02   01   00   99   98   5   4   3   2   1

Library of Congress Cataloging-in-Publication Data

Roorbach, Bill.
   Writing life stories / Bill Roorbach.—1st ed.
      p.   cm.
   Includes bibliographical references and index.
   ISBN 1-884910-36-X (alk. paper)
   1. Autobiography—Authorship. 2. Report writing. I. Title.
CT25.R66   1998
808'.06692—dc21   98-20993
                                                                CIP

Designed by Clare Finney
Cover illustration: *Menemsha* by Juliet Karelsen

For my mother and father, Reba and Jack,
and for my brothers and sisters, Randy, Carol, Doug, and Janet,
and in memory of Robert Towers, my teacher.

ACKNOWLEDGMENTS

This book has a lot of makers—all the writers I've read, all the teachers I've had, all the students, all the editors, all the workshop peers, all the colleagues, all the friends, all the family.

To name but a few, and with apologies to the rest:

Thanks to my writing teachers for most of what I know: Max Apple, Harold Brodkey, Daniel Halpern, Edward Hower, Joyce Johnson, Stephen Koch, Richard Locke, Phillip Lopate, Frank McShane, Ron Powers, Susan Richards Shreve, Robert Towers.

Thanks to my writing-and-teaching colleagues for the rest: Lee K. Abbott, Andrea Barrett, Alice Bloom, David Bradley, David Citino, John Clayton, Stephen Dobyns, Paul Doiron, Kathy Fagan, Daniel Gunn, Michelle Herman, Barbara Hope, Nicolas Howe, Robert Kimber, Georgina Kleege, Sebastian Knowles, Anthony Libby, Liesel Litzenburger, Peter Lourie, Daniel Lusk, Wesley McNair, Jeredith Merrin, Pat O'Donnell, Pamela Painter, Vince Passaro, Sandra Prior, Kenneth Rosen, Richard Russo, Lore Segal, Deborah Sobeloff, Edward Tayler, Melanie Rae Thon, Tom Wicker.

Thanks to my editors, past and present, for many lessons learned: Darlyn Brewer, Bill Buford, Stephen Dubner, Lee Gutkind, Colin Harrison, Jay Heinrichs, Betsy Lerner, Laurie Muchnick, Speer Morgan, Lewis Lapham, Jack Schwartz, Abigail Seymour, John Sterling, Peter Stine, Jean Tolle.

And of course, thanks to Jack Heffron, Amy Jeynes, and Lois Rosenthal of Story Press, for their smart help and sure sense of direction and clear vision with the book in hand.

Thanks to my agent, Sloan Harris, and to Amanda Urban.

Thanks to the Department of English, The Ohio State University, for research support and time to write, and to Christopher Griffin, the world's greatest Administrative Assistant.

Thanks to the generous readers for this project: Jennifer Cognard-Black, Lisa Dush, Kristina Emick, Beth Lindsmith, Tom Moss.

Special thanks to Maureen Stanton, who helped compile the reading list at the end of this volume.

Thanks to my brave students whose work is included herein: Jacki Bell, "Janet Bellweather," "Gow Farris," Wendy Guida, Nancy Kuhl, Jane Renshaw, Tim Rushford, Vicki Schwab, and "Chuck."

And most of all, and always, thanks to Juliet.

CONTENTS

INTRODUCTION

> In most books the *I*, or first person, is omitted; in this it will
> be retained; that, in respect to egotism, is the main difference.
> We commonly do not remember that it is, after all, always the
> first person that is speaking. I should not talk so much about
> myself if there were anybody else whom I knew as well. Unfor-
> tunately, I am confined to this theme by the narrowness
> of my experience.　　　　　　　　　　　—H.D. Thoreau

Gow Farris had a lifetime of stories and ideas. He surely had something to say. Yet when he sat down at his keyboard to get it written,
nothing came, or nothing he cared to show anyone, certainly
nothing like the stories he'd always told at family parties, the stories
his kids said he'd better write down, the stories his grandchildren
were starting to ask for.

The surprising thing was that Gow had been a newswriter for 45
years: 45 years of writing other people's stories; 45 years of a confident professional approach to the facts; 45 years of successful
writing for a major newspaper. Retirement brought this: silence.
Silence when he'd expected his life and humor and lessons to pour
out whole, short memoir after short memoir, essay after essay,
article after article, book after book. What was going wrong?

He needed a change of place, that's all! He kissed his wife good-
bye (his third wife, truth to tell, quite a story there: death and heart-
break in the first marriage, betrayal and loneliness in the second),
called a rental agent he knew on Cape Cod, hied himself for an
amazingly inexpensive, off-season ten days to Nantucket, where
many writers had gone before him. Perfect. The surf pounded
distantly, no phone to ring, no visitors, no pressures upon him, not
even mail.

"My brother died when I was eighteen," he wrote. Always, he'd
wanted to write a memoir of his brother. But nothing followed, just

ten straight mornings staring at his notebook. Guilty walks (longer each day), hourly snacks, resharpened pencils. Occasionally he wrote lame sentences of description (his brother's great size, his brother's big teeth, his brother's favorite expression) that did nothing to bring his clear memories of the lost sibling to the page, and even less to shape those memories into something someone else might enjoy reading—a memoir—much less into anything resembling literature. Afternoons he roamed the October beach in writerly despair.

During the night before his last day on the island, he woke to a fit of inspiration, clicked on the bare bedside bulb, took notes for a different project, a memoir of his career. Next morning he didn't pause for breakfast, rushed to the kitchen table (he'd come to distrust the little desk his landlord had provided), wrote: "I was a newspaperman for 45 years" and kept going, ten pages, a rush of words, great relief, something to show for his trip and the lonely days of his vigil.

Home the next night he pulled out his pages and read. This didn't take long. He read fast and with growing embarrassment. What he'd meant triumphantly to show his new wife he tucked into his desk drawer beneath a stack of similar pages. The day's ferry ride and drive home had given him enough perspective to hear clearly how the opening of his journalist's memoir came off: pompous, puffy, wordy, nostalgic, nothing like what he'd envisioned in that moment of wakefulness, as far from the truth as Pluto from the Sun! Gow was a reasonable, humble, reserved person; Gow was a precise and no-nonsense man. Why couldn't he get that on the page?

I know Gow's story because after a couple more months of false starts and increasing discouragement, he signed up for a summer class I happened to be teaching at the University of Vermont. First day of class he sat there glowering at me. Gow Farris was pissed.

And Gow, of course, is not alone.

Janet Bellweather had taught writing for nine years to high school kids, knew all the rules, knew what she liked when it came to student work, knew how to get even the most challenging kids to pull off their Walkman headphones and write. Her particular pride came in helping her young students see that what they had to say mattered, that their lives were important, that they could reach readers. She had wonderful exercises. The kids had a blast. She'd march around the room giving praise and advice, urging and scolding, reading passages aloud. Janet was a great teacher, funny and smart and eloquent, passionate and caring, maybe even a little eccentric.

She had no trouble turning out the pages. She wrote short memoirs of her youth, many poems, an essay a month, even a column for the school district's award-winning newsletter. Her writing was sometimes funny, but seldom eloquent or passionate, and never eccentric. She showed it to friends, but few said much of anything when they were finished reading. A wan smile here and there. But never the praise and approval she wanted, except from her mother, who didn't understand why *The New Yorker* didn't buy every word. Janet didn't expect miracles on that order, but she couldn't understand why smaller magazines didn't seem interested in her. She had a folder of rejections thick as the phone book in Manhattan, where she lived. In rare moments of clarity, Janet knew why the magazines didn't take her work: It just wasn't as good as she knew she could make it. What was the problem? Why couldn't she do for herself what she did for her students every day?

She turned up in a memoir class I taught for the Riverside Writers Group in New York City and right away—first night's class—raised her hand to make a comment, and in the course of this comment (ostensibly about writing memoir), she made it clear that she, too, was a teacher, that she, too, had written plenty, and, finally, that she didn't really need a class or know what had possessed her to sign up. She knew all the rules, she'd read all the books, she certainly didn't need us. Her intensity was both charming and frightening. She was nearly shouting: "I only want this class so that I might have an audience." She had a truly great essay subject: being single and wanting to stay that way.

Okay, Janet, okay! You're in the right place!

Other writers who have turned up in my classes: a physician with an amazing story—not getting told—of an internship in the Amazon; a holocaust survivor whose book on his teen days in Warsaw, then Auschwitz (including a miraculous escape), was crawling past nine-hundred pages with no end in sight; a technical writer who wanted to find escape from aircraft manuals to write about his love of flying, but who—in his clinically self-aware way—

knew his writing was dull, flattened by years of mechanical sentence making; a college professor in bioethics who wanted to dramatize bioethical case studies for a lay audience, but who couldn't get characters to emerge from the people he'd known; a former nun who wanted to write about her faith, how it was broken, how it lately had come to be restored; a businessman who wanted to combine tales of his travels with advice about commerce in Asia. The list goes on and on. Good people all of them (well, all but one or two), with wonderful ideas and compelling stories and fascinating lives not coming to the page quite as simply as they'd hoped.

Welcome, welcome. You're in the right place.

A NOTE ON THE EXERCISES

This book is designed to take you by way of exercises through a series of approaches to certain branches of the vast field that's come to be called creative nonfiction, and especially to the making of memoir. The usefulness of any one exercise may not seem apparent at first, but if you trust yourself, and trust the exercise, if you do the work on a steady (preferably daily) basis, you'll soon find what you're looking for: access to memory, access to material, access to ideas, access to the unconscious, and, finally, access to meaning.

John Gardner, the extraordinary teacher, novelist, controversial medievalist, and all-around literary luminary and daredevil (he died in a tragic motorcycle crash), thought exercises were valuable because of the low stakes. And it's true, it's easier to set out to make something small rather than set out to make something large (like, say, the story of your life). Then again, Norman Mailer has said that exercises are worse than useless, even damaging, precisely because the stakes are so small. Why waste time on something that doesn't count? All writing should be out there at the edge or in close to the heart, vital and urgent and necessary.

I'm in between these titans (and in mortal danger of being crushed by huge ankles). I do think drills are a waste of time, the memorization of rules. But when exercises discover material, or open the vaults of memory, or give access to real emotion, or offer points of entry into the massive story that is a human life and mind, the stakes are high indeed, and what may seem at first mere practice turns out to be writing of the most urgent kind.

To be taught, one must be willing to learn. One must be willing to change, sometimes in fundamental ways, because to learn *is* to change. A writer who really wants to make the next step, to grow, must give up the idea that she's already arrived (remember Janet Bellweather?), must give up the idea that he already knows what to do (think of Gow Farris).

Here's a Confucian aphorism: "If you don't know where you are going, get there by a way you don't know."

And here, Shunryu Suzuki's famous observation from his peaceful and important (and perhaps puzzling) book *Zen Mind, Beginner's Mind*: "In the beginner's mind are many possibilities, in the expert's mind there are few."

I like Donald Hall's one and only exercise, which he recommends in his essay "On Ambition," and which I'll freely paraphrase here: *Write something better than the best thing ever written. Take all the time you wish.*

The exercises in this book are meant to discover mounds of juicy material for you, of course. They're meant to give you practice, for sure. They're also meant to help you develop and then further develop your critical eye. But quietly, they are meant to challenge the ways you already write, the ways you already find material, the ways you have settled into and that—if my own experience and the fact that you have read this far are any indication—are no longer producing satisfactory results, much less *great* results.

Nancy Kuhl, one of my graduate students at Ohio State (and already a well-regarded and much-published poet), included a note when she offered the use of some of her writing for this book.

> I was a little resistant doing these exercises. When I examined that resistance, I learned some very valuable things about my writing process. So, for me, part of what was important about these exercises was paying attention to my own response to the assignments and thinking about what my response revealed about me as a writer.

Yes!

We all want to get to the masterpieces of our writing lives by the shortest route possible. Trouble is, the shortest route possible is always the road ahead. Honestly examining whatever resistance you find in yourself and overcoming it (by just doing the exercises is the best way) is going to be a key step in your improvement as a writer. In fact, it's the surest shortcut. Most of my students, and by extension most of the readers of this book, and probably you, gentle reader, are already good writers. It's certainly hard to turn the clock back, be a beginner again, a learner. I'm glad you're willing to try.

YOUR FIRST MILLION WORDS

R.V. Cassill, in his classic book of instruction, *Writing Fiction*, says a writer's apprenticeship isn't over until his first million words have been written.

Time to get to work.

ONE

GETTING STARTED

I never wanted to write an autobiographical work, being averse to anything autobiographical. The fact is that at a certain moment in my life I conceived a curiosity about my childhood. I said to myself, "I haven't much longer to live, so why not try and record my life down to the age of nineteen? Not as it really was—there's no such thing as objectivity—but as I see it today." I set to work, intending to write a small volume. This was followed by a second. Then by a third . . . until I reached the point where I began to get bored. After all childhood always remains childhood. After the fifth volume I decided to call it a day.

—Thomas Bernhard, quoted in the
translator's note to *Gathering Evidence*, a memoir
made up of the five volumes mentioned

I certainly don't (enjoy writing). I get a fine warm feeling when I'm doing well, but that pleasure is pretty much negated by the pain of getting started each day. Let's face it, writing is hell.

—William Styron

Why is it so hard to sit down and write?

Great expectations, for one thing. Our favorite high school English teacher, Janet Bellweather, is infinitely patient and caring with her charges at P.S. 239, thinks with pleasure of all the years of their learning, but from herself expected excellence (yes, *The New Yorker*) instantly.

Our friend Gow Farris thought he'd take on a new kind of writing and an entirely new subject (his own life!) and get it perfect—prize-winningly publishable—the first time he tried. But ease and instant excellence are illusions, illusions that successful writing conjures up, illusions that make it hard—maybe impossible—for Janet Bellweather or Gow Farris (or perhaps you), to believe that their (or your) favorite writers have gone through anything like the struggles Janet pretended not to have, and that made Gow so furious, and that discourage you and me.

To compound the problem, partners and friends and parents are caught up in the old myth of talent: You have it or you don't, and there's no sense in struggling along if your first efforts aren't Shakespeare or (more to the point, since we're talking about memoir here) Annie Dillard or John Hersey or Mary Carr or Frank McCourt.

So often what's missing is compassion: compassion for the poor soul who turns to writing after a long day of less satisfying work; compassion for the creative one, who can't rest till the story is made, even while those around him play; compassion for the learner, too, the person who at any age sits down to write thinking she already has what it takes, only to discover, as all good writers continually do, that there is still a lot to learn; compassion, in the end, for you, gentle writer, you yourself.

Exercise One: A Clean, Well-Lighted Place.

Of course the name of this exercise comes from an Ernest Hemingway story, but I can't help but think of Virginia Woolf when I give this assignment, which is about compassion, really, about having compassion for yourself as learner and seeing to the needs of that learner.

In her series of lectures and subsequent book, *A Room of One's Own*, published in 1929, Virginia Woolf points out the unhappy fact that women often didn't (and don't) have a place where they might get some thinking and work of their own done, away from the duties of the mother, the wife, the housekeeper.

The idea here—male or female—is to set yourself up in a decent writing environment. Not too beautiful (lest you get distracted by the view), not too Spartan (lest you find it a place best avoided), but a place you can hope to be uninterrupted for the blocks of time available for writing.

In my Maine house I write in a small attic room (hot in summer, but so be it) with a window looking on grapevines and bird feeders, a spruce tree, a lilac, a tamarack, the porch roof, our clothesline. My wife's studio (she's a painter—one of her early pastels is on the cover of this book) is at the other end of the house and downstairs. I have two old doors on spindly legs to make desks, two chairs, a light, a small bookshelf, a trusty laptop, two printers (one broken). And a lot of other junk: seashells, a softball, stacks of old manuscripts, cancelled checks, piles of letters, cassette tapes, posters from readings I've done, maps on the wall, postcards, a calculator, floppy disks, a big fan, scissors, empty notebooks and full.

If there's nowhere obvious to set yourself up, be like Crazy Horse, who said, "This is my lodge," wherever he had to stay, even when finally imprisoned. (Since we're on the subject of writing nonfiction—and since in chapter five I'll quote from the book—I think it appropriate to let you know that I learned about Crazy Horse in Ian Frazier's work of memoir and history and journalism and geography, *Great Plains*).

Say out loud: "This is my office!" Over the years I've had my table in the corners of my various bedrooms, in the front of a one-room cabin, in the loft of a barn, at picnic tables in campsites, in the mushroomy basement of an insanely busy house in Martha's Vineyard. I've looked out windows at alleyways and river valleys, brick walls, backyards, playgrounds, forests. But always I had a particular place to sit when it came time to write, a recognizable place, even if temporary, and always it's been the same place: my office.

Don't get fancy; just give yourself some continuity.

I'm thinking of Mario Puzo, who, flush from the success of his novel *The Godfather*, decided to build himself a beautiful office off the back of his house, a large, bright room with two huge desks and everything a writer could possibly want. Trouble was, he couldn't write there, and before long he went back to the kitchen table, where, amid the bustle of his household and in the midst of the lives of his children, he got back to work.

MEMOIR IS MEMORY'S TRUTH

Let's try for a working definition of the word *memoir*: A memoir is a true story, a work of narrative built directly from the memory of its writer; in memoir, the writer is also the protagonist—the person to whom the events of the story happen—or at least an observer closely involved with the protagonists. Memoir arises in and exists only because of the first-person singular: the *I* remembering.

When I say memoir, I don't mean one's memoirs in the sense of one's whole life presented as a historical artifact. That's for the famous—heads of state, Nobel prize winners, heroes, celebrities—tomes not infrequently ghostwritten (and not infrequently written badly, come to think of it).

I mean memoir in the sense the word is used by the editors of, say, *Harper's Magazine*, when they publish narratives of real lives. I mean memoir in the sense that Frank Conroy's publishers use when they characterize his classic story of youth, *Stop-Time*.

Phillip Lopate (an important teacher of mine, whom I will certainly quote again) has wryly called such work "half-life memoirs," works created before much of the story can be known. But, of course, the ambition of memoir (as opposed to memoirs) isn't very often historical but literary. Information is almost never the first goal of memoir; expression often is. Beauty—of form, of language, of meaning—always takes precedence over mere accuracy, truth over mere facts. The successful memoirist respects facts, uses them, rigorously represses the human impulse to lie or embellish, but knows that truth is different from facts, and greater than facts, and not always their sum.

Memoir is a report to others from foreign territory: the territory of the writer, of the self, of an *I*. When I say memoir, I only mean memory put to the page and carefully arranged. I do mean a true story, unadorned, but always a true story laid down with the understanding that memory can be faulty, that images fade, that the *I* itself is a construction, a kind of fiction, only capable of representing part of the writer at any given time.

Tobias Wolff said it well in the small acknowledgments paragraph to his first memoir, *This Boy's Life*.

> I have been corrected on some points, mostly of chronology. Also my mother thinks that a dog I describe as ugly was actually quite handsome. I've allowed some of these points to stand, because this is a book of memory, and memory has its own story to tell. But I have done my best to make it tell a truthful story.

In fiction writing, the contract with the reader has to do with "That willing suspension of disbelief which constitutes poetic faith"

(Samuel Taylor Coleridge's memorable and oft-quoted line). The writer implicitly says, *I'm making this up, but please go ahead and pretend all of it really happened. Enjoy.* In memoir, the writer implicitly says, *Hey, this is factual. You can believe it. Enjoy.* Both fiction writer and memoirist, of course, may be fudging a little or a lot: The fiction may be based absolutely in fact; the memoirist may be a liar. Dishonest, honest, the contract remains the same, and thus readerly enjoyment remains the same. Every writer of memoir has his own conscience to grapple with, his own ethical stance when it comes to matters such as invented dialogue, compound characters, telescoped time. What constitutes artistic license, and what constitutes lying? The border shifts writer to writer, story to story.

Memoir is not journalism, though journalism relies more heavily than many journalists like to admit on the same faulty human memory—that subjective sieve—as memoir. (Old Russian insult: "He lies like an eyewitness.") This is a fact that need not repeatedly be apologized for by the memoirist. The vagaries of memory are a given, accepted by readers of memoir, and might be stated once and for all as follows: *I'm going to have to fill in some of the details where memory or my photo albums or my journals don't help me; to get to the truth, I'm going to have to make up certain things or disagree with the memories of others.*

But a readerly indulgence of your making things up in specific instances doesn't mean you'll get indulgence for lying in big ways. Approximating the words from a lecture attended long ago at your modest college is something quite different from saying you studied under Robert Lowell at Oxford. Fiction is fiction, and if you have half a conscience, you'll know where the line is, always, and always you'll earn for your work the name nonfiction.

Still, facts or no, if your reader doesn't believe you, you're sunk as a memoirist. And weirdly, sometimes it's easier to capture readerly belief when you're consciously making fiction. At readings, people will come up to me after a short story or novel excerpt—pure fiction—and say confidingly, "I *know* that was you. . . ." I can't tell you how many people believe I have teenage children, all because one of my characters in a short story did. People believe I have driven a truck for a living, that I have worked selling antiques, that I have crashed a Subaru station wagon through a hardware store.

And after I read true stuff at some bookstore or college podium, people always come up and say, "I *know* you made that up."

Can't win.

Here's a sort of corollary: When I ask students in fiction classes for more drama in a given scene, they will often say, "But that's the way it really happened!" Conversely, students in nonfiction classes: "But that's not the way it happened!" To me the first goal, the first excellence, is artistic. The needs of other excellences, such as mere accuracy, must follow the needs of drama in a kind of hierarchy that helps me make decisions as I write.

Other obstacles: When you announce that you are working on a memoir, the unknowing (perhaps a voice in your own head) will smirk and ask what makes you think anyone would be interested in *your* life. "The chief danger memoirists face is starring in their own stories, and becoming fascinated," as Annie Dillard writes in her introduction to the anthology *Modern American Memoirs*. She's making the point that most good memoir turns out not to be about the memoirist at all. *Survival in Auschwitz* cannot be said to be primarily about Primo Levi, though it is his memory and experience that brings light to dark days. Isak Dinesen's *Out of Africa* is certainly more about colonialism than about Dinesen. Then there are the hard cases: Is *A Moveable Feast* more about Hemingway or the people he dishes? Some memoir is more about place than person: Think of *Desert Solitaire*, by Edward Abbey. But always the reader becomes a stand-in for the *I*, and the life of the *I* becomes the life of the reader, so no matter who is speaking, the sucessful true story is always the reader's story. Much more on this as we go along.

AUTOBIOGRAPHY NEEDS AN *I*

When I think of autobiography, I think of big, staid, honorable tomes, like Henry James' autobiography, which he called *Autobiography*, as if it were the last word on the subject forever. In truth, of course, the word just means self-biography and covers a lot of ground. I use it primarily as a generic term to mean any writing wherein the writer's self and history take on importance.

In the introduction to a special all-autobiography issue of *Witness* (a quality quarterly literary magazine out of Farmington Hills, Michigan), editor Peter Stine quotes the letter Rick Bass sent with his submission: "I don't know if this is autobiographical, but there's an I narrator and it's true."

"I was grateful," Stine says, "for a definition of the genre that might encompass [a] wide range of writings—private journals, meditations on nature, anecdotal reminiscences, acts of moral witness."

That *I* narrator is at the heart of things: one person, remembering. And this *I* appears two ways: as a lead character in a narrative and as that ineffable quality called *voice* in exposition. With voice there is the sense of someone speaking to us, perhaps as intimately as over a candlelit dinner, perhaps jovially as at a loud cocktail party, perhaps pontificating as if at a banquet. But voice doesn't come easily in a culture that assiduously teaches its young not to have voices. Think of all the years American schoolteachers forbade the use of the first-person singular in any writing, ever!

Times change. The first person is *in*. (In fact, for writers it's been in since ancient Roman times. It's not for us to worry that teachers and op-ed page pundits are just now noticing.)

To have a voice is to have a self, and to have a self is powerful. Perhaps this sense of power is why so many critics are so threatened by the act of memoir, the act of autobiography, and put it down as something less than literature on the one hand, less than journalism on the other, as self-indulgent in any case.

The critics haven't been and won't (and shouldn't) be silenced, but in recent years readers' (and therefore publishers') interest in real lives has bloomed, and good writers have rewarded that interest with real books mining real lives: "the literature of fact," in John McPhee's apt phrase.

THE ROLE OF MEMOIR IN THE PERSONAL ESSAY

When I use the term *personal essay*, I mean an informal essay, a discursive essay, a wandering self in words. The personal essay is an old form, painstakingly and exhaustively defined by Phillip Lopate in his introduction to and his selection for his anthology *The Art of the Personal Essay*. This is an essential book for the autobiographer of any stripe. The personal essay is an old form, yet no form, since under its rubric writers have ranged over huge territory for centuries. The starting place, once again, is the self. But the personal essay strides past storytelling, past simpler memoir, to offer counterpoint in exposition, quotes from other writers, arcane knowledge (How many rivets in the skin of a Boeing 767? What was the hometown of Paul Lynde? How do blue crabs shed their skins?), odd comparisons, grand metaphors, in short, whatever's in the writer's head, whatever's in his library, whatever's relevant in the world. From these juxtapositions of the funds from the writer's "well-stocked mind" (as Elizabeth Hardwick called it in a class I once took) comes meaning.

One's life becomes evidence, and the evidence is examined until it's plain just what's evident. Abandon the outline, all ye who enter this territory! Discovery is the thing. Too firm a plan, and you miss the digression that takes you where you didn't know you wanted to go. Essays written from outlines can succeed, but what's the surprise in arriving exactly where you planned? More on this subject anon (in chapter four, to be exact).

Remember Socrates: "The unexamined life is not worth living."

Exercise Two: Reading and Writing. After diligent study and many conversations and a lot of beer with smart people, I've come to the following observation: There are two things good writers always have in common.

1. Writers write. (Most do so every day.)
2. Writers read. (Ditto.)

We'll deal with number one in an exercise coming right up. But let's think about number two. First of all, writing *is* reading. Think of that. But reading is also writing.

Lately I've come to the realization that I need to schedule special time for hard reading. I can't count on clear blocks of quality time, time when I'm not half asleep or entertaining company or mired in life's poignant details. So I claim the first hour of the day for reading. My wife knows; my friends know. Most important, I know. Magazines don't count for this hour (they come later), "fun" reading doesn't count, books read for book reviews don't count: For this hour—just after breakfast, just after a walk—I carefully select one difficult book or series of books after the other, day by day, week by week, month by month. Amazing what you can get done in an hour (or even less) a day. I try to choose harder stuff for the reading hour, stuff I've been meaning to get to for years. (George Eliot has been my project lately. She's changing my life, rearranging my brain cells.) And doing this work doesn't mean I don't do my usual obsessive reading at other times of the day (always I've got several books and ten magazine articles going); it just means I can count on a solid hour a day when I'm fresh and rested and ready to grapple with the difficult stuff, ready to learn.

Oh, yes. You want an assignment. Here it is: Read every day. Make it part of your job as a writer. And since that's easier said than done, let's make it more formal: For the next week (and every week hereafter), schedule into your days and evenings a little time for reading, as much as is necessary to finish at least a book a week. An hour a day isn't hard to find (though you might have to forgo something else you value, like television).

I've included a long reading list in creative nonfiction at the end of this book, but make your own list especially for your reading hour. Make it eclectic. Read stuff you don't normally go for. Haunt the used-book stores, browsing the sections you normally avoid. Probably there's just the book in the art history section or psychology or engineering. Don't always head (as is my habit) to the literature section (but head there often enough). And search your own bookshelves for those good volumes you bought or borrowed with best intentions to read and haven't quite yet cracked. Sunday night, pluck a difficult or important or intriguing book and assign it to yourself (sternly if necessary) for the seven days ahead. And see to it the job gets done.

Exercise Three: First Lines. One of my favorite experiments in getting started is first lines. How did other people do it? I ignore the fact that most first lines weren't first till after much revision, and I walk around the bookstore or library pulling down volumes and examining how chapters and essays and stories and memoirs commence. What makes each opening compelling (or not)? How is my readerly interest caught (or lost)?

One of my favorite first lines is from a novel, Joseph Heller's *Something Happened*: "I get the willies when I see closed doors." Another is from a personal essay by Scott Russell Sanders called "Under the Influence": "My father drank." I didn't have to look up either of these lines—they are caught forever in my head, along with a long list of others.

Your assignment is to look at first lines, as many as possible in an afternoon's browsing. Head to the library or bookstore or even your own shelves, and read—first lines only. Type up a list of your ten or twenty favorites. What makes them work?

Exercise Four: A Writing Schedule. Writers write. But one of the big challenges is finding and defending time to do the writing. Any craftsperson knows that a regular work schedule makes for consistent production. Writers credit consistency with greater access to the unconscious (if you're working consciously every day, you'll be working unconsciously every day, too, and all night). The most popular excuse for not writing is this: *I just can't find the time.*

I have all kinds of sympathy for busy people (new parents tops on the list!), but if you look into successful writers' lives, you'll find unbelievable burdens: full-time jobs, children, multiple deadlines, car trouble, weddings and funerals, family expectations, illness, exhaustion, depression, imprisonment, on and on. Yet the work gets done.

Here's how it gets done: every day. A little or a lot, but every day. Okay, maybe a day off every seven or so, and two weeks vacation a year and a little sick leave, and time for goofing off. Otherwise, *every day*, if you're going to call yourself a writer.

Your assignment here is to make up a reasonable writing schedule for yourself. I'd suggest making a fresh schedule every week, say on Sunday evening. Even if you can only manage fifteen minutes on Monday (what with the kids' activities and all), schedule it in. Twenty minutes Tuesday, fine. Wednesday, two hours. Thursday, fifteen minutes. Friday, two hours. Saturday, four hours. Sunday, off. For example.

Then, *use the time.* For creative writing. No letters to agents. No reading (your hallowed reading time is scheduled separately). No submitting or printing stories. No reorganizing your computer files. No wedding announcements. No column for the church bulletin. Just creative writing. Be at your writing place. Even if you daydream or fret the hour away, be there.

Don't be surprised if that little fifteen-minute block before dinner Mondays and Thursdays turns into a half hour, then an hour. The regular schedule will help words start to flow, make writing blocks dissolve.

Perhaps most important, your schedule becomes your shield. With schedule in hand, you feel (and are) fully justified in saying to family members or old friends or insistent temptations, "I can't. I have to work that night." There it is, right on your schedule.

GO EASY

Now that you have your schedules set for reading and writing, don't be too harsh a boss! What's it going to hurt if sometimes you daydream on the job a little or goof around in the kitchen? As long as your working hours are clear, you at least know you *ought* to be working. A little guilt is a good thing sometimes.

Onward.

TWO

MEMORY

Initially, I was unaware that time, so boundless at first blush,
was a prison. In probing my childhood (which is the next best
to probing one's eternity) I see the awakening of consciousness
as a series of spaced flashes, with the intervals between them
gradually diminishing until bright blocks of perception are
formed, affording memory a slippery hold.
>   —Vladimir Nabokov, *Speak, Memory*

When you use memories as a source, they're no different from
any other source—the composition still has to be made.
>   —E.L. Doctorow

All my stories have been written with material that was gathered—no, God save us! not gathered but absorbed—before I
was fifteen years old. —Willa Cather

Gow Farris said, "I don't do that kind of thing." He looked at me
and the whole class looked at me and it was as if he were talking
about mugging old ladies or shooting dope, as if I'd suggested something he found immoral. Worse yet, several heads nodded.

What we were talking about was an exercise I'll outline a little
later on in this chapter, an exercise in mapmaking. What Gow was
saying was, roughly, this: *I have written daily newspaper stories for
forty-five years and never once done an exercise of any kind.*

All I could really say was, "Gow, you'll have to trust me." And
that's what I said.

As a newspaperman Gow had learned not to trust anyone, of
course, especially those with benevolent smiles. He just looked at
me. I wanted to say more but didn't. Wanted to give a little speech

about how it was time to disconnect that scolding part of the brain that demands to know where you're going before you start in all endeavors. Wanted to say how writing isn't a trip up the Amazon. Not exactly. How you won't die if you get on the wrong tributary. You'll maybe revise at worst. Or maybe have to admit to being stuck. But any poison-tipped blow darts that pierce your hide in this particular jungle are going to be fired by yourself, and some might have "I don't do that kind of thing" printed right on the side.

Just, "Trust me," that's what I said, kind of lightly, as if it were a joke, and people took it that way, including Gow, and we all mildly laughed, breaking the tension.

CHALLENGING THE LIMITS OF MEMORY

One of the many curious things about the act of writing is the way it can give access to the unconscious mind. And in the hidden parts of consciousness lie not only hobgoblins and neurotic glimmers, but lots of regular stuff, the everyday stuff of memory. The invisible face of your grade school bully is in there, somewhere, and the exact smell of the flowers on vines in your grandma's backyard, along with most everything else. Some of it is going to be painful, to be sure, but some of it pleasurable, too. An awful lot is just informational, the stuff of lost days.

And—I'm just realizing this—memory is what people are *made* out of. After skin and bone, I mean. And if memory is what people are made out of, then people are made out of *loss*. No wonder we value our possessions so much. And no wonder we crave firm answers, formulae, facts and figures. All are attempts (however feeble in the end) to preserve what's gone. The present is all that's genuinely available to anyone. Even facts distort: What's remembered, recorded, is never the event, no matter how precise the measurement.

If you've written fiction at all, you know that detail is required to make a vivid scene. What's in the room? What sort of day is it? Who exactly is in the scene, and what exactly do they look like? All well and good for the writer of fiction: You make it up. But for the maker of nonfiction, the challenge is different: how to *remember*. For, of course, if we're going to call it a true story, the details better be true, right? Then again, we all know memory is faulty. Don't forget Tobias Wolff: "[M]emory has its own story to tell."

My sister Carol likes to tell the story of the time our younger brother, Doug, sucked on a hollow toy bolt till it suctioned onto his lips. He was maybe four. She and Mom and Doug were at Roton Point, our beach club, end of the day, marching to the car carrying blankets and towels and pails and toys. Doug was a stocky little kid (we sibs meanly called him *The Bullet* till he shot up into a slim young man), and he looked cute as hell stumbling along carrying the Scotch cooler with this big blue bolt suctioned onto his lips. In the car he still wore it, all the way to the guard booth, where he liked to say good-bye to the genial old guard who watched the beach gate. Carol tells the story at Thanksgiving and Christmas about every year. And I believe she told it at Doug's wedding: rehearsal dinner. Anyway, at the gate, Bullet Boy tried to pull the bolt off to say hi to the guard, but it wouldn't come. He'd sucked on it so long and so hard he couldn't unstick it. So Carol grabbed hold of the threaded end of the thing, wrestled with it a little till *pop* it came loose.

And Carol looked at Doug and Doug looked at Carol and then Carol said, "My God!" and so Mom turned and said it, too: "My God!" Doug's lips—poor Doug!—were ballooned up like some character's in a cartoon, so big even he could see them. Doug freaked! Carol freaked! Mom freaked! Doug cried and cried, even though it didn't hurt, but before they could even get near the doctor's, the swelling had disappeared.

That's it. Cute little family story. But the trouble is, Carol wasn't there! *I* was there. And the bolt wasn't blue, it was *yellow*. And that guard was a nasty old guy. I can still see him, all crabbed in his cheap uniform. And Mom didn't freak; she laughed. She laughed despite herself, because poor little Doug looked so comical, and because—this is important—she knew he'd be all right. And I laughed and laughed, "Bwaa-ha-ha!" because I was a big brother, and big brothers laughed at the misfortunes of younger, at least they did in 1963.

I let Carol tell the story at meals, only occasionally challenging her, and now that's part of the family story, how we both claim the memory. I *know* she's wrong. She *knows* I'm wrong. Whom do you believe? Does it matter? Maybe we're both wrong. Is something more important than swollen lips at stake here?

Memory is faulty. That's one of the tenets of memoir. And the reader comes to memoir understanding that memory is faulty, that the writer is going to challenge the limits of memory. One needn't apologize. The reader also comes expecting that the writer is operating in good faith, that is, doing her best to get the facts right.

Listen to Darrel Mansell, a teacher of writing, in his article on nonfiction in the *Associated Writing Programs Chronicle.*

> You just can't tell the truth, the whole truth and nothing but the truth about that amorphous blob primary substance— language with its severely limited and totally unrealistic rules and regulations won't permit it. Furthermore the aesthetic and rhetorical demands of writing won't quite permit it either. The best you can do is to be scrupulous about facts and conscientious about what you and only you know to be the essential truth of your subject. That way you have a shot at telling one modest aspect of what really happened—something true, up to a point.

Exercise One: Mapmaking. Please make a map of the earliest neighborhood you can remember. Include as much detail as you can. Who lived where? What were the secret places? Where were your friends? Where did the weird people live? Where were the friends of your brothers and sisters? Where were the off-limits places? And so forth.

MAKE THAT MAP

Go on, go make your map. Notice the ways (if any) you resist doing so, but make that map, no matter how simple (one young guy made an X with a pencil and wouldn't go further—ah resistance!—at least not until he saw the maps of others). Or no matter how complex (another student, over fifty, reverted completely to childhood, went to work on a huge sheet of poster board with colored markers and tempera paint, magazine cutouts, bits of cloth to represent lawns, complete lists of house occupants, dioramas of two school yards, three churches, and her grandparents' house. She spent so much time that she came to our workshop all exhausted and without any writing to show).

However you approach your map, enjoy yourself. Then come back and read on. See you in fifteen minutes, an hour, a week. But do make that map, or drawing, or $15,000 fiberglass scale-model relief complete with working grain elevator and talking puppets.

DISCOVERING LOST WORLDS

We're back. Remember Gow Farris? Our retired journalist? Well, Gow surprised me with a wonderfully detailed map, stiffly drawn, showing his childhood neighborhood in St. Louis, Missouri. His family had left there when he was ten. A squiggly line behind his house denoted a ravine, he told us, and the ravine, judging by his small smile as he pointed it out, seemed to hold fond memories.

You may have used maps before in your writing. They work well for fiction, especially as a way of delineating territory, aiding imagination, creating a world. But maps can aid memory, too, unlock memory, re-create a world.

And that's the thing, isn't it: The world of your map is gone. In the introduction to his collection of short memoirs, *Excursions in the Real World*, William Trevor writes: "Places do not die as people do, but they often change so fundamentally that little is left of what once they were. The landscape of the Nire Valley that spreads over a northern part of County Waterford is timeless, but the Dublin remembered here is the Dublin of several pasts."

My own map would be that of a neighborhood in Needham, Massachusetts, where I lived till I was five. Only five. Young, young, the earliest rosy light at the dawn of my memory. But I remember Fuller Brook Road (or is it Fuller Brook Avenue—it won't be hard to find out, when the time comes). Fuller Brook curved into the woods from a busy main road, made a crescent sweep, then turned back out to the highway.

After sketching a rough crescent, I'll draw a little box for Ellen's house across the street. I remember the big picture window of that house, and the name Ellen, though not Ellen herself particularly. I'll draw the sidewalks, and in doing so images will come to me unbidden, images of chalk and crayons and cracks one best not step on. Few cars passed by there. I'll draw our short driveway and our enormous brown station wagon, which suddenly I can picture so clearly I know it's a Ford, though I wouldn't have known that then. Oh, let's see, the year is 1959. We moved to Connecticut that year in August, which I know because Douglas was born just before the move, his birthday two days after mine. So now I'm five. That car smelled a certain spicy way, and the headliner—the material on the ceiling—was soft and crushy as felt. Of course drawing the confines of our yard I think of my older brother, Randy. And I think of the older of my two younger sisters—you've met her—Carol, and see my toy bass drum and Mom's garden taut with strings to make the rows straight and certain adult neighbors and a rusty wagon. The more I draw, the more comes to mind, lost stuff: The second corner of the crescent had a dirt road off it. The houses ended and there was this dirt road and big fields and then a lot of woods. I draw, I draw. Heroic Randy (who stabbed the head of my bass drum repeatedly with a fork) was stung by bees in the edge of one of the fields. I was tagging along and didn't get stung. I can clearly see the place he stepped and the wasps—yellow jackets—coursing out of their ground nest. And thinking of this fear makes me remember another fear: the Nike missile base. Yes, of all things there was a cold-war Nike missile base. I draw it on the map at the other end of the crescent of Fuller Brook Road (or Avenue) and remember the high fence and barbed wire. Am I really remembering this? Later (chapter seven, to be exact), I can be a reporter and check. One call: *Hey Mom.* And while I'm at it, I'll ask about Dougie's lips. But for now memory's the thing.

Nike missiles? Yes, and Sputnik went over—you could see it—a moving star in the night sky. Checking (I can't wait for chapter seven, I guess) I find out I'm not quite right about Sputnik: The first sputnik was shot to the heavens in 1957—the one I saw that summer was part of a series of uncapitalized sputniks (the word being a generic, like satellite). But hey: Without bothering Mom I remember our windows rattling with sonic booms (research note: how come there aren't any sonic booms anymore, yet far more supersonic activity up there?) And school, the Dwight School, was over that ridge. I draw the ridge and recall Randy and some other bigger boys climbing the missile-base fence: a shortcut to school. I recall some man in a uniform yelling at us. I recall (and draw) the approved route to the Dwight School, out Fuller Brook (among my first jokes was to call it Fuller *Brush* road—I remember my dad laughing and seeming impressed with my humor) on the sidewalk along the busy main street, a long walk. Then take a left. The classroom is clear to me. And Mrs. . . . Mrs. . . . Can't get her name, though I bet my mother knows. Mom would have been thirty-two. Last I'll draw some rudimentary bulldozers in the fields. Just before we moved they started development on those pastures. I loved the bulldozers. They were dinosaurs.

Exercise Two: Map Story. Once you've made your map, it's time to write. Here's the assignment: Tell us a story from your map. "One day back in Anchorage. . . ."—and off you go, elaborating on your recollection that you and Ellie Tottenhammer used to throw frozen fish through garage windows. Don't edit yourself much; don't try for anything finished. The story needn't be long. A couple of pages is fine (but keep going if you get inspired).

Perhaps it will help to broaden the definition of the word *story* for yourself. Here's a quote from Flannery O'Connor: "If nothing happens, it's not a story." That makes a pretty simple definition, and very broad: In a story, something happens.

Now, go write. Stop reading this book right now, and get to work. Yes, even if you're in bed or on the subway or at the coffee shop or seated on a jet. Pull out that notebook you've got with you always and get started.

A SAMPLE MAP STORY, COMPLETE WITH DISCLAIMER

Here's Gow Farris' response to the map story assignment, written quickly and in longhand, no cross-outs.

> It's July in St. Louis, 1936. My younger brother Frank and I want ice cream, but we're not allowed.
>
> I am ten and Frank eight.
>
> If we go off down the street there's hell to pay.
>
> We have a plan. Climb down through the ravine. Down there we will be hidden. Then sneak out to Four Corners along the tracks.

I don't remember what we thought we'd do at Krock's store for money. I don't remember being in the store. The store I remember all right. Large jars of candy. Licorice, is the one I remember. And Mr. Krock. I remember him, he was very far off and quiet, but friendly enough. He was sad, I now see. Or maybe depressed. That may have been the time we stole. Anyway, we would walk down there along the tracks and take our time, even though we knew we had to be home by supper. Oh, we would walk to the road and then down to Krock's and get candy. We would do this daily right up until the time we stole. Then, of course, Mother got into it.

Those were days when kids thought about candy instead of Nintendo and TV.

That's it. Nothing finished about it, obviously, or meant to be, just a pencilled draft written on the busy front stoop of a great stone house in the twenty minutes between lunch and a lecture at a summer writing conference in Maine (Gow had no trouble shutting out distractions!), but full of life and possibility nevertheless, and the force of memory.

He read it to us the next morning, but not before apologizing profusely for how rough and unfinished it was going to be. He'd had little time. He hated writing with a pencil. He wasn't trained in this sort of writing. Lots of self-doubt. (Imagine having to read your exercise to a group!)

Gow didn't know it, but he was speaking for all of us. Most people have something similar to say just before presenting new work to a group. In fact, it's so similar that I have come to call it the generic disclaimer, or even Generic Disclaimer, or better yet GENERIC DISCLAIMER. We save a lot of time in the workshop just by raising a hand and saying, "Generic disclaimer," when the impulse to apologize for our work strikes.

Exercise Three: Generic Disclaimer. Make up a little card, or maybe a big one. Write GENERIC DISCLAIMER across the top in big letters, then write a paragraph or so apologizing profusely for how rough and unfinished your exercises and first and second drafts are going to be. Talk about how little time you had, how tired you were, how ornery your computer is, how dull your pencils, how you're not used to doing exercises, how you just couldn't think, how you write and work and think differently than other people do. Get it all down, all your best excuses and reasons, all your self-doubt and blaming and delusions of grandeur. Make it a nice card, and pull it out and have a look at it whenever you feel discouraged about your writing, whenever you feel everyone in the world is farther along than you are.

Having given the GENERIC DISCLAIMER, Gow turned red and stammered a little. Then he read his piece. We all sat quietly when he was done, drawn, despite the roughness of the writing, into the past. Then we talked. A young woman said she liked the part about the candy: She could really see those jars. A fellow, not young, but not yet Gow's age, said, "I can relate to the wanting to get away."

Other people in our group noted the shift from direct narrative to the "I don't remember" stuff.

Gow (a touch defensive) said, "I won't and can't write something I don't remember."

I don't know who said it, but I hope it was I: "But, Gow, you remember so much!"

We all agreed to that: the ravine, the store, on and on, even in such a short piece.

Next, the woman across from Gow noted the terse short sentences, one or two per paragraph.

Another workshopper said, "Newspaper style, ma'am," in a kind of Joe Friday voice. And he knew a little more: Those narrow newspaper columns make single sentences look like paragraphs, and the eye needs those breaks. But Gow was entering a new world, one in which long paragraphs are welcome alongside short ones.

He seems to know it, too, judging by that last block of his effort, the "don't remember" block. Here Gow lets the paragraph get longer, makes at least some of his sentences longer.

Despite his writerly protestations, we all agreed that Gow had managed to evoke Krock's store and Depression-era St. Louis pretty admirably for twenty minutes' scratching in a pad of paper.

Exercise Four: Sentence and Paragraph Length. You'll want to learn to look at your own writing the way our class looked at

Gow's. We'll talk about language more as we go along, and especially in chapter nine, but since language is so important, let's start now. Note without judgment the length of your standard sentence, the length of your standard paragraph. Where do odd lengths turn up and why? Is there a dearth of short sentences? Do you never make long paragraphs? The next step as you do your daily writing is to consciously experiment with sentence and paragraph lengths, using more of whatever you avoid now.

TAKING DOWN THE SCAFFOLDING

Perhaps you noted the important who, where, what, why, when, and how information Gow spins out in his first lines, not a bad habit by any means, though first sentences probably need to do more than offer basic information. Gow's working to a formula that's so familiar to him (and to many of us) it's become unconscious.

The truth is, we're all working to formulas that have become so familiar they seem handed down to us by God himself, or by Mother Nature. Even if we're not writing for newspapers, we've been taught, for example, that essays start with introductions.

If you look at the end of Gow's effort (and probably at your own), you'll find the traditional conclusion, too. The question is, Does it add much here?

We've all been told from first grade that a good essay has an introduction, a body, and then a conclusion, and we've been praised for delivering, even when our introductions were too neat, our conclusions pat (or clever mirrors of introductions that repeat language to form a frame: a tired structural cliché). That structure—or formula—made it easy for our teachers to teach large groups of students, but there's nothing inherently wonderful about it.

Man oh man, when I think of my college essays: "In this essay I will show that William Faulkner's use of the first person . . ." Then to the body of the essay, where I'd talk to the assigned page length about Faulkner's brilliant use of first person. Then, hallelujah, the ringing conclusion: "In this essay I have shown that William Faulkner's use of the first person . . ." Arghh! Forget all that. No matter how painful it is to do so, chop those intros and conclusions away. Just for now. Just for an experiment.

This will help you become aware that the *introductory impulse* (let's call it) runs deep, that the *conclusion compulsion* (ditto) has been carefully beaten into all of us.

But introductions and conclusions aren't necessary. Good stories, good essays, leap right to their subjects, perhaps not in draft one, or draft six, but at some point, the introductory apparatus is cut, seen for what it is: scaffolding. You put up the elaborate and complicated and even beautiful scaffolding and build the cathedral. When the cathedral is complete, well, you take the scaffolding down.

Why not take the advice of Aristotle and start *in medias res*, in the middle of things. And keep in mind it's possible and permissible (what a word!) to *end* in the middle of things, too. Often conclusions are neat but redundant, extra. Sometimes they just lead us off in a new direction that as readers we didn't want to go.

Have a look at Gow's piece. What would you identify as introduction? What as conclusion? Where's the story?

Exercise Five: Point of Entry, Point of Exit. Have a look at your own map story with the same critical eye you turned on Gow's. Have you built an elaborate introduction? How about a subtle one? I know you meant it to be there, but—just as an exercise—delete your introduction. Where does the story really begin? Where do you stop explaining? Now delete any conclusion you find. Is there a story left there?

Sometimes I've deleted my introduction and conclusion and had nothing left: I was so busy making scaffolding, I never got to the cathedral.

Finally—we spent probably twenty minutes talking about Gow's piece, not long—I pointed out the switch to generic mode in the last paragraph. Instead of something like "We walked down there," Gow gives us "we would walk down there," that *would* meaning that over time and probably in several summers, Gow and his brother walked down those tracks many times. Generic mode is a great way to condense time to move a story along, but in this case it puts distance between the reader and the action. It also creates a safety net for Gow: He doesn't have to remember any particular day, just a set of similar days. Fine, fine. But notice how one particular day is emerging despite him: the day he and Frank stole.

A Neighborhood in Brooklyn

Let's look at some more responses to the mapmaking exercise, points of comparison for you to use with your own work. Here's one from Wendy Guida (she's a cheery, very hip high school English teacher from Brooklyn and was in one of my summer workshops in Vermont), which I'll type up from her rough handwriting on pink notebook paper, skipping the cross-outs and the false starts (though the cross-outs and false starts are interesting, too, of course).

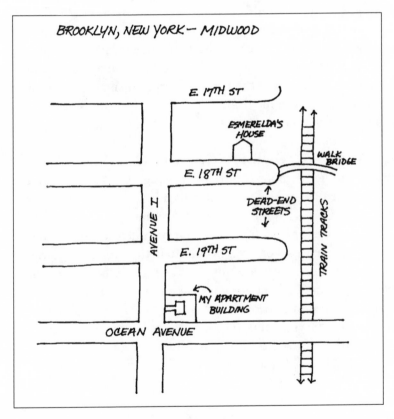

Esmerelda's house was way better than mine. It was better in all ways, which is hard if you consider all the possible ways there are, but it was. Most of my childhood was spent coveting. Esmerelda had a house (not just an *apartment* like ours), with a sprawling, cluttered porch. She had cats, where I only had a dog. She had Ralston cereal and my family only had farina. Her things were, by definition, better than mine. I figured any time my family was different we were low class.

Somehow I believed that song lyrics were maps to my future, not lessons to be learned from to avoid pain. I mirrored Esmerelda's taste in music, adoringly purchasing Carly Simon's *Greatest Hits*, James Taylor's *White Album*, every Barry Manilow album. I could probably still sing my way thorough every Barry Manilow song. But Carly, Carly was our love.

Obviously, this is a response to an exercise, quickly rendered. Wendy, I'm sure, would certainly like to invoke the GENERIC DISCLAIMER at this time. Of course it's not a finished or polished or structured piece. There's quite a jump here from feelings of lower-caste unworthiness to the record collecting. Some of the sentences are a little ungainly. But there is no abstract opening, no scaffolding. We get right to the point and quickly arrive at a promising discussion of a kind of musical nostalgia. Material is arriving.

EXAMINING YOUR PRECONCEPTIONS

Here's another response to the map assignment, by Nancy Kuhl. You'll remember her note about resistance, from the introduction. This is the first assignment she wrote for me, and you'll see signs of her resistance, which I hope will help you detect any resistance of your own. Nancy's work was produced in the course of an academic quarter, when she was a graduate student at Ohio State. She had five days and a weekend to work, so another thing you'll see is the result of more time spent than Gow or Wendy had, perhaps more the kind of time you yourself have been able to spend. Before reading what follows to the class, Nancy invoked the GENERIC DISCLAIMER with vehemence.

THE BIKE

The house I lived in until I was five sat on the corner of a street that dead-ended into an elementary school parking lot. The lots nearest my backyard were still meadow from which you could see the square, skeletal frames of new houses.

I have no story from that neighborhood or that house; I have only disconnected bits of memory. For instance, I remember a green bedspread, and a baby, named Evelyn, born to the couple who lived across the street.

Though my memories of my life in the house are few and flawed, I think of one fragment often. My brother is pulling me in a wagon. The wagon tips over and I crack my front teeth on the pavement, knocking one of them out. That's it. The whole thing. Yet, like a piece of cloth between my fingers, I worry that memory, until it is only bare threads. I was four, Schuyler was eight. He was wearing blue tennis shoes. It was a Saturday in late spring. The wagon was bright yellow.

My mother would have stepped outside in response to my brother's calling for her, which I also remember.

This memory stays with me, perhaps, because of the question it poses. If this memory is impossible, as it surely is, how then can I trust any memory? That I remember this, of all the falls and bumps and scrapes I must have suffered as a kid, makes it remarkable. My memory of the moment stands as the middle ground, somewhere between what could never have been and what is.

Wow. Nancy declares there is no story, then produces a story, then proceeds to analyze her memory and challenge the assignment. Wonderful! Yet evasive, too. Note the concluding paragraph; observe her instincts toward making a rounded essay with beginning, middle, and end. All good. But the assignment was to tell a story from the map, not to write a traditional essay. Part of the explanation for such a remarkably intellectualizing response is just more resistance, no doubt. But part of it—the greater part—is Nancy's half-unconscious insistence on a preconceived notion of what nonfiction is or can be. I asked for a scene; she gave me the first draft of a taut little essay. What gives?

Well, she's a writer.

I'm not trying to box her in, or you. Any response to the assignment is of intense interest to me, and your own should be of intense interest to you, not only as a piece of writing but as evidence of your notions about nonfiction, as example of your eye and ear for sentence and paragraph, as evidence of your modes of resistance, as a small laboratory in which to begin the work of growth. Try hard to give the same tough scrutiny to your own writing exercises. That's why they're there: to help you develop your critical eye.

Right now we're just trying to tap into memory. Right now we're just learning to trust our sub- or preconscious minds. Think of all the material in those vaults, all the subjects. Anytime in the next months or years, you might make more maps of other neighborhoods you've lived in, tell stories from all the eras of your life. Always, rich material will emerge, especially if you do the exercise without thought of making publishable work. Not yet, okay? For now we're just bringing ore out of the mine and into the light.

Remember Janet Bellweather? Janet didn't do exercise one at all. Nancy Kuhl only became aware of her resistance gradually. How about you, gentle reader? Have you read this far without writing anything? What? You haven't even drawn a map? Well, as I said to Gow, trust me. And as I say to all my students: Get to work.

COLLECTING MATERIAL

Here are some exercises to try after the map: I wouldn't spend huge amounts of time—though perhaps one will catch your imagination and keep the keys clicking. Just write and collect a nice pile of pages—rough, polished, good, bad—it doesn't matter at this point. The important thing is that you're writing every day, creating a file of material. Forget the introductions, the conclusions, the impulse to round stories off, the powerful need to make completed pieces: Just get things that happened when you were however-many-years younger onto the page for possible future use. And don't forget that practice is always one of the main objectives of all these exercises. Allow yourself to be a learner. Practice, practice, like a kid at the piano. We'll get to the finished product in good time.

Think of what you are making as good, clean rocks for an eventual stone wall. When the time comes to make the wall, you'll want a big variety of rocks to choose from: all sizes, many shapes, many colors or subtle shades, many textures. Most of the rocks you collect in preparation for the wall won't be used in the final product. Some may be discarded, some used in a different project. And then again, some rocks are beautiful all on their own.

Exercise Six: Time Lines. Life goes by in such a tumble of events that it can be hard to reconstruct even the big picture, much less remember particular days. "Time Lines" is akin to the map exercise, in that it not only provides a frame for remembering, but provokes memory. And it's simple. You just make a chart for any year of your life. Not quite a calendar: a box for each month of the period will do (detail beyond that—weeks, days, hours—is up to you, and certainly beneficial). Then fill in the boxes with what you were doing. Last year will be pretty easy. But what if I pick, say, my sophomore year of college? 1972. What was I doing then? Ithaca, New York: Ithaca College. But when exactly was it that I went to Maine to work on Mike's cabin? When was it that I worked for Dave Conway, the electrician? When was it that I met Bob Meyer, who would later become such a good friend? When did my not-quite girlfriend Gail and I break up? Harder than it looks, but one clue leads to the next, and after a couple of days of puzzling over it, I figure out that Dave Conway was a year later, Bob Meyer and I met November of *freshman* year, Gail and I broke up in January, and Maine was that summer, in August.

Once you've got one year figured out, you might want to go on to the next year, or the year previous. My book *Summers With Juliet* covered eight years of my life; eventually, my time line—much revised and recopied—covered all eight years, full of notes and arrows and surprises. It helped immensely in keeping time straight, for sure, but helped me remember lost days and events and people as well.

And one of my students in Vermont—a minister, seventy-six years old—spent a whole year and made a chart of her entire life, color coded. What a catalog it was, the uneventful alongside weddings and funerals and relocations and religious awakenings. And what a valuable tool the chart became as she worked on her memoir. (In chapter seven we'll dig deeper with a little personal research, but for now the idea is simply to see what memory will yield.)

Exercise Seven: Time Lines, Part Two. Back to the writing: Look for the stories in your time line and tell some of them in quick versions. The idea isn't to produce finished stories, not yet, but to create a collection of rendered memories. Chances are there'll be a lot of stories—truckloads—far too many to write. So make lists, more or less detailed. This is enjoyable work, great on a day when you are otherwise stuck, or not sure what's next for your writing.

Exercise Eight: Idea Notebook. This is something you might already have going, in one form or another, a common writerly habit, used in varying ways by different writers. I've got a loose-leaf notebook that's almost a scrapbook, full of ideas I've had—bad and good—for essays and stories, full of odd sentences that have passed through my head, full of cryptic phrases and snatches of conversation. I settled on the loose-leaf book years ago, because I can punch holes in any odd piece of paper I've written on and file it away. I tape napkins in and staple in notes hastily made on the backs of credit-card receipts. It's a wild mishmash but gives me a place to go when I can't get started. Scott Fitzgerald went so far as to keep his ideas in file folders, alphabetized by subject.

I also have an absurdly large collection of miniature notebooks for various pockets and glove compartments and desk drawers. I'm crazy for these things, buy them in threes and fours whenever I see a cool one for sale. I also keep a pen in my pocket always, always, always, just like my keys.

Got an idea? Write it down.

Exercise Nine: New Leaf. You must have heard about Ernest Hemingway's young first wife, Hadley, packing a suitcase full of the only copies of his early stories in order to surprise him on a visit in Europe. She lost the suitcase on a train. At first, of course, old Ernie was displeased, to say the least, but in the end he said it was the best thing that ever happened to him.

So here's a painful exercise: Collect all you've written (well, at least up to the day you started reading this book; keep your exercises for now, okay?), published or not (whether on paper, on floppy disk, or downloaded from that hard drive), and put it in a box or boxes. Next, tape the boxes shut dramatically. Now, take a thick marking pen and write PHASE ONE on the side of the box, or APPRENTICE WORK, or perhaps OLD LEAF. Do all this theatrically, with lots of moaning and shouting, keening and weeping. Ululate. Tear your hair. Pound your chest. Put the box of retired work in the attic. Or leave it on a train. Then take yourself out to dinner and celebrate.

Next morning, dawn of a new era, get to work.

THREE

SCENEMAKING

Others please us by particular speeches, but [Shakespeare] always makes us anxious for the event, and has perhaps excelled all but Homer in securing the first purpose of a writer, by exciting restless and unquenchable curiosity and compelling him that read his works to read it through.

—Samuel Johnson

When I think about my existence, any stretch of it—any month, any year, any minute, really—I'm thinking in fragments. Perhaps a meadow comes to mind, and a stone wall, and my high school girlfriend Linda sitting on the stone wall kicking her feet waiting for me. The snatch of conversation I can hear is Linda, too, but seems to take place in a room imbued with a certain light . . . morning sun . . . her parents aren't home. But the meadow was later, wasn't it? Yes, college years. I can immediately start spinning vignettes, and those quick stories of my life come so fast I can't believe it. The more I think, the more I remember. The more I write what I remember, the clearer it all comes to me.

True stories depend on memory, of course, but what do you do once the great gates are open? It's a painful truth of memoir making: You can't tell it all.

The secret is in scenes; scenes are one kind of rock for that stone wall we spoke of last chapter. Scene is vital, sits at the heart of all dramatic writing. And scene is nearly always what's missing when a piece of creative nonfiction fails to come to life.

SCENEMAKING IS SHOWING

A good scene replaces pages and pages of explaining, of expositional excess, of telling. Instead of a passage about your family's socioeconomic status, you show your dad pulling up in the brown Ford wagon, muffler dragging. Or does he pull up in a shiny Mercedes? Or does he walk up the hill with his jacket over his shoulder, car traded for shares in a new invention? Let the reader write the passage about class. In one house the furniture is polished wood. In another, it's painted metal, showing rust. Trailer park? Butler? Ranch house? Elvis Presley clock? Trust the reader to gather all that's implied, and get on with your story.

And trust the reader to discover emotion in your real-life character's actions. Instead of a lot of explaining about how much you loved a boy or a girl and how good-looking he or she was to you, and how awful it was that he or she never paid much attention to you, show the beloved. Give a whiff of the orangy scent you associate with him or with her. Show him smile at the prom queen just the way you'd hoped he'd smile for you, or show her hug the football captain when she thinks you can't see. The difference between telling and showing is life. And life is the root meaning of the word *vivid*, the highest praise a scene (or any writing) can garner.

I'll define the word *exposition* in some detail in the next chapter, but for now let's just oversimplify and say this: Exposition is telling. Scenemaking is showing. And you know what Aristophanes said (and every creative writing teacher since): "Show, don't tell."

Exposition is good at giving the facts ("I had a serious girlfriend named Linda for a year in high school back in Connecticut"), but emotion, when presented as a fact ("I was in love with her"), starts to fade, dies on the page. When presented as scene ("Linda stood up when she spied me coming through the tall grasses. She fixed her blouse, inspected herself, looked up and grinned, then frowned. I wanted to look serious, too, but my heart leapt; I grinned—couldn't help myself—hurried to her, almost running, though I'd meant to walk cool and slow"), emotion fills the reader's head and heart as well.

A good scene can succinctly exemplify and illuminate whole sections of a life, give the reader all she needs to go on, make a writer's point clear, make further discussion unnecessary.

Listen to this from *Going to the Territory*, a memoir by Ralph Ellison. The writer (author of the stupendously great and poignant and funny novel *Invisible Man*) is recalling a time he heard some men arguing heatedly (behind a closed door) over who of two Metropolitan Opera divas was the best soprano. Curious, he knocks.

> For a moment there was an abrupt and portentous silence; then came the sound of chair legs thumping dully upon the floor, followed by further silence. I knocked again, loudly, with an authority fired by an impatient and anxious urgency.
>
> Again silence—until a gravel voice boomed an annoyed "Come in!"
>
> Opening the door with an unsteady hand, I looked inside, and was even less prepared for the scene that met my eyes than for the content of their loud-mouthed contention.
>
> In a small, rank-smelling, lamp-lit room, four huge black men sat sprawled around a circular dining-room table, looking toward me with undisguised hostility. The sooty-chimneyed lamp glowed in the center of the bare oak table, casting its yellow light upon four water tumblers and a half-empty pint of whiskey. As the men straightened in their chairs I became aware of a fireplace with a coal fire glowing in its grate, and leaning against the ornate marble facing of its mantelpiece, I saw four enormous coal scoops.
>
> "All right," one of the men said, rising to his feet. "What the hell can we do for *you?*"

Ellison tells the men what he's doing—collecting signatures for a petition (significantly, at least for our purposes in thinking about the nature of memoir, the writer tells us he can't remember what the social cause was: Some things don't matter to the drama). They rib him and make jokes and decide to trust him, then deign to sign his petition. But something else is at stake here.

> Then I blurted it out. "I'd like to ask you just one question," I said.
>
> "Like what?" the standing one said.
>
> "Like where on earth did you gentlemen learn so much about grand opera?"
>
> For a moment he stared at me with parted lips; then, pounding the mantelpiece with his palm, he collapsed with a roar of laughter. As the laughter of the others erupted like a

string of giant firecrackers I looked on with growing feelings of embarrassment and insult, trying to grasp the handle to what appeared to be an unfriendly joke. Finally, wiping coal-dust-stained tears from his cheeks, he interrupted his laughter long enough to initiate me into the mystery.

"Hell, son," he laughed, "we learned it down at the Met, that's where . . ."

"You learned it *where?*"

"At the Metropolitan Opera, just like I told you. Hell, we been down there wearing leopard skins and carrying spears or waving things like palm leafs and ostrich-tail fans for *years!*"

Now, I have no way of knowing how the writing of that scene went for Ellison, no way of knowing except my own experience: It was hard. The natural flow, the vivid description, the humor all came piece by piece till the scene was whole. He remembered imperfectly a scene from his youth, did his best to recreate it, complete with feelings. I've left out most of the fine dialogue he creates (knowing you'll be heading to the library later), but the dialogue, too, came with many revisions, much testing of memory, much willingness to *re*-create.

Let's look at Ellison's passage more closely.

First, note that it's all scene. Every word. Even the expository stuff, the explaining. Ellison opens with a knock: we feel that knock on our knuckles, we hear it, we see the hand hitting the door, the youth waiting. The grown man—the writer—doesn't intrude here. Now's not the time. The reader is as involved in the silence as the teenager was, so long ago. We hear chairs move. More silence. Ellison is carefully remembering the particulars of the event, the full sequence, confidently getting it all in. Some details will have been pure in his memory, some will have been filled in—stuff he knows would have happened after such a knock.

The last line of the first paragraph I've reproduced ("I knocked again, loudly, with an authority fired by an impatient and anxious urgency") looks a lot like exposition. That, of course, is because it *is* exposition. But it's exposition that doesn't interrupt the reader's picturing the scene but heightens it, giving a picture of the youth's nature: impatient, urgent. And those aren't exterior words: "Impatient" is a feeling in the breast and not just the mind. "Anxious," "urgency": These are gut feelings, even if offered expositionally.

Then a voice. Dialogue is always immediate, always takes place in *time*, as narrative must. The door opens (how clearly we see this!), and the room and men inside are revealed. Here Ellison spends a whole paragraph setting the scene and giving us the characters. The room details he chooses are deeply significant, not the least bit arbitrary: sooty lamp, pint of whiskey, water tumblers (note the specificity of word choice: *tumblers* over, say, *glasses* or *cups*), four coal scoops leaning on an ornate fireplace (analogous, of course, to the four laborers when they turn opera extras). He uses the five senses: yellow light, rank smell, warm fire, a heard voice. Sight, smell, touch, sound. Not a few readers will taste the whiskey, too. Some writers would have put in creaking chairs or any of a number of other sensory details, but Ellison knows when enough is enough, when to let us imagine the style of the chairs, the size of the table, and so forth.

There's character development going on here, too: the men straightening in their chairs, their scoops at rest, the use of the mild curse "hell" in dialogue. The class issues being investigated live in the coal dust; nothing else need be said. These are working men. The author—destined for a life in letters—is distinctly other, despite shared race.

All this in what amounts to a single typed page!

CUTTING TO THE CHASE

I talk about scene a lot in my classes and in critiques of manuscripts. I talk about it because it's crucial to the enterprise of creative writing. But one danger of my accenting scene is that some students get the idea that I'm saying scene is the only way to go, the only tool we've got, that scene is tops on my list, king of the realm. Listen: Expository passages play as big a role in memoir as they do in fiction. And an even bigger role in the making of essays. But it seems to me that exposition—let's call it telling—has come to play too large a role in the making of nonfiction.

It's perfectly understandable that people come to creative nonfiction and think in terms of exposition. Still, I used to be surprised when able fiction writers in my classes approached nonfiction as pure *telling* (sometimes as pure *pronouncement*, though years ago they'd learned the mantra I don't mind repeating: Show, don't tell). These were makers of vivid and intense scenes who seemed to forget all they knew when it came to memoir. If it's going to be true, they seemed to reason, it has to sound like, well, like a *newspaper article*. Or an *essay*, that word used in the restricted sense that so many of our schoolteachers still tend to use it: exposition, argument, dry formality.

Exposition is vital, of course, to any writing enterprise, and, in the next chapter, I will give it its full due. But here, let's think about exposition's counterpart (not to say opposite): narrative. And don't forget we're still experimenting: actively trying to change our writing. You may want to say, "I *like* my style, exposition and all!" Good, good! Say it! But give purer scenemaking a go. And don't worry. Your style's not going to go anywhere while you try something new and different.

Narrative. That's not going to be easy to define. Go ahead and make the attempt. Pencil and paper: Go!

Last chapter we said a story is something happening. Dictionaries aren't going to be much help here, talking about narrative as the result of narration, and narration as the act of a narrator, and a narrator as someone who narrates, that is, one who tells a story or gives an account. Of what? Of something happening.

Definition may be difficult, but no one's found better words for the *effect* of narrative than John Gardner did in his landmark book *The Art of Fiction*.

> ... whatever the genre may be, fiction does its work by creating a dream in the reader's mind. We may observe, first, that if the effect of the dream is to be powerful, the dream must probably be vivid and continuous—*vivid* because if we are not quite clear about what it is that we're dreaming, who and where the characters are, what it is that they're doing or trying to do and why, our emotions and judgements must be confused, dissipated, or blocked; and *continuous* because a repeatedly interrupted flow of action must necessarily have less force than an action directly carried through from its beginning to its conclusion. There may be exceptions to this general rule—we will

consider that possibility later—but insofar as the general rule
is persuasive it suggests that one of the chief mistakes a writer
can make is to allow or force the reader's mind to be distracted,
even momentarily, from the fictional dream.

The reader is made to dream by the writer: She sees characters in
her head, she pictures settings, almost as if watching a movie.

Let's run with the movie comparison for a moment. Think of all
the work that's done by the camera before the actors ever say a
word. There's the church; there's the main street of the town. And
there are the actors, mouths agape in surprise, or whatever. If narrative is what the characters are up to, the stuff we're seeing and inter-
preting as viewers, then what is exposition? For one thing it's stage
directions. For another it's advice on the settings. Necessary stuff.
But let's think of exposition as *voice-over*. You know. The credits
are rolling, the camera is dollying in on the village in the
Appalachians, our protagonist's voice comes in out of the blue, kind
of quavery, saying: "Life was sure different in those days. Why,
America was in a depression, the papers said, but in West Virginia,
we didn't feel a change at all. In fact, people felt a little better
knowing it wasn't only us poor as mice." Exposition. Then the little
boy pops out of the general store, his arms full of clearly stolen
baseball mitts: Scene. Soon enough we'll figure out that the mitts
are for his town league team and that he's destined to be a star
pitcher. No one need tell us now—we're too busy watching the store
clerk lose a comic chase (mitts flying) past the town's three churches.

When you are engaged in scenemaking, know it, and get to work
removing anything that interrupts Gardner's dream. Exposition is
interruptive in that it doesn't make us see or dream or feel, but rather
makes us intellectualize. Not a bad thing for words to do, but when
we're talking about scene, poison. It's like lying in your hammock
dreaming peacefully of tropical island breezes and found money and
perfect love and having someone lean over you to say, "Are you
asleep or what?" Bad news.

Here's a rule of thumb to help you weed out what's not needed:
Scene occurs in a place and at a time. Exposition has no place and
is out of time.

Action!

Exercise One: Cracking Open. Please go back to any of the exercises you've written from this book so far—perhaps your map exercise—and look for a sentence (or even a phrase) of voice-over or other exposition that condenses or skims over or rushes past a possible scene.

Now, get to work writing. Build the sentence or phrase you've identified into at least two pages of *scene*: pure narrative, no voice-over, no exposition. The idea is to start to develop an eye for scenes that can move a memoir forward or provide evidence better than any amount of dry explaining or argument. Also, cracking open will help you begin to clearly see the difference between scene and exposition, always a fuzzy distinction.

A Scene Grows in Brooklyn

Remember Wendy Guida's map story about her friend Esmerelda? Let's look at the scene Wendy cracked open. The sentence she found rich with meaning was this one: "Somehow I believed that song lyrics were maps to my future, not lessons to be learned from to avoid pain."

I don't think it's coincidence at all that the sentence she picked is rather awkward. She's trying to do so much, say so much that needs to be shown. For Wendy, this exercise really took off. I'll just reproduce the opening page or so here, but Wendy's cracking open took up five pages, and then grew further into a tight little essay that proceeds from the childhood confusion and dreams about sex and romance and power displayed below to a clear-eyed (and yet entertaining) analysis of a failed marriage.

THE VOCABULARY OF LOVE

Esmerelda and I learn the vocabulary of love as we sing "Haven't Got Time for the Pain" on the way home from P.S. 152. At least, I am learning. Esmerelda already has a stockpile of useful terms from her 16-year-old sister, Malerie, such as "hand job," as in, "if you don't want to sleep with a guy, you just give him a hand job." I figure this is something like lanyard, something to keep the guy's hands busy while you make your escape.

I reassure Esmerelda about the safety of my own virginity: "If Starsky ever comes to my house, I'll just give him a hand job," I tell her.

"Hutch is cuter."

"No he's not."

"Is, to infinity," she says, raising the stakes so high I fold.

Esmerelda is shorter than I am, but she's taller as we walk because she wore Malerie's clogs this morning without asking. We wear our hair in long braids, hers dark blond, mine brown. I do our hair alike each morning before school so people will think we're sisters. Our bodies are soft and rounded yet strong from gymnastics; we have been in the eight-week beginner class for six months. I do sloppy cartwheels so we can stay in the same level. When the instructor tells Esmerelda to do a series of rolls, she retorts, "My mother is paying you. I don't have to do anything."

One thing Wendy's cracking open shows is how much material hides beneath the most unassuming sentences. Note, though, that Wendy hasn't absolutely stayed in scene. Have another look. Where has Wendy gone back into voice-over? Where is she most purely in the realm of the senses?

The scene is two girls walking home from school. Wendy interrupts the scene—nothing wrong with this, as I keep saying, nothing wrong when the time comes to make an essay, but in this exercise I just want you to be aware of such interruption—to fill in some history for us: Sometime in the recent past, Esmerelda has given Wendy some curious advice. She tells us how the girls look: "soft and rounded yet strong." This isn't an interruption (although it's exposition—try cutting it; how might you get the information provided in it into purer narrative?), because that's how they look during the time frame of the scene. The interruption comes when Wendy goes on to tell us how the girls got strong: gymnastics class. The interruption escalates as Wendy tells us more about the class.

To stay in scene is to stay in the moment. Very difficult, of course, not always necessary for readerly satisfaction, but a sense of the moment—knowing the temporal boundaries of your scene—is critical. (*Temporal*, of course, means *of time*.) After you've given Wendy's cracking open a good inspection, after you've thought about her use of exposition and interruption, inspect your own work. Where have you gone into voice-over? Where are you most firmly operating in the realm of the senses?

Another Example for Comparison to Your Work

Janet Bellweather. She's a little behind the rest of us by now, but eager to make up for her lack. Janet came to the second class with a simply drawn map and, having heard the other writers read their stuff, was visibly less threatened, less worried that everything she wrote had to be perfect. She showed her map around, shrugging, invoked the GENERIC DISCLAIMER to especial hilarity, and read.

> Mother carried Great Aunt Ellen's famous quilt hugged up in her arms like it was Great Aunt Ellen herself. She asked us to lay down on the blanket she's brought and she wanted us to wait until after we ate to swim. Which we did, then we walked a mile along the beach and I always think of that mile. That's when I learned what a mile was walking it. To Grandfather's house where we visit, then walk back. This is on the Cape. And the blanket had blown away. Its into the water, we guessed. And Mother yelled at us in an explosion and called my sister several very serious names and blamed us for losing the blanket and that was like the mile, I always think of it that's when I learned that mother was not well.

So much in this passage, so roughly written. In class I decided not to mention the differences between the verbs *to lie* and *to lay*, and the difference between *its* and *it's*. Not yet. Also, there's plenty to say here about run-ons and fused sentences and fragments and verb tenses. Later, later. Janet had already shown she was pretty defensive, after all. And the truth is, we're all defensive when well-meaning readers start in on the grammar stuff and seem to ignore the important content of our pages. Heck, this is a rough draft, not even a first draft! Better to just note her (extremely common) grammar and usage difficulties in pencil in her margins, then talk to the class about such things later, when no one is in a defensive position.

(But you, gentle reader, you are not in a defensive position at the moment. So go look up a few things, right now. You might even mark Janet's paragraph, naming precisely each problem you find. Use a handbook if you're not clear on a given problem. To name it is to know it, and all that. Are you sure you have the difference between *it's* and *its* straight, for example? A lot of writers, even accomplished writers, don't. The point, of course, is to make you an expert on your own sentences. But more on that in chapter nine.)

In class, we didn't say much about Janet's small errors at all. What we did first was praise what's good here. Someone pointed out what a great line that was about the mile! Janet "learned what a mile was walking it." And the picture of her mother, hugging that blanket, then yelling. The admission at the end that mom was mentally ill. As for setting, we only have "the Cape." I think of Cape Cod. Someone else might think of Cape Canaveral or Cape Ann or the Cape of Good Hope, on and on. Turned out it was a cape in *Oregon*. So "the Cape" is probably not precise enough, at least for first mention.

We talked about what Janet might crack open. And folks, by the time we were done, we'd highlighted *every* line as rich with promise. The writer—Janet—was going to have to pick out her own line to work with. As will you. Use your reactions to Janet's writing as a way of calibrating your reactions to your own writing. Where are you more successful than she? Where not?

Gow Cracks a Scene

Gow Farris was infuriated by his faulty memory as he worked on cracking open a line from his map exercise, refusing to add one word that he couldn't safely testify (before the hanging judge in the court of his mind) was true and correct. First, he told us, he tried cracking open this line: "Those were days when kids thought about candy instead of Nintendo and TV." Even on his own, Gow came to see the evasion in picking the line the group had singled out as *conclusion compulsion* stuff and expendable. His cracking open of this line rendered a bunch of sentences, all right, a kind of rant about kids and TV, an editorial, at best, but not a story, which is what he was after.

So, taking advantage of the fact that writing is endlessly erasable, he tried again, cracking open "Then, of course, Mother got into it." Let's see how he did.

Mother was on the back stoop when Frank and I got home. We saw her as we came up out of the trees from the ravine, and she saw us. My pocket was purely bulging with candy, two kinds I'd stolen. Jawbreakers and rootbeer barrels.

We were caught, no way around it. My knees about gave out.

Frank marched right up to the porch and without a second thought he just lied. He said, "We have bought some candy at Krock's." I remember that line clearly. Mother said, "I see." I remember that line, too. Unforgettable.

She saw, because around Frank's neck were licorice whips, maybe a dozen he'd liberated, a penny each. You see, mother knew how much money we had to spend. A nickel apiece on the very richest day.

Next thing we knew we were on our way back down to Krock's. This time, however, we arrived in a pony cart, one ear each pinched in Mother's sharp fingers.

After Gow read, we in the workshop told him what we admired about his cracked-open piece: Mother's sharp fingers, the image of Frank with the incriminating licorice whips around his neck, the strong sense of the place, the strong feeling we all had that a story greater than the vignette is just beginning to unfold. And all without lying.

Someone around our workshop table pointed out the expression "purely bulging," saying she loved it, that it was an example of the success of Gow's voice.

Gow said, "Oh, heavens," at this compliment. He hadn't even noticed that "purely." He said he never talked like that anymore, had spent years purging his vocabulary of such old-time expression. I just grinned: Gow had unintentionally remembered something very important as he recreated this scene—his childhood voice. How wonderful that this bit of truth had slipped by all of Gow's prodigious controls and rules.

Then we talked about the idea of voice-over, the author interrupting the reader's dream. Do you find any voice-over in Gow's piece? Where exactly? Where does the author sitting at his desk writing intrude himself into the reader's "dream"?

What we picked out as voice-over in Gow's piece is the stuff our favorite retired reporter has included about how clearly he remembers, and the forgettable "Unforgettable" that he throws in, trying to convince the judge in his mind of his veracity. But readers aren't like judges, really. They just want to believe. No need to wake them up to tell them to do so: Their dream is proof of their belief!

And then, some joker (I'm afraid it was I) had the temerity to say that there was still much to crack open here. How about "she saw us"? How does a boy know when his mother sees him? How did Gow? Did she stiffen? Wave? What exactly?

Or how about "Next thing we knew"? Hidden in that entirely conventional phrase is Mother's entire response to the boys' crime. But how did she act? Is she a mother who shouts? Who smoulders? Who is entirely understanding? We know she pinches ears! What else? (We'll do a lot more with this kind of consideration in chapter five, which is about characters, but for now, let's simply note how closely character and character development are related to scenemaking.)

We talked, too, about language in Gow's exercise. I took the liberty of pointing out one small construction I would have liked to change: "Mother was on the back stoop." A simple verb switch can do a lot of work here. How about, say, "Mother *loomed* on the back stoop"? Or any verb (as long as it's just right: Gow's job) except that pesky verb *to be*.

Now it's time to closely inspect your own work. Can you give yourself the same clear-eyed look we've given Wendy, Janet, and Gow?

DIGGING DEEPER: BE YOUR OWN BEST READER

Exercise Two: Voice-Over Patrol. Examine your own "Cracking Open" exercise for voice-over. Where are you interrupting the reader's dream with pronouncements and explanations and analysis from your writerly desk? Try cutting all the voice-over you find. What's left? Scene, that's what. Things happening.

And remember, I'm not trying to turn you into a voice-over cop. Voice-over has its place. It's just that that place isn't here and now.

Look for the places you're speaking as a writer and not acting as a movie camera. And just for now, for the sake of the exercise: Cut.

Exercise Three: Cracking Open II—The Sequel. Please go back to your "Cracking Open" exercise and see what's still there to crack. There's always something. For the sake of this exercise, try cracking a phrase that doesn't look very promising, something transitional, like Gow's "Next thing we knew." Or try cracking open pronouns. Who do you mean by "we" exactly or "it" or "they"? Almost any sentence or phrase (or even word) will yield not just verbiage but important surprises.

Exercise Four: Day of the Week. Sundays aren't like Mondays aren't like Tuesdays. Find a passage in your "Cracking Open" exercise (or your "Cracking Open II") that's set in generic mode. You know: *"When I was a kid we would* go to Jones Beach." Or *"In the months* before our trip we *would* sing with father." Try starting with a particular day of the week: "One Sunday . . ." The idea is to go from generic exposition to a specific day and time, and therefore firmly into scene. And the day of the week is vital. Did our writer sing with father every day? Or was it in reality only on Saturday nights? Perhaps from there our writer will recall that Dad wore jeans on Saturday night only: "One Saturday Dad couldn't find his dungarees." And now we're in the midst of a scene. If it's Monday, a certain mood prevails, no? Fish on Fridays? Choir rehearsal Wednesday? Board meetings Monday? And so forth. Note how the expression *One day* puts your work and therefore your reader in a particular time and not only a particular place: Both are necessary for scene.

MORE SCENEMAKING EXERCISES

Exercise Five: To the Movies. Rent two or three movies you've liked a lot and watch them, thinking about scene. How does the director manage scene? What exactly is the starting point of a given scene? Where does it end? Are there interruptions of any kind? If you were to convert the scene to writing, what would be necessary to provide a similar mood? What information comes from the actors? What from the cinematographer? What from the director? Try blocking out a favorite scene from a film on paper, then try writing a section of it in prose.

Now turn back to your own writing. How would a director (and her huge staff) film *your* scene? What directions would you have to give to have it come out just the way you see it? Try turning your scene into a film script, including not just dialogue but camera directions, advice to the actors, and set notes. What's needed? What's extra?

Last—back to memoir mode—revise your original scene to reflect what you've discovered.

Exercise Six: Apology. Think about Gow Farris. How might someone who will under no circumstances lie manage to make a vivid scene—including dialogue—that is true despite relying on re-creation?

Try this: Start a vignette by confessing to your reader that you simply cannot remember all the details of, say, the day you fell in the well, then apologize profusely for your memory. I'm sorry, I'm sorry, I'm sorry, but I can't remember what people said. Then apologize further: I'm going to have to make a few things up. Now make the scene. You aren't deceiving anybody, right? The idea is to free you of ethical baggage—just for the moment—so you can attend to drama.

Exercise Seven: Telling the Goddamn Truth for Once. If, unlike Gow Farris, you have tended toward easy fiction in these exercises—lying, Gow would call it—you might want to try this exercise. Gow Farris is a journalist. You, perhaps, are a fiction writer. No one has to tell you how to make things up, or when. If it's more convenient for your story that Grandma live in Seattle, by God, she lives in Seattle. (Journalists, please go back to exercise six. Go on, shoo.)

If you're still reading this exercise, you must belong here. Embellisher! You know who you are. Here's your special assignment: Look back to your map or your cracking open or other exercises and pick a scene to dramatize. Only this time the first line is "For once, I'm going to tell the truth."

And go on to write (or rewrite) the scene in a way Gow Farris would approve. It might help to imagine that a team of fact-checkers from *The New York Times* is going to investigate every single word. I've worked with these people. They're very, very good, and very, very stern; not even mild exaggerations are going to get by.

Exercise Eight: Seeing. My wife, Juliet Karelsen, is a painter, and one of the things she's begun to teach me is to *see*. Oh, you know, I've always been able to look out over the backyard in Maine and see the green forested hills, but what if I had to choose colors and shapes and values of light and dark to represent those hills? These days I look and see that the more distant hills are not green at all, but blue. The middle hills are *lavender*. This lavender startles me every time, but there it is. Only up close is anything green, but it's a multitudinous green: The grass is one shade, the pine trees another, the maples a third, and on and on. The leaf in front of my face folds in two, the right half one shade of green, the left half another; every shadow holds a new hue.

Here's the exercise: Go sit someplace—an office, a park, any-place—and just really look. How are trees put together? How are chairs made? How is this rock different from that rock? How do shadows and distance affect color? And so forth.

I always think of an Edward Hopper retrospective I saw some years ago at the Whitney Museum in New York. His early work was good—showed his great talent—but was different from his later. The early paintings tended to use hundreds of small and rather fussy strokes, many shades of color carefully smoothed and blended. In one painting—a seascape—I took notice of a seagull for some reason, examined it. Loosely represented by about twenty small brushstrokes, the bird had a stiff quality, but no mistake: It was a seagull.

Gallery to gallery in the Whitney I followed Hopper's growth. Across one large room I spied another seagull in a painting that came thirty years after the first (the painting newer, the artist older), very plainly a herring gull, standing proudly gazing the way herring gulls do, this one on the peak of a barn. Up close I could see the artist's hand motion—flick flick—and see the amazing fact that the seagull was a matter of two quick and well-controlled dabs of paint, one white, one gray. Two strokes. Hopper was learning to see precisely and to simplify his work into mastery.

How would you put what you see into words? Take some notes as you look; try out some sentences. How few words can you use to get an exact impression of, say, a stone wall? Get a good drawing pencil and make sketches with words, thinking of words as strokes.

A variation is to look at people, preferably from a distance. Just see. What exactly are the visual clues that tell you someone is angry or intelligent or old or unhappy or high or a potential friend?

Exercise Nine: Hearing, Smelling, Touching, Tasting. This is just exercise eight adapted to all the senses. What's to be sensed in a room? What's to be sensed in a field? How exactly are these sense impressions apprehended, and what effect do they have? To disconnect overpowering sight, you might try a blindfold.

One caveat: When it comes to smelling, touching, and tasting people, discretion is advised, and, at the very least, permission.

Exercise Ten: Practical Seeing. Pull out one of your cracked-open scenes (with luck and hard work you already have an accumulation growing). Now that you've spent some time seeing (and hearing and tasting and so forth), how might you revise? Don't be afraid to double or triple the length of a passage in this draft. Later you can cut and shape till your seagulls are two strokes. All in good time.

Taking Time to Grow

Before you move on in this book, I'd suggest a period of studious reading and writing. Analyze the scenes of favorite writers. Think about how good writers separate scene and exposition (sometimes line by line). Then make scenes from various parts of your life and the lives of others—this can be a lot of fun when the pressure of making a finished piece is off your back—just make scenes for the sake of making scenes. Notice the connections between scenes, the emergence (perhaps) of themes and subjects and ideas, but don't work these up just yet. For now, just crack those scenes open sentence by sentence, revise the cracking open, make rocks for the beautiful stone wall that's coming.

If you can make a vivid scene, a scene full of action and image and light and sound—life itself—then you will catch every reader, every time.

Go and write. Take all the time you wish.

FOUR

BIG IDEAS

If you can't explain your theory to a bartender, it's probably
no good.   —Ernest Rutherford, astrophysicist

Believe those who are seeking the truth; doubt those who find it.
                                        —Andre Gide

In the last minutes of the last session of a two-week summer course
I taught at the University of Vermont a couple of years ago, I turned
with mock gravity to one of my favorite students ever—Jane
Renshaw—and asked her a tough question, not expecting an
answer, not at all. I said, "Jane, tell us, what's the secret of life?"
    Jane was eighty-five. Within a few months she would pass away,
succumbing to a condition she had told us much about in a very
short and blunt essay called "On Illness," which she'd written in
fulfillment of an exercise I'll give later in this chapter.
    The secret of life. Some question! I was making a joke about the
process of our course, I guess, acknowledging a bit too sardonically
that there weren't going to be any final answers, that the questions
we'd raised about writing were going to have to be the answers.
    Jane had arrived each morning in the van from her modest retire-
ment home, had presided patiently at her end of our conference
table, listening to my foolishness, asking for clarification when the
younger troops (their ages ranging from twenty to sixty-six) were
nodding their heads as if what I said made perfect sense. She was
quick to smile and had a sweetly wandering laugh. Always her criticism of the other students' work was gentle; always it was tough
and wise: "I wonder why a man would act like that," she'd softly
say, getting to the exact heart of a memoir by a classmate about his

rotten father when our writer hadn't really thought through that all-important *why*. And once, after I'd given one of my impassioned speeches about the need to care strongly about our material, Jane nodded to indicate a young man at my right and softly said, "That young fellow doesn't understand." She was right, of course—Chuck looked 100 percent dazed and confused—but she'd also picked up the quiet fact that it was that young fellow's callow and careless work that had got me speechifying.

So, last session: "Jane, tell us, what's the secret of life?"

Jane smiled benignly, forgiving me my sardonic nature, tilted her head, and said without the slightest pause: "Searching."

An indignant Chuck said, "Not *finding*?" quite sure he had it right.

"No, no, no," Jane said emphatically, letting her beatific smile spread. "Searching."

FROM IDEAS TO ESSAYS

Ideas are abstract by nature. Unbidden, ideas arrive in our brains in pieces: a bit of evidence, a blast of emotion, a sentence of logic, a shot of paranoia, a visceral reaction to film on the news, a vision descended as if from heaven. The pieces float around, coalescing in various and partial shapes, wrapped and then rewrapped in layers of preconceptions, blankets of family custom (or pathology), clear sheets of wisdom, sturdy pockets of knowledge. The problem is getting what seems whole and vital in our brains onto the page whole and vital. Seldom as we sit with pencil in hand will the idea come at once (though many experienced writers are skilled at doing earliest drafts in their heads). Most often, an idea will reveal itself fully—move from amorphous blob to elegant artifact—only in the writing. Honest first drafts often look like the mind as described above: aswirl with conflicting notions, half-baked insight, generous impulse, hackneyed platitude, opinionated surety, brilliant strings of words, silence.

How often have you had a heated argument with someone about a subject the two of you gradually come to realize you substantially agree upon? Or left a pleasant conversation and understood only slowly that you have nodded your head to erroneous thinking and said things you don't believe? In conversation, as in drafting, ideas take shape sentence by sentence, retraction by retraction, statement by revised statement.

Ideas. What I'm talking about in this chapter is sometimes called theme, sometimes called thesis. But theme seems too one-dimensional to cover what I want to cover here, too purposefully invoked by the writer, too easily grasped by the reader.

Thesis, as you know, is the *point* of a traditional essay (which point is traditionally made in a succinct thesis sentence, then supported). The term *idea* as I use it is a little broader: Idea is the deep and cool well from which the waters of theme and thesis are drawn. When I talk about idea in an essay or memoir, I'm talking about the underlying conception or conceptions that give a piece of successful nonfiction its unity—the kind of unity that plot sometimes brings to fiction.

To convey an idea you must *have* an idea. Where do ideas come from? How to get from the whorled mists of the mind to the straight lines of the page? How to develop *belief* into the background for a rich and convincing essay? How to build the vignettes of memoir into evidence that supports an idea?

Read on.

Exercise One: Automatic Writing. Automatic writing was a tool of Gertrude Stein's and has been used by everyone from clairvoyants to psychoanalysts, philosophers to statesmen. It's a simple way to disconnect the overweening editor in our heads, to let what's in our heads hit the paper raw so that we can *see* what's in our heads. All you do is pick a prescribed time limit (start with one minute, work up to ten or more), get your notebook in hand, and say, "Go." And then go. Write. Don't stop, don't think, don't worry, don't edit; just go go go, till the time limit is up. Ding! If you get stalled, just write anything, any nonsense—I hate you Bill Roorbach for making me do this, I hate you Bill Roorbach for making me do this, I hate you Bill Roorbach for making me do this—but do not stop writing.

The goal is simply to see what comes out. Often, the issue at hand will be defined: You're about to start a new job; you're in the throes of grief; you're pregnant, you're in love. So that's what appears. But how you feel about the issue at hand turns up, too, often in surprising ways. And, so frequently as not to be coincidental, a new way of saying and seeing arrives. And often a key turns up for that lock you've been yearning to open.

This one is best done daily over time, perhaps when you first wake in the morning, and has the distinct excellence of not requiring excellence.

THE *I* IN IDEA, THE *I* IN THE ESSAY

I think (and dearly hope) things are changing, but I was taught as a schoolkid and in high school that an essay was an argument of a particular kind. It had to have the thesis sentence we've mentioned earlier, clearly stated, and all the stuff you wrote had to support that thesis. And, of course, I learned that an essay had parts—a beginning, a middle, and an end—and that these parts had names. This format is the soul of what's commonly called *expository writing*, the kind of writing that makes a category and a term like *creative nonfiction* necessary. For me as a kid and well into college, one of the defining characteristics of expository writing was that it was no fun. You couldn't be yourself but had to be someone else, someone deathly serious, someone formal, someone who shared the moribund and officious voice of an encyclopedia. A conformist, in other words, someone who wouldn't challenge the overburdened teacher.

There is, ladies and gentlemen, another kind of essay out there, the kind that you find most often in *The Best American Essays*, or in the work of writers from E.B. White to Adrienne Rich, George Orwell to James Baldwin, and contemporaneously in all the best literary magazines. It's a more wandering sort of essay, an essay in which one gets the sense of a person, a person who is, well, *searching*. And learning, discovering something that the reader will discover, too. As I noted earlier, the term Phillip Lopate uses for such work is the *personal essay*. (Please see his anthology *The Art of the Personal Essay* for not only examples of the genre, but for the genre's history and for Lopate's illuminating and defining introduction. Read his personal essays, too, for strong examples of the form.)

When I say personal essay I don't mean that the work contained therein is private or somehow small; I don't mean that it's work only one's family should read or that there's nothing universal there; I don't mean that there is no argument, no thesis; I just mean that the author speaks as a person rather than as a disembodied voice of knowledge, that the writer speaks from the heart, with no great worries about objectivity or faked fairness. That is, the writer speaks honestly; he admits that he is there behind the words—prejudices, interests, passions, hatreds—warts and all. The writer writes something that only he could possibly write.

Objectivity? People pretending to be objects have never interested me much. And people who think and write of others as objects are aligned with the forces of evil.

TAKE BACK THE ESSAY!

A little history:

The origin of the term *essay* to mean a particular kind of writing is usually placed in Renaissance France and attributed to Michel de Montaigne (pronounced in English to rhyme with Fontaine, and not to be confused in either person or pronunciation with the Italian artist Andrea Mantegna, who died in 1506).

In *The Art of the Personal Essay*, Phillip Lopate lovingly calls Montaigne the "fountainhead," and goes on to say that Montaigne "may well have been the greatest essayist who ever lived." You might want to read Donald Frame's wonderful biography of our man, but here's the way-too-quick version: Michel de Montaigne was born in 1532, son of a patient and doting father (Montaigne himself tells us quite a bit about his father in his *Essais*), who gave him the best education money could buy and set his son up as a lord. Montaigne loved the Latin poets and philosophers and statesmen, Seneca and Plutarch and Virgil, Tertius, Martial, Catullus, Horace. He was a practicing lawyer, a member of the *Parlement* of Gascony, and later, mayor of Bordeaux. But it was at *Parlement* that he met Etienne de La Boetie, a poet and thinker and statesmen with whom Montaigne talked endlessly. According to Frame, "La Boetie satisfied [Montaigne's] deepest need, for complete communication."

But after five years of a deep friendship, ideal conversation, and constant companionship, La Boetie died, aged "32 years, 9 months, and 17 days" (in Montaigne's tellingly obsessive reckoning), of a sudden intestinal ailment. Frame fills in many details of La Boetie's life, but readers of Montaigne already know much of the story from Montaigne's *essai* "On Friendship."

Donald Frame: "There is much to show that the *Essays* themselves are—among other things—a compensation for the loss of La Boetie."

Phillip Lopate: "Indeed it has been suggested that Montaigne began writing his book so that he could talk to someone; the reader took the place of La Boetie."

So the *Essais* of Montaigne are an ongoing conversation with Etienne de La Boetie. And years and centuries after Montaigne's death, a reader feels in Montaigne's presence: his essays separately and in total remain a conversation with readers—readers who become stand-ins for La Boetie, one at a time.

Exercise Two: The Conversation. What if you were to begin to think of your writing as a conversation with a reader, just one? Two people intimate over a meal, say, or over a cocktail, head-to-head. What if your audience was not a huge roomful of frighteningly various souls but one single person, the king or queen of good listeners, always nodding in interest, always with you, *and* a genuine friend, always ready to question your logic? What if you started to think of your writing as a conversation?

Here's the exercise: Pick a dear friend with whom you enjoy conversation and argument, and picture that friend reading over your shoulder as you sit down to revise any of your exercises to date. What must change? Will your friend admonish you for a certain pomposity? Will your friend yawn as you repeat old information? Will your friend take issue with some of your facts? Argue your opinions? Where will she laugh? Where will she grow sad? Where will she nod her head in understanding and agreement? Tailor your sentences to the needs of one reader, and you'll tend to make your work more accessible to all.

If you find it hard to *imagine* your friend listening, why not bring the work to the actual person and read it aloud to her? What reactions do you get? Why? Again, what needs to change?

And if as yet you are (understandably) too shy to read your stuff aloud to anyone, take heart: Even contemplating such a reading will result in necessary revisions.

YOU ARE AN EXPERT, TOO

Montaigne is said (by himself) to have worn a medallion around his neck inscribed with his motto, which I will render in modern French: *Que Sais-Je?*—What do I know? And indeed, when it came time to write, he would look into himself and report what was there—good or bad, ugly or beautiful. He was an expert on himself (as we all are, or should be) and so reported confidently, as an authority (note the word *author* lurking in that common word).

It's difficult, these days, to ascribe much value to our own thoughts on, say, friendship. The editors of *Newsweek* call a psychologist or a sociologist if they wish to report on friendship. Yet we all are experts on the subject, just as Montaigne was. Even if you have no friends, you know something about friendship, perhaps more exotic stuff than the rest of us! So look in yourself. What do you know? The answer is that you know a lot, about a myriad of subjects.

If I asked you to write on, well, let's say *ants*, you'd have plenty to type: You've dealt with ants all your life. And your take on ants would be different from anyone else's. Sure, someone like Edward O. Wilson, the renowned myrmecologist (and fine memoirist, by the way), knows more about ants than you do, but you know more about the day the ants carried away your Great-Aunt Minnie. And you could always study up to add to your knowledge, bolster your authority (but more about that in chapter seven).

Here are a few titles from Montaigne's essays. Note that anyone—even you, especially you—could write about any of these subjects: "On Sadness," "On Idleness," "On Liars," "On Prognostications," "On Fear," "On the Power of Imagination," "On Drunkenness," "On Books," "On Cruelty," "On Valour," "On Anger," "On Smells," "On Experience."

Other writers have taken over and made use of this form of title, too, for books as well as for essays: *On Love*, by Stendhal; "On Shaving a Beard," by Phillip Lopate; "On the Morning After the Sixties," by Joan Didion, "On Embalming," by F. Gonzalez-Crussi; "On Living Alone," by Vivian Gornick; *On Becoming a Novelist*, by John Gardner; "On Coffee House Politicians," by William Hazlitt (the elder); "On Failure and Anonymity," by Mira Schor;

"On Ambition," by Donald Hall; "On Apprenticeship," by yours truly.

Let me forthwith reproduce in its entirety Montaigne at his most basic, as translated (with probable debt to John Florio) by Charles Cotton in 1685–86 and revised by William Hazlitt (the younger) in 1842.

OF THUMBS

Tacitus reports that amongst certain Barbarian kings their manner was, when they would make a firm obligation, to join the right hands close to one another, and twist their thumbs; and when, by force of straining, the blood mounted to the ends, they lightly pricked them with some sharp instrument, and mutually sucked them.

Physicians say that the thumbs are the masters of the hand, and that their Latin etymology is derived from *pollere*. The Greeks called them *antichier*, as who should say "another hand." And it seems the Latins also sometimes take them in this sense for the whole hand:—

> *sed nec vocibus excitata blandis*
> *Molli pollice nec rogata, surgit.*

It was at Rome a signification of favour to depress and turn in the thumbs,—

> *Fautor utroque tuum laudabit pollice ludum*

> "Thy patron, when thou mak'st thy sport
> Will with both thumbs applaud thee for't,"

and of disfavor to elevate and thrust them outward:—

> *converso pollice vulgi Quemlibet occidunt populariter.*

> "The vulgar with reverted thumbs
> Kill each one that before them comes."

The Romans exempted from war all such as were maimed in the thumbs, as having no longer sufficient strength to hold their weapons. Augustus confiscated the estate of a Roman knight, who had wilfully cut off the thumbs of two young children he had, to excuse them from going into the armies. And before him, the senate, in the time of the Italian war, had condemned Caius Vatienus to perpetual imprisonment, and confiscated all his goods, for having purposely cut off the thumb of his left hand, to exempt himself from the expedition.

Someone, I forget who, having won a naval battle, cut off the thumbs of all his vanquished enemies, to render them incapable of fighting and of handling the oar. The Athenians also caused the thumbs of those of Aegina to be cut off, to deprive them of their precedence in the art of navigation.

In Lacedemonia, pedagogues chastised their scholars by biting their thumbs.

[Note that Cotton and then Hazlitt have decided not to translate the first Latin passage. John Florio, 1603, was not so shy: "It will not rise, though with sweet words excited / Nor with the touch of softest thumb invited." And if that's still too cryptic, how about this 1987 translation from M.A. Screech (he titles the essay "On Thumbs"): "Neither sweet words of persuasion nor the help of her thumb can get it erect."]

Note the lack in "Of Thumbs" of introduction or conclusion. Note the quotes, the bits of history. What does Montaigne know about thumbs? Our man reaches into his well-stocked mind and lets us know. When he can't remember the thumb-chopping general's name, he says so and goes on contentedly. Of course he could have looked up this information, but he sees (even through multiple revisions) that the name is not the important thing. But translators like Hazlitt Jr. simply cannot let Montaigne's insouciance about sources go: There's often a footnote and the general named.

THE TRUE NATURE OF THE ESSAY

Montaigne called his chapters *essais*. This term, as you may already know, comes from the French verb *essayer*, which means to try. So an essay is a try. That's all. An attempt. An effort to get some little bit or large chunk of thought into writing. (Sir Francis Bacon brought the word to England and to English during Shakespeare's lifetime, publishing some of his own writings as *Essays*.)

So an essay, dear reader, is just a try. Doesn't that take some of the pressure off?

Exercise Three: Trying. One more conceptual exercise: Think of each day's work as a try. Nothing more, nothing less. This may be a radical bit of thought restructuring. And instead of applying the labels *memoir* or *essay* or *piece* or *article*, say, "Try." Just to yourself. Just for now.

Remember Jane Renshaw: "Searching."

And Chuck: "Not *finding*?"

"No, no, no. Searching."

A GENTLE GOAL

One more note: My talk in Jane's class about essays as *tries* reminded another student—Joe Deffner—of his days in the Peace Corps, teaching English in Kenya. One of the many cultural differences between Kenya and the United States became apparent as Joe taught: The greatest compliment, the thing his students told each other and most wanted to hear from him, was, "You have tried."

Exercise Four: "On . . ." This one's easy to start. You just write the word *On* at the top of a piece of paper (or type it at the top of your screen), then add an abstract noun. One I like to do in class is "On Separation." Everyone seems to have something rich to say about that subject. Montaigne's list of titles or Bacon's may give ideas, too. But go with the word that popped into your head first (it's probably hanging there right now, worrying you with the honesty it's going to take to discuss).

This exercise should be as close to automatic writing as you can make it: Pick your title, think for a minute, then *write*. No pausing, no editing. Just tell us what you know about, say, humiliation, or ecstasy, or what have you, that word that's in your head right now. And don't pre-edit by searching for an easier word to use. The word now peeping its name from the depths of your cerebral cortex has great value in itself. Why that word at this moment?

But please be sure it's an abstract noun. Not a concrete noun (like *ant*), not a proper noun (capitalized, like *Joe* or *New Jersey*). Abstract. Note that many students try jokes: "On My Husband." Ha ha. "On My Way to Work." Ha ha. But the joking interferes with the purpose of the exercise, which is to get you saying true things about abstract notions. That is, to get you working with ideas. Oh, by the way: no narrative.

One page is fine.

Go!

PURE EXPOSITION

How'd it go? Not so easy? Piece of cake? Either way, this is an exercise you can try again and again. It will help you find ideas— even if you struggle mightily with it—and ideas, as we've said, are the main engines that power an essay or a memoir. What you write in this exercise might not make its way verbatim into your finished work but may explain to you what's at stake, or what you're getting at. Always and at the least, it will leave a flavor. Often it will provide your essay or memoir with a sentence or two, sometimes the very pivot of your piece.

In the previous chapter, I asked you to make scenes: pure narrative. Now I'm asking you to make pure exposition. Both are nutty propositions, since the two forms can't be so absolutely separated. When I say, "No narrative," people sometimes go into shock. Certain writers (I'm like this) are *made* out of narrative—characters doing things, dialogue, action—that's all they really know or care to do. But, let me repeat something I said earlier (and let it become a refrain): Learning is changing.

Then again, some readers of this book will have struggled more with the narrative exercises, the cracking open. Maybe you. Just dying to write exposition? Well, here's your chance.

Some definition, or redefinition is probably in order: Narrative takes place in time. Exposition is out of time. Narrative tells a story. Exposition explains. Narrative portrays events. Exposition analyzes events. Narrative exemplifies ideas. Exposition expresses them directly.

High exposition is exposition that's aphoristic (an aphorism is a saying, an adage). Some examples? Here's a classic, from Jane Austen, her opening sentence for the novel *Pride and Prejudice*: "It is a truth universally acknowledged, that a single man in possession of a good fortune, must be in want of a wife." Or how about this sentence from the opening of the chapter called "Reading" in *Walden*, by our friend H.D. Thoreau: "In accumulating property for ourselves or our posterity, in founding a family or a state, or acquiring fame even, we are mortal; but in dealing with truth we are immortal, and need fear no change nor accident." Or this, from Katharine S. White's *Onward and Upward in the Garden*: "For gardeners, [spring] is the season of lists and callow hopefulness. . . ." Kathleen Norris, from *Dakota*: "Dakota is a painful reminder of human limits, just as cities and shopping malls are attempts to deny them." High exposition has a quality of grand truth, of universal applicability. God probably thinks in high exposition when He or She is not making up the stories of our lives.

Other forms of exposition include informational exposition (the facts—newspaper journalism is mostly this); exposition of opinion (op-ed pages, columnists, polemicists); observational exposition (description); personal exposition (the grand *we*, speaking for us all, is replaced with a humble *I*, speaking for itself); and narrative summary (what happened over longer periods of time).

Have a look at this passage from Diane Ackerman's *A Natural History of Love* (which book might as easily have been titled *On Love*).

> Many lessons about whom and how to love, and what's sex-
> ually chic, bombard us from the media. Whenever I open a
> magazine these days, I half expect steam to rise from the pages.
> Perfumes war in the visual Amazon of the ads. To make their
> zest more potent, one rips a slit open, smears the all-but-
> invisible, exploded beads of scent along one's wrist or inner
> elbow, and inhales the aroma. We crave sensory experiences.
> In that, we're no different from most people.

It's all exposition, of course, but note that the first line and the last two are high exposition, and use the grand *we*. The rest is good writing, of course, but note the differences in sweep and grandeur, the different styles of exposition, sentence to sentence.

Exercise Five: High Exposition. Please look back at your "On . . ." exercise. Have you written any sentences of high exposition? No? Try to add a couple. Not easy, I know. A lot of first stabs at saying something grand about love, for example, will get you slogans from drugstore greeting cards. But keep going. Use the grand *we.* Say a great truth. Don't get embarrassed; no one's looking. It might take many tries, but keep going till you get a sentence you can use, even if it means making stabs at your "On . . ." exercise ten minutes (or more) a day for two weeks.

The acid test for high exposition? It should be unarguably true, and unequivocal.

Jeez, is that all?

MORE EXAMPLES FOR COMPARISON

Gow Farris, you'll be glad to know, used the opportunity of the "On . . ." exercise to blast me as a knee-jerk liberal and a general clown with an essay called "On Ponytailed Professors." I would gladly reproduce it here, but for some reason Gow hasn't offered it for my use. Suffice it to say, it was very funny; the class roared with laughter. You have never seen so many red faces and teeth and tonsils. I took the piece as proof that Gow was falling in love with me. My response after laughing a long time was to ask him to do the assignment over.

He did.

ON GRIEF

Time heals nothing. Those that are gone, stay gone. Your heart like a balloon with it, a gloomy balloon. The kind that rolls on the floor after bad parties. Swollen and dejected. Might explode at any minute. Lord help us. We are made of dust and ashes and to dust and ashes shall we return. That's not original with me, by the way. I am TRYing to get the exact feeling. O, liberal professor, I am essaying (do you know that word?). In grief the air around us is filled with the heaviness of loss and our chest is filled like a rising balloon. A sinking balloon. Our chest is filled too full with some gas heavier than air.

Gow is getting there, folks, battling his defenses, battling me, battling memory, working toward the idea that has made it so important that he write. And sometimes the search *is* a battle. In fact—let's face it—sometimes searching is the whole damn war.

Jacki Bell on Memory

Let's examine another student's response to the "On . . ." exercise. Note that a lot of fine things can happen even while no high exposition or very little turns up. Look for traces of narrative, for examples of high exposition, for examples of other expositional styles, especially personal exposition, where the humble *I* replaces the grand *we*.

Here's a try by Jacki Bell, a talented writer of fiction, working in creative nonfiction for the first time.

ON MEMORY

There should be more choice in memory. It should be a kind of video store where we can go and choose what we want to remember clearly—and obscure, no *delete*, that which we no longer need or that which serves no good purpose.

Memory should be reliable. Like the lungs or the heart.

A child's happiest moments should be preserved absolutely in memory, emotional responses intact—both for the parent and the child—and readily available any time they are needed.

The opposite should be true for the worst moments.

People who love you should have only fond memories of you. People who don't should have no memory of you.

Memory is too inaccurate to have so much power over our lives.

Jacki is playing with the concept of memory in grand terms, but, clearly, personal terms are emerging here. Which of her lines would you consider to be high exposition? Which might more appropriately be called personal exposition? Is anything here unequivocal or unarguable? How might Jacki rephrase certain sentences to get the more universal sound of high exposition?

Perhaps it will help to think in terms of bumper stickers: *More Choice in Memory!* perhaps, or *Make Memory Reliable!* I love this line (let's revise it into one sentence): "Memory should be reliable as the lungs or the heart." It's so plaintive. And complex, too. Jacki doesn't say "reliable as the sunset"; she invokes our mortal and thereby unreliable human organs, seat of much suffering and many deaths. Lovely depth there. And clearly Jacki's take on memory indicates struggles in her own childhood.

Janet All Alone

Now an excerpt—the last paragraphs of a long piece—from Janet Bellweather's try, "On Solitude."

> Solitude is the only natural state for a human to live in. In Solitude comes peace. The patter of little feet to me is like hailstones knocking my head. Alone, we face the edges of the Universe more squarely, and know the eternal more fully.
>
> So where's the peace?

The early portion of her try was six pages of aphorisms about solitude. Some sounded awfully familiar. Many had the sharp tone and edgy meanness that Janet brought to class; many had the humor that went with all that. But look at that last line. Something's happening. In the effort to make high exposition, some marvelously revealing personal exposition is emerging. The first cracks are appearing in Janet's armor, her castle wall.

Gow Leaves the Joking Behind

As for our friend Gow Farris, I'm trying by not analyzing his "On Grief" till now to reproduce the silence that filled the room after he read his paragraph. Note that the angry stabs at "professor" aren't the least unusual in students at this phase. Note, too, how well he's done at leaving the joking and teasing behind, getting at something important to him.

THE EXAMINED LIFE

Difficult as it is to begin to see Janet's and Jacki's and Gow's defensive armor, and then to see the cracks therein, it's more difficult still—exponentially more difficult—to see our own armor. Sometimes the cracks are what we see first—those places where the stuff of our lives oozes out, perhaps embarrassingly, perhaps painfully, perhaps joyfully. But turn from Jacki and Janet to your own work now; see if something formerly invisible is taking on ghostly outlines. No right answers here—it's enough for now to begin to take serious looks at the ideas that power our lives, that lurk behind jokes and defensiveness and vagueness and facility and laziness.

Exercise Six: Left-Brain Workout. For this exercise, I'd like you to pull out a passage of pure (whatever that means!) narrative, perhaps one of the rocks you cracked open in the last chapter. Read it once or twice, then ask the following difficult (and sometimes obnoxious) question: What's this try about? Make a list of ten possible answers.

One student of mine in Maine, Shermaze Lawrence, had written about a camping trip. Her list was roughly as follows: (1) camping, (2) scenery, (3) my ex, (4) my father, (5) my brother, (6) my son, (7) my husband, (8) different tempers, (9) marshmallows, (10) anger.

Shermaze was surprised. She didn't clearly see that her piece was about relationships with men till she made her list. And—wow!— the word *anger* seemed to come out of nowhere, since the piece was just about a pleasant excursion to the hills of Michigan.

Once you have your list, write a paragraph or so analyzing your scene. What's it about? What's going on in it exactly? Think of the scene you made as evidence; then, in your paragraph, tell us just what is evident. Keep going till you've got it right: true and elegant and hard as a diamond.

Difficult work.

Exercise Seven: "On . . ." Again. Pick the most compelling or most mysterious abstract noun from your list above, whatever word intrigues you. Write a page, "On . . . ," using that word. Then go back to your narrative and revise according to what you have learned.

Shermaze wrote "On Anger." It isn't a fabulous piece of writing— not at all—and nothing she'd want anyone but her teacher to read, but when she went back to revise her narrative, she knew the subtext of the charming marshmallows-over-the-campfire scene, and suddenly a piece of narrative that had been slight—light, humorous, and adequate—was poignant, deep, layered, meaningful.

Yet somehow still funny.

Exercise Eight: Write Something Awful. My friend Van Santvoordt is a fine set designer and a smart, subtle actor. Also a generous friend. Years ago a couple of us lived with him (and, okay, various girlfriends) in his loft in SoHo, New York City. We did lots of projects in the place, built walls, painted, added plumbing. Sometimes it took Van a long time to get a project done. Sometimes a very long time. Why? He wasn't lazy, that's for sure. He worked twice as hard as I did, yet (for better or worse) I finished my projects twice as fast. The problem was he wanted things *right*. He'd reject warped 2×4s, he'd sand knots endlessly; he'd strip paint off old French doors till there wasn't a speck left. This kind of obsessive exactingness, he realized, was alive in his acting practice, too, was holding him back. So he wrote a message on the loft wall in dark black charcoal (later adding a red border).

A JOB WORTH DOING IS WORTH DOING BADLY.

Your exercise, if you find that some form of perfectionism is holding you back, is to write something bad. I give you permission. Write something horrible, some awful exposition, and put it on the wall for a day or two. Resist all temptation to fix it up. At the end of a suitable display period, revise it. Or throw it away. So what?

You might even make yourself a facsimile of the permission slip below, which I hope you'll pull out when necessary, especially during the making of rough drafts.

> I, William Forsyth Roorbach, being of sound mind, do hereby grant and concede permission for _____ , who resides at _____ , to write something horrible, and to display this miserable verbiage upon the living room wall for a period of _____ days.

Exercise Nine: What Do I Know? Simple: Make a list of subjects upon which you are an expert. Faint expertise is fine for our purposes here. The list should be long. The idea is simply to uncover subjects meant for you, good stuff to write on.

Exercise Ten: Loaf and Invite Your Soul. This exercise will be very difficult for most readers (except perhaps certain college students I know, who had better skip it), but I recommend it highly. Spend your writing time this morning or afternoon or evening just doing nothing. You'll want to pick a place where no one will bother you at your task, because people hate to see someone doing nothing and they will do their best to see you doing something. To them, quote Walt Whitman:

> I loafe and invite my soul
> I lean and loafe at my ease observing a spear of summer grass.

And let me quote Brenda Ueland, from *If You Want to Write.*

> So you see the imagination needs moodling,—long, inefficient, happy idling, dawdling and puttering. These people who are always briskly doing something and as busy as waltzing mice, they have little, sharp, staccato ideas, such as: "I see where I can make an annual cut of $3.47 in my meat budget." But they have no slow, big ideas. And the fewer consoling, noble, shining, free, jovial, magnanimous ideas that come, the more nervously and desperately they rush and run from office to office and up and downstairs, thinking by action at least to make life have some warmth and meaning.

The Secret of Life (and Ideas), Redux

Learning to write about ideas is largely a matter of learning to *have* ideas, learning to see the ways experience contains ideas. I'll give Jane Renshaw the last word: "Searching."

And good old Chuck the second-to-last: "Not *finding?*"

"No, no, no. Searching."

FIVE

CHARACTERS AND CHARACTER

> . . . I had all this stuff about the kid not going to sleep, and it
> finally occurred to me, about the billionth draft, well, [The
> *Cryptogram*]'s about why can't the kid sleep? It's not *that* the
> kid can't sleep, but *why* can't the kid sleep?
>
> —David Mamet

My first spring in Maine I got to work making a garden. My parents—especially my mom—had had gardens all my life, and to me a garden was a form of love.

I started at the corner of a hayfield where no garden had been before, so the first task was breaking sod. I got blisters on my thumbs. I worked the dirt up with a borrowed rototiller. Blisters on my palms. I raked and added manure and dug out stones until the full moon at the very end of May, which full moon our prickly and unsuperstitious neighbor Mrs. Bailey said would mark the last frost. She was exactly right. I planted cucumber and squash and radish seeds along with a couple of flats of tomatoes and peppers from the makeshift nursery down the hill, and a little basil.

The dirt of the garden worked its way into the healing on my hands where blisters had been, darkening the coming calluses. My nails broke and got so much black under I couldn't get them clean. My hands had gotten awfully soft in the new life: full-time professor, full-time writer at his desk. Pol Pot's brigade of children would have shot me for certain.

My hands were starting to look and feel as they had not many years past (but a different life) when I had worked in New York City renovating bathrooms, demolishing old kitchens, running pipe, laying tile. Standing there in the gentle, sunny garden in Maine, thinking of my hands, my new life, my old life, I had the vague notion that all this could be some kind of essay. Then I had a vision of the essay, clear as the view from our hill of the White Mountains, and as complete, as satisfying.

I picked up an empty seed packet and scratched HANDS on it with a broken pencil, stuffed the packet in my pants pocket, forgot about it.

And carried on with my life, finishing up my first year of tenure-track teaching at the University of Maine at Farmington: stressful. I'd just published *Summers With Juliet* and was struggling to get started on the next project, a novel (I'm still finishing that novel now, five years later). The seed packet (radish) made its way from the table in the laundry room of our rented farmhouse to the trash, where I retrieved it—pure luck—on recycling day, thence to my desk, and after a month or so more into my idea notebook.

Since the novel was such hard going, I hit on the idea of writing on it five days a week, then giving over Saturday mornings to work on something else. I'd work on a short piece instead of the novel: a story maybe, or a memoir, possibly an essay, something I could get done in a couple months.

Saturday morning. What to work on? I got out my idea notebook, an old black three-ring binder I've had twenty years, a huge thing, overstuffed with a mess of bar napkins and matchbooks and scrap paper and typed scenes and cryptic phrases: GAS STATION. THE TIME YOU FELL THROUGH THE HEDGE. SOMEBODY STEALS SOMETHING. Stuff like that, appalling handwriting.

Somewhere in there I found the seed packet with its scratched notation: HANDS.

What was that about? I spent half a morning leaning back in my chair, picturing myself in the garden, trying to remember what I'd been thinking. I remembered the clarity clearly, but not really the idea.

But started in writing. "Our hands make our worlds." No way. "My hands used to be tough." Nah. I don't want to start with exposition. I want to start in the middle of things—a scene—but I don't know what things I want to be in the middle *of*. What scene? What people? My hands, my hands. I'm certainly not going to start with me standing in the garden! My clarity that day must have been an illusion.

Somewhere in the last hour of my writing time, I managed to write a bar scene that described the time I barely dissuaded a rough drunk in a Berkshire dive from his project of killing me for being a yuppie by showing him my cracked and grimy and calloused hands.

Just that much: I walk into a bar in the Berkshires, get into a small argument with a large man, show him my hands and I'm saved. Plenty for one morning.

During the week I worked on my novel, but that true scene tumbled around in my head. Come the next Saturday I seemed to know a little more: The issue here was *class*. I was a suburban kid, raised in a well-to-do town by well-to-do parents. I was different from the bar fighter, my beat-up hands, work boots, and construction job notwithstanding. But in the rough draft of my scene, I'd made myself out to be as tough a tough guy as my tormentor.

So. My reluctance to be myself—college educated, privileged in definite ways, headed away from construction, strong but not particularly tough—became one of the things I was writing about. And class in America.

How'd I get such split sensibilities? How'd I end up in shop class in high school, for example? Why had I taken wood shop over and over again? I started a bit of a scene about shop class that Saturday. Couldn't sustain it past about lunchtime. Beautiful summer day.

Saturday by Saturday the essay grew. At some point, it (yes *it*, the emerging essay) realized that my father was a big factor in my youthful need to seem and even be working class. My relationship with my father became, very gradually, the subject of the essay. And my father, poor guy, got translated from walking, talking human being to a character on typed pages, a dual existence. Suddenly, the man had a doppelganger.

And one Saturday, perhaps the seventh, the emerging essay took on life, and I kept working past lunch, and kept working on it daily through the next weeks, pushing the novel (not for the last time . . .) out of the way.

I certainly never worried what my dad would think of his portrayal, his transformation into literary character. This, he'd never see. If I were spectacularly lucky, it'd be published in, say, *The Iowa Review*, and my dad does not read *The Iowa Review*. Much less the

Eenie Weenie Teenie Quarterly, where the piece was much more likely to appear, if at all. Totally safe.

I got the essay written.

And to make a long story a little shorter, I'll just tell you that *Harper's Magazine* took the piece, which the editors confidently labeled a memoir and titled "Into Woods." With your permission, I'll include it in this volume, as Appendix One, page 187.

Harper's! One of my favorite magazines! Now, of course, the first thing you do when you get good news like that is tell a few people. Your wife. Your colleagues. Your parents. Gulp. I called home, told my dad that *Harper's* had taken a piece I'd written. "Oh, chief, wonderful," he said. "When's it coming out?"

PEOPLE AREN'T WORDS, AND WORDS AREN'T PEOPLE

Characters are the soul of creative nonfiction, whether it's memoir, new journalism, or personal essays you're making. And characters in nonfiction present special problems: They're not only based on real people (as is sometimes true in fiction), they *are* real people.

A lot has been written about characters and character in many good books about making fiction. Don't ignore that advice in your quest to be a writer of nonfiction. If you're not coming at memoir from a fiction background, you owe it to yourself to study the techniques of fiction, especially as regards characters. I'll list some good books in the bibliography at the end of these pages. Read up.

But in this chapter we'll talk about the best ways to bring real people to the page, to transform them into characters. Because it *is* a transformation: People aren't only words, and words aren't people. Along the way we'll talk about ethics a little, and think about dialogue and the other dramatic and scenic elements that make memoir successful. Remember that it is through *action* that characters most successfully and fully emerge, and seldom mere description.

Always in memoir (and really in all creative nonfiction), the most important character is you. Even if you hide yourself from view (as many New Journalists do, with an odd preference to be flies. On the wall. Or odder, to be couches. In the room), your language reveals you. I'll get to this aspect of character—you and the character you must make of yourself when you write—in the next chapter.

For now, let's talk about other people, the people whose stories you mean to turn to your use.

WHAT DO WE OWE OUR CHARACTERS?

Right off the bat there's an ethical problem. Janet Malcolm says it well in her controversial book *The Journalist and the Murderer*.

> Every journalist who is not too stupid or too full of himself to notice what is going on knows that what he does is morally indefensible. He is a kind of confidence man, preying on people's vanity, ignorance, or loneliness, gaining their trust and betraying them without remorse. Like the credulous widow who wakes up one day to find the charming young man and all her savings gone, so the consenting subject of a piece of nonfiction writing learns—when the article or book appears—*his* hard lesson. Journalists justify their treachery in various ways according to their temperaments. The more pompous talk about freedom of speech and "the public's right to know"; the least talented talk about Art; the seemliest murmur about earning a living.

Memoirists don't have the same immediate and practical need to exploit the stories of others, yet others come into our own stories in unavoidable ways. What do we owe our families? Our friends? Our lovers (past and current)? Our enemies?

I once sat on a panel to benefit the Graduate School of the Arts at Columbia. On the panel with me were other, more accomplished alumnae of the writing program there—Mary Gordon, Kim Wozencraft, Rick Moody—all of us writers who have written memoir or autobiographical fiction. The title of our talk was, I think, meant to be a little tongue-in-cheek: "Autobiography and Guilt: Managing Your Loved Ones."

We the panel took our seats. The crowd hushed. Some latecomers found seats, then some more. Then a nicely dressed couple, who found seats where they could see me clearly, and I them: my *in-laws*. Did I say that my parents-in-law live in New York City? They'd promised to come. I had discounted this promise. But there they were.

The novelist Rick Moody spoke first. He had used parts of real people in fiction, was delightfully unremorseful, looked archly over his glasses at the crowd as he read. Kim Wozencraft, author of *Rush*, was next. She was very serious. She had written her fine novel based on events that had landed her in prison. The stakes were getting higher. When my turn came I was nervous but managed as planned to quote Scott Russell Sanders (from his essay "The Singular First Person"): "The I is a narrow gate." And explain that what Sanders meant by that is that you can't—impossible—put your whole self on the page. Always, you pick and choose, construct an *I* that has a select and manageable few of your traits and quirks and inconsistencies. Generally, you make the best self you can out of the raw material of reality; generally, you are careful to put in a humble flaw or two.

My point when I finally made it (I'm a rambler) was that *all* the people in our true stories are narrow gates. It's possible—every journalist knows this—to make the person you wish, picking and choosing amongst perfectly real facts (and traits and quirks). You can make someone bad look worse; you can make someone good look better; you can make someone bad look good and vice versa. Every writer's ethical stance is going to be different: How far do you go in the service of drama, for instance, or of your idea? How can you tell when you're going too far?

Let's see if I can come up with a rule about using real people as characters . . . just give me a minute . . . hey, how about this?

DO UNTO OTHERS AS YOU WOULD
HAVE OTHERS DO UNTO YOU.

At the panel (and lots of other times before and since), I was asked what my wife thought of *Summers With Juliet*. Did she feel exploited? Exposed?

Well, no, she didn't. Not really. I didn't include anything I knew would embarrass Juliet or bother her. I left out many facets of her personality in order to focus on one: her directness, her outspokenness (one of her teachers at the Art Institute of Chicago called her "the most charming pushy person" he'd ever met), traits she was proud of. Also her beauty. I left out her sorrows, for the most part, her bad-hair days. I left out the leather whips and her extensive collection of masks and handcuffs . . . no, no, no.

I left out things that weren't needed for the story. What I put in was all meticulously true. And I let Juliet read the book as I made it. She was a great help: "I didn't say *that!*" And we'd figure out what she *did* say. (She also helped with chronology and told me when my jokes were bad and when I got too cutesy, which she hates—she'll hate the handcuffs gag above, for example.)

I made a Juliet out of words. And that Juliet *perforce* is not *my* Juliet, is not and cannot be, though from what I managed to get on the page her friends recognized her, as did her folks.

Her folks: sitting politely and listening to me with evident pride but quietly thinking of their portraits in *Summers With Juliet*. Which had bugged them. Of course their portraits bugged them, even the fond renditions I had made. It's seldom you like your own photo. (Then again, the reviewer for *The Boston Globe* said my sketches of them were "merciless.") They did not raise their hands, thank God, though I introduced them to the crowd. Much laughter.

When I finished my monologue, Mary Gordon spoke. She was articulate and impassioned, said how awful she thought the phrase "managing your loved ones" was, how we ought more think about respecting their privacy than managing them. Further, said she, we as memoirists ought to remember that our characters are people and that we owe them not only the truth but every courtesy, ought to manage ourselves, if anybody. She said she's never shied away from writing about people very close to her. She writes. She writes it all. Then—simple solution—she doesn't publish.

IT'S MY STORY, TOO

I agree with Mary Gordon, and of course I agree with myself. But there's another twist that only Kim Wozencraft really touched on: What about bad people?

Some of the most dramatic stories, some of the stories that most need to get told are about bad people. In criminal activity, in conspiracy, the rule is *Don't rat.* In abusive families, one of the primary slogans is *Don't tell anybody. Don't tell anybody*: That's what pederasts tell their victims (adding, "You'll get in trouble, too"); that's what violent husbands tell their wives; that's what we all say at different times and in different ways about any weirdness at home (insanity, violence, deformity, perversity, venality): Don't tell anybody. And it's not just negative stuff that gets hidden under blankets of enforced shame; sexuality, illness, bodily functions, sadness, and lots more are hidden, too. Why? There are cultural answers to that fine question, of course (good subject for an essay), but every case of secrecy has its own whys and wherefores. And not all (not even many) secrets are big, obvious ones (murder, addiction, unfaithfulness): Some secrets are so subtle, we are able to keep them even from ourselves.

So now you want to write about your life. And I want to write about mine. Are we going to write the sanitized versions with which we and our families face the world, or are we going to write the truth? Are we going to flinch when the subtle stuff arrives in the course of writing? Or are we going to stare it down? Probably, if you're like me, you're going to flinch. At least in the first drafts. And those places where you do so will be the places that hold your essay back, the places where your essay is dying to teach you something.

Exercise One: Your Life—The Cast. Get a big piece of paper. In a small circle at the center, write your name, or *me*. Now draw a circle for each friend and family member and co-worker and on and on, placing the circles near or far from *me* as is appropriate to their importance in your life. Where might you draw a larger circle to enclose those names that could be called the inner circle? Who's in there? Who's just on the line? And who's not in there?

Try different versions of this constellation: One for family. One for friends. One for co-workers. One for your childhood. One for now. One for the people who give you the most trouble. One for angels. The idea is simply to get thinking about who's important in your life and why.

It's the usual dilemma for the writer, the always fine line: Do I lie and damage my drama, or do I risk hurting people?

Lying leads to inconsistencies that a reader will pick up instantly, just as an observant doctor might see the truth behind a child's unusual bruises, just as all of us know that only a snob could say the sentence, "I am not a snob."

Lying adds a layer of distance thick as fog between reader and writer, and worse, between writer and text.

My vote is to tell whatever story you have to tell exactly and truly, leaving nothing out, at least in a first draft. And those places where you catch yourself changing the facts should be alarms, grand signals, signposts saying here's the place to examine most closely for meaning. Dig in. Tell the story right. Later you can adjust so as to protect privacy, if necessary (though if you want privacy, why are you telling your story?). Later you can change names (of towns, of states, of characters). Later you can choose to leave out part of the story that doesn't bear on the eventual focus your essay takes. Later. In a rough draft, let it all arrive.

If you have half a conscience, there will be the urge to protect people in your life. They never asked to be put on the page. You're not a journalist, exploiting others for their stories. But listen: *It's your story, too.* If, like Scott Russell Sanders, you had a parent who drank, *that drinking happened to you.* If, like Mikal Gilmore, your brother was a murderer, *those murders happened to you.* Do you have a famous grandfather? *That fame happened to you.* Was your father crazy? Your mother a master of guilt? Your brother a big success? Your old lover manipulative? Your wife preoccupied with career? It's your story, too. Negative emotions and traits, such as jealousy, greed, misery, and meanness, are all part of the story—your story—and shouldn't be left out any more than the good stuff should be left out: generosity, love, happiness, health. The truth is the whole story, never half.

When the voice in your head (or the voice of an actual person) says, "Don't tell anyone," that voice (or person) is taking away your story, and your story is *you*, baby. It's your life.

In the end what we owe our people is exactly what we owe ourselves (and this is exactly what we owe our readers, what readers will demand): the truth.

But what is the truth?

The truth will arrive and will announce itself character by character, some of them kind and sweet and good, some of them mean and bitter and bad, most of the rest in between. And you will have to shape those characters so as to serve the truth, and not some sense of propriety, or revenge.

Exercise Two: Characters as Traits. From your constellation of characters, pick a friend. Type her name, or his, at the top of your screen, and make a list of traits. Include absolutely anything that comes to mind. What bugs you? What's endearing? What kind of humor? What kind of clothes? What's her favorite movie? What time does she hit the hay?

Next, do the same for a family member. Then an enemy. Then an employer. How well do you know each? What kinds of things do you know about one person in your life and not about the other? What traits would you leave out of a portrait? Which would you include? What traits would your subject like left out of a portrait? Which traits are needed for the story but uncomfortable for the person you portray?

The idea is simply to start seeing the people in your life as characters, for as soon as you write about them, that's what they turn into.

RULE NUMBER 872

As you go about bringing your people to the page, remember this: Human beings are enormously complicated. Characters are enormously simple.

Exercise Three: Relationships and Drama. For each person you reduce (I use this word quite purposefully) to traits in the previous exercise, try a paragraph or two explaining the central drama between the two of you. Drama can be defined as conflict, conflict as tension, but not all drama is negative, nor is all tension. This should not be a story or an event but a discussion of your relationship. As you do two and three and four of these discussions, the phrase and idea of a *central drama* will take on more meaning for you. Note how reducing a friendship or romance to one central thing simplifies, clarifies. And note how drama arises from character.

Would the person you're writing about agree with your assessment? Why not?

Again, the idea is to start to see yourself and your people as characters and the life between you as drama.

CHARACTERIZATION THROUGH DIALOGUE

Making characters of real people (most of whom you know well) is difficult business, and quite different from making fictional characters. As a memoirist, you can't presume omniscience, can't read your brother's mind, can't but guess or intuit motives (unless you ask). Your reader must be made to forget your presence as the creator of his readerly impression of a character, must be made to forget the filter of your bias. Your reader comes to trust you only slowly, is quick to take the side of your mother, say, if your portrait feels too bitter, quick to disbelieve you if your portraits are too sweet.

So a good place to start thinking about characters in nonfiction is with dialogue. In dialogue, your characters, your people, are speaking for themselves, and if your characters are speaking, the reader can look over your writerly shoulder, have the feeling he's seeing past you to the person herself.

Dialogue in nonfiction poses the same problems as in fiction—drama, verisimilitude, intensity, surprise, storytelling—with the added burden that (to whatever extent your ethics demand) it must really have been said, or be representative of the kind of talk that did occur. When I'm engaged in journalism (and when the talk isn't merely straight quotation, an easier case), any dialogue I use is verbatim, though at times I have condensed a conversation, or moved a sentence, or edited for sense and grammar. That's as much as my journalistic ethics will allow.

I give you preeminent writer of literary journalism John McPhee (as quoted by Norman Sims in the introduction to Sims' anthology *The Literary Journalists*): "The nonfiction writer is communicating with the reader about real people in real places. So if those people talk, you say what those people said. You don't say what the writer decides they said. I get prickly if someone suggests there's dialogue in my pieces that I didn't get from the source. You don't make up dialogue."

I get prickly, too, when we're talking about journalism. But in memoir I give myself more leeway. Writing about events twenty or thirty years gone, I use dialogue more freely than in my journalistic pieces, letting my people talk as characters in the rough drafts to aid my memory, then carefully editing their talk to make it as close to that of my real friends, family, and other characters as I can, to make the speeches I can't quite remember not only plausible but probable.

Amazingly, though, much of what I report as dialogue I *do* remember well, some of it very well indeed. I can hear my father as clearly as I did the day he caught me puffing at a cigarette (stolen from him) in my bedroom thirty years ago: "You'll be a lucky bird if you don't start smoking."

I don't remember my reply, but you can be sure it was a squirming promise (unkept, by the way). If I were to write about my former smoking career and my quitting, I'd probably reproduce that promise, knowing the kind of words I used for such things, and not feel badly about it, or unethical. And if I'm really going out on a memory limb, I'll say so: Admit to making plausible dialogue, then carry on.

New writers of memoir will sometimes let problems of memory—especially in matters of dialogue—freeze them up. And if nothing gets written, what difference does a high ethical stance make? If your first goal is verifiable accuracy, you're better off as a scientist or historian or traditional journalist than as a memoirist. Successful memoir requires drama. Readers demand it. The form itself demands it. Drama—characters in action—must be the first excellence. Accuracy comes in a very close (and very important) second, but second.

Like other defenses, the refusal to write plausible dialogue (even in a memoir's rough drafts) gets in the way of discovery. Memory holds a lot more—even in matters of dialogue—than we may at first examination credit. You probably do remember what was said: Let yourself hear it. And if you don't quite remember, let yourself write anyway—your rough draft and your first drafts are yours alone. What matters is that your last drafts are as true as memory can make them.

Exercise Four: Your People, Talking. Pick a character from your constellation, and write two pages or more of the two of you talking. You might use as a starting point a remembered conversation, but don't get too technical at this stage. Just let the two of you talk about one of your usual subjects.

Do four or five or more dialogues, different characters talking to you, a page or two each. See if that central drama I spoke of in the previous exercise starts to emerge in each one. If not, see if you can't make it emerge. See if you can't get your people talking about stuff that matters.

Make at least one of your characters a person you could easily ask to read the dialogue you come up with, and show it to him. Does your friend feel well represented? Make sure, too, that one of your characters is someone you could *never* ask to read it. And think about why not.

DIALOGUE TO AVOID
Wooden

> "Doctor Smith has just called, Jonathan, and says the tumor is not malignant after all."
> "Well, that is good news, Marilyn. I did not want to die so young."
> "Yes, Jonathan, that is good news to me as well."
> "Marilyn, our life insurance agent, John Strauss of Wilton, called last night to say you have quintupled the policy upon my life. Is this true, Marilyn?"

These people sound too formal, inhuman. They are a couple, yet they use each other's names excessively. They speak without contractions.

Small Talk (and Lost Sequence)

> "Doctor Smith called, and you're going to be okay!"
> "That's good news!"
> "Isn't it?"
> "Quite good."
> "I'm so pleased."
> "Me too."
> "Darling."
> "Darling."
> "I'm going to live."
> "Yes, you are."

"Ah."

"Ah."

"Oh, honey!"

"Relief!"

Real talk consists of a lot of filler and repetition. Your dialogue doesn't need to. All the relief here takes too much time, grows boring. And did you find the lost sequence? The speakers change places somewhere in the middle, not an uncommon problem in long stretches of unattributed back-and-forth.

Information Dumping

"Jonathan, Doctor Smith, who lives just down the street, phoned while you were at your office in the most expensive building in Dallas and said that the tumor in your gizzard has turned out to be benign."

"Darling, that is good news. Come here with your ample figure and long blonde hair and give me a hug!"

"Watch it, your black eyeglasses that you've worn since the skiing accident in Tahoe are gouging my prominent forehead."

Information dumping is a matter of the writer trying to give readers important information through dialogue. These characters are telling each other stuff they certainly ought to know. Better to just say it in exposition or show it in scene. Let the characters speak for themselves.

Too Much Dialect

"I kin a' ha' na see a kenning tha' bless kinna wooffle nok."

"Aye, an' is trey, matey, an is trey!"

Okay, how people talk is important, but all that's needed to indicate accent is a suggestion here and there to give the flavor of it. Trust the reader to add the rest. In this case, our writer might have said, "He's Scottish and sounds it." An "aye" here and there and selected unusual vocabulary will do the rest.

Mimetic Comedy

> "I uh-uh-uh-uh-uh d-d-d-d-don't k-k-k-k-know, Ch-Ch-Ch-Charlie."
> "Uh, you, uh, don't, uh, know?"
> "N-n-n-n-no."

Again, the suggestion of a stammer is all the reader needs. She'll add the rest as part of her readerly dreaming.

Dumb Tag Lines

> "I guess we can cancel that insurance policy now," he enthused.
> "Perhaps it can wait till Monday," she encouraged.
> "But we'll save eleven dollars if we do it now," he misered.
> "Who's we?" she queried.
> "Why you, darling, and I!" he exclaimed.
> "I'm more inclined to cancel *you*," she chortled.

I know your high school teacher told you to vary your tag lines. But there is nothing whatever wrong with repeating *he said* and *she said* over and over. Every great writer does so. *He said* and *she said* provide fine rhythms, and repeated, they fall into the background of readerly consciousness. Fancy, verby tag lines shake a reader out of his dream. Note that a question mark *means* "she queried," and that an exclamation point *means* "he exclaimed." "Chortled"? That's a marvelous word, coined by Lewis Carroll for *Alice in Wonderland*, but how do you laugh and talk at the same time (if it's possible, show me, don't tell me . . .)? "Enthused"? What's said ought to *sound* enthusiastic. "Misered"? Please! I'm not saying never use anything but *he said*, *she said*, just use anything else sparingly and carefully.

Adverbial Insanity

> "I'm going to live," he said gratingly.
> "Where?" she said mysteriously.
> "Why, I mean, I'll be alive!" he said meaningfully.
> "What makes you think so?" she said menacingly.

"What's that in your hand?" he said realizingly.

"A hunting rifle," she said explainingly.

BANG, went the weapon loudly.

Your story ought to have provided enough context that only very rarely should you need to add an adverb to your tag line. As a matter of policy, try cutting all of them in your work. Which, if any, turn out to be really necessary?

Exercise Five: Read It Out Loud. Gather all your dialogues from exercise four in this chapter, and any dialogue you've written as part of other exercises, and one by one, try reading them out loud. One of the characters is supposed to be you; do you sound right saying what you've written? If you've got a patient friend, try reading together a dialogue meant to be between you two.

I always read all of my writing out loud at some stage of the drafting, often at many stages. Visitors think I'm nuts up there ranting to myself in two or three voices. But anything I can't say right, a reader is not going to hear right in her head.

Exercise Six: Monologue. I use a lot of long speeches by single characters, particularly in my journalistic work. Try re-creating five or ten minutes of someone giving a talk or someone passionately explaining an opera or someone giving you complicated directions. The trick is taking fast notes while you listen, writing them up immediately afterward, no putting it off.

Of course, a tape recorder will help, but the point of this exercise is training your memory. Use your tape only as an aid to check yourself.

Exercise Seven: Real Talk. Take a tape recorder to a gathering at which you know lively conversation will result: your poker night, a dinner party, reading club, family outing. You probably don't need to hide the machine; people forget it's there very quickly, and certainly you'll feel more honest (don't you think?) operating openly. Unless you can't operate openly. Or don't care about feeling honest.

Pick a section of the talk where things were going well conversationally, and type it up. That is, transcribe it. Get it all correct, and add tag lines.

Chances are, you'll have a lot of pages before you're through, and chances are even the most scintillating conversation you remember won't flow smoothly, won't hold tension, won't work as dialogue.

The assignment is to *make* your transcript work as dialogue. What must be cut? How do you set off one character from another? How different are the voices? Can you get the funny way Aunt Esther coughs before each pronouncement? Can you get Charlie's lisp? And so forth.

The idea is to think about how different actual conversation is from written dialogue, how much artifice is required to capture the truth of the mood and timbre of lively talk.

LOOKING AT EXAMPLES

As with every other writing skill, when it comes to characters talking, it's a good idea to look at the work of fine writers.

So, let's look at some dialogue from a master, Philip Roth, this from *Patrimony*, a memoir of his father (and particularly of his father's death).

> When finally my father seemed to remember Benjamin's presence, he looked up and said to him, "Well, Doctor, I've got a lot of people waiting for me on the other side," and with his head jutting out toward the bowl, he dropped his spoon into the Jell-O and resumed the attempt to eat something.
>
> I walked out into the corridor with the doctor and his aide. "I don't see how he could survive two operations like that," I said.
>
> "Your father is a strong man," the doctor replied.
>
> "A strong eighty-six-year-old man. Maybe enough is enough."
>
> "The tumor is at a critical point. You can expect him to have serious trouble within a year."
>
> "With what?"
>
> "Probably with swallowing," he said, and that, of course, evoked a horrible picture, but not much worse than envisioning him recovering not from one eight-hour operation on his head but now from two. The doctor said, "Anything can happen, really."
>
> "We'll have to think it all through," I said.

> We shook hands, but as he and his aide started away, he
> turned back to offer a gentle reminder. "Mr. Roth, once some-
> thing happens, it may be too late to help him."
> "Maybe it's too late already," I replied.

The drama here is certainly clear. Between the doctor and Philip
Roth is the imminent death of Roth's father. No problem finding
the dramatic center. I've plucked this bit of talk out of the middle
of a scene in the middle of a chapter in the middle of a book, but
note how much sense it makes; note the tension, the urgency. And
note the parts that aren't talk. Roth's father says his poignant piece
about people on the other side, and then there is silence. No one's
talking. Everyone is silenced by the first line of speech. Roth fills
this silence with his father trying to eat Jell-O. The silence lasts long
enough for Roth and the doctor to get out into the corridor. Their
talk fills in the facts, which we get as Roth gets them. His concern,
his surprise, his worry become ours. "Probably with swallowing,"
the doctor says. Then there's another silence. Roth fills it this time
with his thoughts at the time. His worry about his father's swallowing has been made visceral and visible to us by the earlier image
of the old man eating Jell-O.

More talk. Then a handshake, and one more silence in which we
get the image of the doctor walking away only to turn and say the
last devastating thing.

Roth's dialogue is never talk; it's always managed as a scene.
How? He doesn't forget the people who aren't talking, for one thing.
He remembers that talkers aren't just mouths, for another. He uses
what's called stage business: characters doing things while they talk.

Exercise Eight: Stage Business. Again, get out one of your dialogues. Does it contain stage business? That is, are people doing
things with their hands? Their faces? Are there silences? Are there
moments when one character forgets to listen to the other? Are there
background activities (traffic, music, wind)? Try adding the things
that are missing. How much adds to the drama? At what point does
too much start to take away?

What people do is as important as (and often more important
than) what they say. The marvelous thing about nonfiction is that

as writers, we already know what our people have done (the story needs only be dramatized, not made up), and even better, how they have done it. We know the way Mom holds her mouth when she doesn't believe a word we're saying; we know the way Mr. Collins lurches when he walks through the office; we know how the gas station kid smirks when we ask him to hurry. That is, we know these things if we've been observant.

Exercise Nine: Write First, Look Later. Pick one of your scenes from earlier exercises, one that portrays someone still in your life, a person you can be with. And then, go observe him or her. Have lunch, play tennis—life as usual—but as soon as you part company, write your person up: Note gestures, typical expressions, stance, quirks of manner, whatever is available. Then go back to your scene. What can you use and where?

GOOD OLD DESCRIPTION

I've saved description for last because a great deal of the work of character description gets done in the course of the scenes your characters make possible, in their dialogue and in their actions. But always, it's vital that your reader be able to see your characters clearly and that the picture in her mind have something to do with the picture in your mind as you write. Adjectives alone won't do the job; in fact, too many adjectives will serve more to obscure a character than reveal him. It's probably most effective to reveal your character in the course of a scene, trait by trait. And it's important to keep quietly reminding the reader of your character's physicality: gesture, hair style, clothing, posture, body English, *affect.*

Let me define that last word the way psychologists use the term. First of all, it's pronounced with the accent on the first syllable. It's not the same word as *affect* with the accent on the second syllable. And, it's very important as we think about making characters. *Affect,* the way I understand it, is the visible and otherwise tangible expression of personality, mood, and attitude. When we talk to a stranger, affect is what we see. Sad eyes, a downcast demeanor, sighs, halfhearted shrugs might be read as a depressive affect. A big smile, bared teeth, bright eyes might be seen as aggressive by one observer, happy by another. Some people—notably murderers in court—seem to have no affect. One's affect will change from interaction to interaction, and day to day.

Affect is what we want to capture when we try to portray one of our people. The depressive affect above I might lay out in the course of a long dialogue: first the sad eyes, later a shrug, and so forth, as my person speaks and is spoken to.

As always, lots of practice is the best way to get better, in this case the best way to simple, evocative description of your people. And, as always, reading as a writer is crucial. Here's a passage from *Great Plains*, by Ian Frazier (not incidentally one of my favorite books of creative nonfiction for the way it mixes so many elements of good writing and thinking, and for its humor). This is the opening of chapter six, and by now we know that Frazier is very interested in and very knowedgeable about the history of Plains Indians.

> One day, on the street in front of my apartment in New York (this was before I moved to Montana), I met a Sioux Indian named Le War Lance. I had just been reading a study of recent ecomomic conditions on Sioux reservations. The authors seemed puzzled that so few Sioux were interested in raising sugar beets or working in a house-trailer factory. As I waited for the light to change, I noticed that the man standing next to me resembled many pictures of Sioux that I had seen. I said, "Are you a Sioux?" He smiled and said, "I'm an Oglala Sioux Indian from Oglala, South Dakota." He said his name and asked for mine. He had to lean over to hear me. He was more than six feet tall. He was wearing the kind of down coat that is stuffed with something other than down—knee length, belted around the waist, in a light rescue orange polished with dirt on the creases—blue jeans lengthened with patches of denim of a different shade from knee to cuff, cowboy boots, a beaded leather ponytail holder. His hair was straight and black with streaks of gray, and it hung to his waist in back. After I saw him, I never cut my hair again. In one hand he was holding a sixteen-ounce can of beer.
>
> "Your name is Lou?" I asked. "*Lou* War Lance?"
>
> "*Le!*" he said. He pronounced it kind of like "leh" and kind of like "lay." He said it meant "this" in Sioux. I had never

before met anyone whose first name was a pronoun. Next to him was a compact woman with straight auburn hair. I had not thought they were together. "Do you know each other?" Le asked. She recoiled just perceptibly.

What is the center of drama between Frazier and War Lance? The center is the fact that Le War Lance is a Sioux Indian (as the scene goes on we learn the amazing fact that he is a grandson of Crazy Horse's, who we learn is a special obsession of Frazier's). Note the luxurious paragraph Frazier devotes to describing Le War Lance as he first saw him. He doesn't need to supply a guess as to the Oglala's age: The gray streaks in the Sioux's hair help the reader make her own guess. Frazier shows his own height and War Lance's by way of a quick comparison. The orange parka, the blue jeans, the hairband all give us the man. That Frazier never cut his hair again is about the power of the presence of Le War Lance, and this power is part of his affect. Le War Lance smiles at the initial question, "Are you a Sioux?" That friendliness is affect, too. That sixteen-ounce can of beer is a stage prop, of course, and has its meaning. It's not an elegant bottle.

Only when the description has been delivered does Frazier resume the dialogue. That long descriptive paragraph represents the moment of observation, that burst of time when we first see someone and gather in all the clues there are as to character. And Frazier gives us as many of those clues as he can.

The minor character—the woman with the auburn hair—gets minor treatment, but not *no* treatment. We see her size, her hair, and an important bit of affect: She recoils when she has to interact with our writer! This lets us see the writer as a character, too. He's been studying the conditions of Sioux reservations in his room so long that women actually *recoil* when they see him. So all three characters are dealt with, none forgotten, even while Le War Lance is at center stage.

Exercise Ten: Description. I don't want to ask you to describe a character, because that will result in a block of description that happens outside a scene, a character doing nothing, a character who's not in the moment (and listen to me, Grasshopper: A person who's not in a moment is dead).

Instead, I want you to work up a clear picture of your character in action, in a scene, talking. So, once again, get out one of your dialogues. (If you don't have more than one, perhaps it's time to go back and write a bunch. Take your time. And quit paving the road to you-know-where.) Pull out one of your dozens of dialogues—you as character speaking to another person as character—and add character traits, give clues as to affect. Help us see the person even as she's speaking, even as she's walking; give us the person *alive*. And while you're at it, find ways to sneak in some description of yourself.

And keep that central drama clear.

MINOR CHARACTERS

A note on minor characters: Use them. Every person you mention should get a quick, sharp, devastingly exact sketch. Help your reader see each person, no matter how minor. If a ticket taker gives you directions, be sure to show us his toupee. If a kid down the street shouts an epithet as you drive past, let's see the kid's freckles and not just the upraised middle finger.

The travel writer and novelist Paul Theroux does remarkable things with minor characters in his travel books. With deft strokes he nails the man on the train, the customs official, the idiot tourist. Joan Didion is magnificent at capturing the small player fast. John McPhee populates his books with unmistakably individual people, no matter how small the role. George Dennison—who lived in the next town from me in Maine—describes neighbor after neighbor with such precision in his journals (edited and published posthumously as Dennison's last book, *Temple*) that I know them and recognize them in town. The best lesson is always to read.

As a matter of revision, come back to your people over and over again. Crack open each person as you have learned to crack open each scene. Talk to those people who are available to speak, telling them or not about your project. Don't let them go till you've got them right, on paper, so right and so true that any complaint will be unfounded. The truth is always your best protection.

A CHARACTER TALKS BACK

I put my feet up and just daydreamed, sitting by the woodstove, home in Maine, teaching done for the week, new snow on the ground, perfect afternoon. My *Harper's Magazine* piece had come out, my novel was going pretty well, life aside from writing was good. The phone rang. My dad.

He said, "I've been checking *Harper's* every month and here it is, here you are! Wonderful, chief! Let me just take it home and read it, and I'll give you a call, tell you what I think."

"Sure, Pop." Oh, man. I'd sort of put off telling him any more about when the piece would come out. I just thought it best if I let life go on as always: My dad never one to read *Harper's*; I never one to insist he did.

My calm afternoon was busted. A *character* had called me on the phone and was about to pass judgment on his portrait. My editor at *Harper's*, Colin Harrison, had called the rendition of my father "loving." But still. I'd said stuff about my dad's and my relationship that I had never said to him, that had gone unsaid. I'd told the world what aftershave he used. I'd confessed to goofing off in school, and much worse!

When the phone rang again, it was my dad. He was crying. Sobbing and trying to speak. I had never heard the man cry before, didn't know really he was capable of crying. I was alarmed. I had done this thing. He cried and sobbed and managed to say he liked the piece; it was a hell of a piece. He said a lot of stuff that hadn't exactly gone unsaid before, but now it got said directly: He was proud of me; he loved me.

He said the piece was true, that he recognized himself, that he was maybe a little sorry to recognize himself. He said I surely over-dramatized a little, that I didn't get everything exactly right. He said, for example, that he didn't ever use Aqua Velva. It was Old Spice. He asked how the car was running.

Here we were nearly forty and nearly seventy, and we were talking as we never had, taking the first firm steps toward a relationship as adults.

I didn't write "Into Woods" to communicate with my father. I just wrote it to say something I had to say, something that turned out to be true. But my dad and I talked. We talked.

SIX

STAGE PRESENCE

> I write the way I write because I am the kind of person I am. . . .
> I am a woman and I write from that experience. I am a black
> woman and I write from that experience.
>
> —Lucille Clifton

Dear reader, I'd like you to do an exercise before I say a word about
stage presence or anything else in this chapter.

Exercise One: Epistolary Discovery. Please write a letter to
someone you haven't seen in a very long time, explaining yourself.
This should *absolutely* not be a letter you intend to send. The person
may be alive or dead. Go, write.

Later, I'll come back to this one with some explanation and rationale (and all that other left-brain stuff). For now, just write your
letter.

HAVING A VOICE

Mick Jagger has a distinctive voice, for example. So much so that
when you hear him in the background of "You're So Vain," singing
backup to Carly Simon in the famous chorus, you know it's Mick
Jagger. Couldn't be anyone else. Similarly for every great or even
really good singer. Ella Fitzgerald is Ella Fitzgerald. Maria Callas is
Maria Callas. Van Morrison is Van Morrison. Liz Phair is Liz Phair.
Louis Armstrong is Louis Armstrong, both voice and trumpet, and
there's no mistaking either. Imitations amuse, but seldom (if ever)
fool us completely.

What accounts for our immediate recognition? In singing it's a
matter of a thousand factors coming together, some a matter of

study and control, others part of an innate gift. There's phrasing (how long do you hold the first syllable of the second line?), there's timbre, there's modulation, there's the simple pronunciation of words, there's breathing, there's authority, there's mood and attitude, there's regional inflection, on and on, some factors a matter of utmost mystery, some of science.

Same in writing. How do you account for voice on the page? How is voice on the page the same as literal voice, the voices of your friends speaking, their unmistakable tones and cadences and enthusiasms, which, even recorded on the cheapest answering machine through static, even with the bar brawl in the background, are plainly their own?

I confess, I don't know the answer.

But every reader knows a false voice when he hears it, knows an imitative voice, knows an unsure voice. Officiousness, tentativeness, coyness, every form of dishonesty, vanity: It all comes through. If an essay is a conversation with the reader, then you must not only have a voice but be able to control it such that most readers hear the exact *you* that you want to project.

A FEW STRONG VOICES

Let us analyze a few strong nonfiction voices. As you read the examples to come, think about what makes the person behind the words apparent to you. Whom are you picturing? What age? What face? And so forth.

Our first example is from *Minor Characters*, a memoir by Joyce Johnson (also a novelist, *In the Night Cafe*, and a journalist, *What Lisa Knew*). *Minor Characters* is Johnson's story of coming-of-age in the fifties. The title gives reference to the fact that she was a minor character in the story of a major literary figure, Jack Kerouac (she was his girlfriend for a time). In her own story, of course, and in her own conception, and very quickly in the reader's mind, she's a major character. The tension of these two points of truth—minor, major—make the dramatic center of this book. Here's the opening paragraph of the second section of chapter three.

> It's the spring of 1949 and I'm thirteen and a half. With my
> best friend Maria, I am sitting in the very front seat of the top

deck of a double-decker bus as it makes its way down lower Fifth Avenue toward Greenwich Village, which I've been assured is the very last stop—thus impossible to miss. Suddenly we see it, the famous arch that's supposed to be the entrance to Washington Square and to lots of other things—perhaps a life of romance and adventure—that I've heard about from four older, very knowledgeable Trotskyite girls whom I've met in the basement of Hunter College High School. Juniors who disdain the bourgeois cafeteria upstairs, they lunch secretly on yogurt deep in the locker room. They carry bags of knitting under which there are copies of the *Militant*, which they hawk around Fourteenth Street nearly every day after school. They have Trotskyite boyfriends whom they make sweaters and argyle socks for and endlessly discuss. They never quite explain to me what *Trotskyite* is, but it seems that if you are one, you're headed for trouble not only with the fascists but with detestable teen-age Stalinists who've been known to harass sellers of the *Militant* and even beat them up. I admire the daring of these girls tremendously, their whole style, in fact—dark clothes and long earrings, the cigarettes they smoke illicitly, the many cups of coffee they say they require to keep them going. Friendly as they are, however, they never invite me on their rounds. With Olympian disinterest, they delineate a territory that it's up to me to explore for myself.

You'll note, I hope, all the background information seemingly effortlessly provided: who, where, what, when, why, and how. But let's think about what makes this brief passage so unmistakably Joyce Johnson. For one there's the length. This paragraph is long, with a calm, rich pace. There's a sense of capaciousness and time, of confidence, of comfortable, adult intelligence. She's going to tell us what needs to get told, and we're going to listen. The tone is slightly ironic throughout—this is a thirteen-year-old self she's writing about, after all, and, of course, all these years later she knows infinitely more about life and knows how silly the longings of youth can be. And yet there's an elegiac tone as well, a whiff of nostalgia, an acknowledgment that for all the silliness of Trotskyite girls there was real romance in the air in 1949, and real possibility. The tone is compassionate, as well: Johnson does not judge her younger self, and only mildly the Trotskyites.

I could go on (and I hope you will continue this analysis), but the most important thing to note is how many layers really exist here, how it is possible to be both ironic and compassionate, how it is possible to mingle the present (the writer sitting at her desk, remembering) and the past (the writer as a present-tense teen), the elegance of these sentences juxtaposed to the awkwardness of young adulthood. *Voice arrives in contrasts.* And voice, please realize, isn't a matter of conscious artifice so much as it is a matter of personality. Of affect, when you think about it (accent, you'll remember, on the first syllable).

When a new writer defends his "style," the teacher smiles (or cringes) because real style isn't an artifice; real style—voice—arrives on its own as an extension of a writer's character. When it's done self-consciously and purposefully, style becomes affectation and as transparent as any affectation (an English accent on an old college chum from New Jersey, for example).

More than anything, voice, the magic of a person appearing on the page, is the result of years of writing practice, of a writer getting so fluent in her medium that the medium itself—in this case words—doesn't get in the way of expression.

But voice is also a matter of urgency. Of passion. Of the clarity of a writer's caring about her subject deeply and deeply caring about communicating it to her reader.

A Stylish Obsession

Let's look at another example, this one from *U and I*, by Nicholson Baker, a funny and poignant and honest and urgent account of Baker's fascination (that's not to say obsession, which Baker admits is a tad bizarre) with John Updike. What follows is the first paragraph of his chapter nine.

> I would never have done it either—drag in *The New Yorker* name so obviously to get his attention—except that *life was too short* not to. Those ticking seconds of signature might be the only chance I would ever get to embarrass myself in his presence. When the excessively shy force themselves to be

forward, they are frequently surprisingly unsubtle and over-direct and even rude: they have entered an extreme region beyond their normal personality, an area of social crime where gradations don't count; unavailable to them are the instincts and taboos that booming extroverts, who know the territory of self-advancement far better, can rely on. The same goes for constitutionally ungross people who push themselves to chime in with something off-color—in choosing to go along they step into a world so saturated with revulsions that its esthetic structure is impossible for them to discern, and as a result they shout out some horrible inopportune conversation-stopper, often relying on a word like "pustulating," when natural Rabelaisians—who afterward exchange knowing glances with each other that say "Sad—way out of his league"—know to keep their colostomy sacks under wraps for the moment. Which referenced sacks bring us to the second time I met Updike—for I did, as it happened, get a further opportunity to embarrass myself.

Nicholson Baker is a stylist, no doubt about that, but style—the choice of words, the speed of phrasing, the grandness or plainness of syntax—is only one of the many layers that create voice. Because, honestly, almost anybody can elevate his language. Almost anybody can reach to the heights of sesquipedalianism. Almost any good writer can throw together a wry passage, full of allusion. But almost nobody (one person in fact) can make a Nicholson Baker paragraph. His sense of humor is alive in there. His irritable and almost microscopic vision of the world (compare this to Joyce Johnson's more sweeping and romantic view) makes us laugh or bridle. His willingness to invoke colostomy sacks alongside mortality, his ability to show himself while hiding—all of it is a matter of voice, all of it uniquely Nicholson Baker.

A Comfortable Intimacy

Now I'll reproduce a much different example, this from *A Childhood: The Biography of a Place*, by Harry Crews.

> My fifth birthday had come and gone, and it was the middle
> of the summer, 1940, hot and dry and sticky, the air around

the table thick with the droning of house flies. At supper that night neither my brother nor I had to ask where daddy was. There was always, when he had gone for whiskey, a tension in the house that you could breathe in with the air and feel on the surface of your skin, and more than that, there was that awful look on mama's face. I suppose knowing what the night would bring, not knowing if it would be this night or the next night, or the morning following the second night, when he would come home after a drunk, bloodied, his clothes stinking with whiskey sweat.

Compare Crews' sentences with those of Johnson and Baker. All of their sentences are beautifully grammatical, all of them musical, but Crews' music is a different kind altogether. That last long sentence staggers and jerks like a drunk coming home. There's the sound of the language of his childhood, and very little of the sound of the writer at his desk, looking back. The imagery is sweaty and bloodied, not figurative (as are Baker's colostomy sacks), not grand and ironic (as is Johnson's invocation of the arch at Washington Square). Daddy is called daddy (this daddy actually Crews' uncle), no caps. There's a familiarity with the reader here, a comfortable intimacy. We're kin as we read.

With all three of these writers, we feel ourselves in their presences immediately, even in paragraphs plucked from the middles of things.

This authorial presence is like the stage presence of an accomplished actor or other performer: The artist comes on stage and captures the attention of everyone in the room with a mere smile, with a plain gesture, with an otherwise unremarkable nod of the head. And the crowd awaits her every move, every word. Stage presence.

When a writer—Johnson, Baker, Crews—comes on stage and within a few sentences has grabbed us, hooked us, called us in, made us ready to listen and listen more, we say that writer has *voice*.

Exercise Two: Letter Work. Cut the salutation from your letter; cut the initial small talk. What's left? (If the answer is *nothing*, you might want to pick another correspondent to write to, and try again.) Read the remaining paragraphs out loud, as a kind of essay.

What's the issue at hand? What's the dramatic center? Why did you pick the person you picked to write to?

I wanted you to make your letter before we discussed the exercise much, because I wanted you to write it truly, without trying to do a job of learning or analysis. It's not too late if you haven't written your letter yet. Go do it, now. Please.

But now that you have a letter in hand, here's the rationale: This is a *voice* exercise. I hope while reading your letter aloud that you noticed how powerful your writing is in it, how it has changed, how close your passion is to the surface suddenly. Then again, I know how hard it is to really hear your own stuff. In my classes, this exercise always produces the best writing of the term up to the time I assign it and leads to better writing after. Really, always. If you haven't felt the power of your letter, find someone you trust (but not the person you addressed, please) and read it to him or her.

Why so powerful? When we address a particular person (think of Montaigne and his friend La Boetie), we know exactly who we are. We know what the other person, our reader, knows about us. We know what the other will find of interest. We know what will bore her. We know what we can leave out. We know what's important. We know what's vital and urgent, and we know what constitutes information dumping. And all this knowing gives us a clear, confident, authoritative voice.

To whom do you suppose Joyce Johnson aims *Minor Characters*, or Nicholson Baker *U and I*, or Harry Crews his memoir? We can't know without asking the writers, of course, but the answers you come up with might be of great help in thinking about your own writing. To whom do you really *want* to be talking?

THE GHOST OF THE WRITER'S PRESENT

Time is perhaps the most mysterious part of voice. I've already talked about the writer, at her desk. Let's call that layer of time in an essay or memoir the *writer's present*. In the writer's present, you can serenely look back on all aspects of your life. The voice the reader hears is you, now, operating with the benefit of hindsight, quietly contemplating even the worst disasters. This is the voice of your exposition, for the most part, the voice the reader most closely identifies as yours.

But your scenes take place in time, back in the past. While the reader is reading about 1928, she's *in* 1928. Let's call this the *story's present*. Now the voice your reader hears is the voice of the scene, a voice in a time, often the voice of the person you were at the time.

The writer may comment from her desk and from another time, but the two voices—past and present—must be carefully separated, carefully managed. To separate and manage multiple voices—multiple layers of time—in a single piece, the writer of memoir (that's you) needs to be aware of multiple voices, multiple pasts, aware of all the selves that may appear and be necessary to do the job at hand.

A SAMPLE LETTER

Here's just a small part of a letter by an Ohio State graduate student named Vicki Schwab. Note the clarity of the voice as it travels through time.

Dear Aliah:

The night your father died, Jim came for us and took us to the hospice. He walked with you hand in hand, back to where your father lay and watched you climb on the bed and felt you kiss him on his cold brow. *He's so white*, you remarked. Psychologists say that children of three do not understand death—its finality, its various aspects, but I know you did. One night, after a visit during which he tried to explain what was happening to his body, you cried hysterically for nearly an hour and I could not comfort you. I was afraid something in you might break.

The night of your father's death, Jim recalled at the memorial service, you asked to return—by yourself this time—and Jim and you once again made the trip down the long hallway. He waited at the door while you scrambled once again onto your father's chest, kissed him once more and said goodbye out loud.

Jim, who rarely cries, did at this moment of retelling.

When you are older, I have a vintage bottle of red wine to give you—very expensive—which your father bought in honor of your birth. The bottle is wrapped in yellowing newspaper

> containing an article about how he was in trial in Cleveland
> and raced home to see you newly born.
> What wonderful gifts we've been given, you and I.

Needless to say, this letter, this *try*, is built in a deep cushion of layers. Written to a daughter too young to read it, perhaps for reading later on in her life, it is really a letter to the dead husband. The grief and all the anger of grief, the sorrow, the shock, are motherly restrained, but all that emotion gives numinous radiance to each sentence.

The voice is contained in the relationships here but also in the layers of time. Vicki scans a whole decade past but looks to the future.

To address the daughter is hopeful, is to address life. To address the husband would have been to address death. The voice of this passage is multiple, arrives in layers of time, of address, of emotion, of luminous mystery.

Exercise Three: Finding a Public Voice. Pick one of your exercises from earlier in this book, or any of your nonfiction writings. At the top, write "Dear _____," adding the name of the correspondent you used in exercise one of this chapter. How must what follows the new salutation change to accommodate this special listener?

Try aiming your prose at different correspondents. Who gets you closest to a voice you recognize as your own? Who lets you say what's on your mind? Let this person into the room as you write.

Who makes you cringe most, censor yourself? Kick this person out of your writing room, forcibly. Write up a restraining order, if necessary. Call the cops.

WHO'S LISTENING?

Voice, of course, is inextricably tied with audience. If the first question is, Who's talking? the second question has to be, Who's listening? If you're going to write about your experiences growing marijuana, how might your essay sound if written for *High Times*? How might it sound for *The Atlantic Monthly*? How might it sound for *State Police Monthly*? Conversely, if you're going to write about being a narcotics officer, how might your essay sound in front of different audiences? Easily, we see ourselves shifting tactics, shifting affect, shifting, shifting, shifting, to accommodate possible listeners. But eventually—this is important—eventually, if you're going to be a writer and not a hack, you will want your voice to be the same for all listeners. As in life, you will want to come to know who you are.

When I was nervous going to a party or a job interview back in high school, my mother would reassure me: "Just be yourself." The advice was good, but I'd walk around doubly flummoxed, trying to be cool and trying to figure out what *myself* meant. Who was I supposed to be? What self?

Selves—wow—selves are awfully complicated. That's what Scott Russell Sanders means (as quoted in chapter five) when he says that for a writer "The I is a narrow gate." I'm a different person in important ways when I speak at some big university function than when I speak at my best friend's wedding, and both are different from the person I am when I sweet-talk my dogs or bark at them. As a professor I'm different than as a husband (and my wife lets me know when I'm not: "Don't get didactic with *me*!"). I'll pooh-pooh the alcoholic excesses of my college students at the same time I fondly remember the beer blasts of my college days (or last week, come to think of it). I'll make fun of sappy musicals, then go home and watch my wife's beloved tape of *The Sound of Music*. Which facets of this complicated *me* do I let into the stuff I'm writing?

And how do I use seemingly inconsistent or contrary parts of me to make my writing jump?

Exercise Four: "Against . . ." One of my favorite essays is Phillip Lopate's "Against Joie de Vivre." In it, he complains about dinner parties and other expressions of sociability and examines his complicated responses to a whole range of life's supposed joys.

Let's go back to chapter four and the "On . . ." exercises you've already done. Try changing the title to "Against . . ."

"Against Justice?" "Against Love?"

Just a try. Write a page or two. See if you are able to arrive at more complicated insights by way of negation, and see if more complicated insights allow for a more complicated—and more human— *you* on the page.

THE SOUL OF VOICE

Objectivity is the enemy of passion. And passion is the soul of voice. Soul, quite simply put, is the eternal and ephemeral difference between one person and the next. Or let us elevate the word to a proper noun: Difference. And Difference for a writer is what makes the artist, distinguishes him from the pack, from the hacks, from those whose facility with language makes them good mimics of what has gone before.

Emotion on the page is a curious thing. We've seen that imagery— scene—puts a dream into a reader's head. Voice adds emotion.

Exercise Five: Get Pissed on Paper. What makes you mad? I mean, really *steaming* mad, mad enough to throw something, mad enough to shout, mad enough to, well, what do *you* do when you're mad?

Some people get very quiet.

The exercise is to write about something that makes you mad and to do your best to *sound* mad. Let it rip. No restraints. I've got friends who will say they are mad but sound quite calm. Come on, man! What are you trying to hide? Other people will immediately resort to cursing, which isn't a bad way to show fury. But try subtler approaches, too. Just be sure anyone reading will get the idea that you're spitting nickels (as a furious secretary once explained to me in a loud voice), that you are *in a rage.*

The idea is not only to communicate but to make your reader feel the emotion you feel. And not just the heat of the emotion but the emotion itself.

Exercise Six: Okay, There Are Other Emotions, Too. What makes you happy? Can you get joy on the page without once men- tioning the word? Ecstasy?

And so forth. Envy, Love, Fear, Excitement, Loathing, Pride. How might you get each onto the page such that a reader will pick it up, feel it?

Exercise Seven: Method Writing. Actors have long used some- thing called the Stanislavski Method, which is still taught at The Actor's Studio in the West Village of New York City and many places elsewhere. Method acting, to oversimplify, is a matter of the actor remembering and really feeling intense emotion before performing a scene. So if he's supposed to be overjoyed at news of a victory, he remembers and sits with a time he felt overjoyed. His heart filled with that remembered joy, he begins to play his part.

I'd like to propose *method writing* for essayists. It's a matter of using remembered emotion to bring fresh emotion to the page. If you wish to write about your love of a particular kind of bird feeder, think first about your love for your spouse, say, or your first steady date. Get that heady feeling in your breast, even writing a little about the beloved. Then switch to bird feeders.

It's easy to get silly with this one. But if you are going to write about bird feeders, do so passionately. And if bird feeders don't matter, don't write about them. If you don't care and care deeply, your reader certainly won't.

Exercise Eight: Yelling in Public.

Exercise Eight: Yelling in Public. Part of the training of certain young Japanese businessmen has to do with shedding inhibition. These young executives have to go out into a crowded urban street and yell, at the top of their lungs, about how stupid they are. Probably you've seen film of them, red faces, open mouths, the crowds coursing past, staring.

Yes, this is your assignment. Go yell.

The idea is (1) to prove that nothing bad will happen to you if you show some extreme emotion and (2) to put you in a *really* embarrassing position so you won't be so embarrassed when it comes time to write passionately.

If you get arrested, well, then the idea is to show that you shouldn't listen to everything I tell you.

Exercise Nine: Imitations.

Exercise Nine: Imitations. In your reading, you've come across some memorable voices. This is an old saw of an exercise but still worth doing: Rewrite a passage of your own in the style of one or more of your favorite writers. But let's change that old word *style* to *voice*. The voice of a favorite writer.

The idea on the surface is to force a close analysis of what makes voice. The quieter result of a lot of work in this area is an unleashing of elements of your own voice. For in imitating others you may find yourself.

Exercise Ten: The Ultimate Voice Exercise. This is one of the hardest exercises I know, and one that can seem daunting. Ready? Voice (like so much of good writing) is a matter of practice. Your assignment is to do just that, for years on end, perhaps comparing one year's output to the next, watching your depth grow, your clarity, your acknowledgment of the complexities of the world. With luck (and hard work) you'll grow in other ways, too, over many years, and along with you, your voice will grow, richer, more beautiful, more irritable, more meaningful, more complex, more entertaining, more you.

WELL, THAT'S ME

I'll end this chapter with a small excerpt from Gow Farris's letter, which he addressed simply to "Brother," and which he read to us with huge passion, losing himself (I mean losing part of himself: that censorious and angry editor) entirely. He read a little then wept copiously while we waited—we were rapt—and then he read some more, lost in the sentences, and not one joke, not one self-trashing aside, not one insult fired at me. When he finished he looked up a little startled and said, "Well, that's me." And it had been. Nobody laughed at the self-dismissive joke he was trying to make. It was as if we'd seen a picture of Gow's thoughts, his most private and most lyrical mind in action. For the first time we'd seen the whole man. He said later he'd never written anything better in his life, never in forty years in the newspaper business. Maybe so, maybe so. I can only reproduce a little, by his permission.

> Dear Brother:
> You know exactly what I have done with my days because you have been with me all along. I have got you in my mind a couple years older than me with a beard and hair white as mine now. I have given you a life past death and you have aged past eighteen right along with me and you have been contrary mostly always and full of advice which I have taken or not taken. One thing you said (*you* said it, even though dead) was, *Do not marry Eloise.* But I did. Remember that river pilot in *Heart of Darkness* that opens the window on the boat no matter Marlow's warning and takes a spear through his chest? Brother, Marlow has to throw his shoes away, the blood is so bad.

SEVEN

FINDING THE FACTS

I know . . . how little I have researched, and what slender
pretensions are mine.   —Horace Walpole

Research. The very word sends my bedeviled undergraduates
groaning into the nearest pub. They want to avoid research because
they see themselves in the dusty stacks looking for ever drier facts,
boring themselves into oblivion in preparation for writing a paper
guaranteed to bore their teachers in turn and guaranteed to go
unread forever after.

I understand why they're wary, and why you might be, too.

But let's get one thing straight: Research is a creative process. And
just like other creative processes, research gets hampered when we
close down its possibilities, narrow too much our definitions.
Research doesn't only happen in the library. And assembling facts
and quotes on cards in advance of writing, as I was taught in high
school and attempted to do in college, just seems nuts to me now.

Well, research papers are research papers, and have their own
mysteries. But you and I, we're engaged in making true stories. Creative writing. The subject is always going to be in some way ourselves. We're searching. So everything we've done so far in this
book—every exercise—is research of one kind or another, though
I've assiduously avoided the word. Yes, research.

Our mapmaking has been research: What do I remember? Our
"On . . ." exercises, too: What do I think? Our scenemaking is
research, of course: Where have I been? Who was there? How did
it look and sound? Work on voice is investigative, too: How do I
feel? All leading to Montaigne's question: "What do I know?"

It's all an investigation. And with any luck our investigations have begun to lead us to the subjects we want to write about. Further, all this searching has begun to make it clear what's missing. What do we *not* know? Often the difference between quite good and publishable is the very stuff that research will produce, stuff you did not and could not predict finding, stuff you didn't know you needed.

By now you've got a subject. You've had at least one and probably quite a few ideas take off. Pages are accumulating. Perhaps you have a draft of an essay. Perhaps you have drafts of many essays. Perhaps some are advanced drafts. This is the perfect time to try some formal research, time to start reaching outside your mind. If we're going to operate in what John McPhee has called "the literature of fact," we better have the facts. Facts give us authority and accuracy, clarity and (believe it or not) heart.

Okay, you've loafed and invited your soul. Now it's time for the legwork. Which, if you love your subject (as you must), will be deeply and profoundly pleasurable, a treasure hunt with guaranteed riches at the end.

The question for this chapter is this: What do others know?

THE LIBRARY, STILL NUMBER ONE

If you're in a good-size city, you have a lot of choices when it comes to libraries. The public library is always a good start. But what about the local university? Some big schools have *dozens* of libraries, built over years by specialists to accommodate sophisticated and specialized needs. Corporations sometimes make their unique (not to say eccentric) collections available to the public. Historical societies, museums of all kinds, churches, planetariums, government bureaus, all of them may have libraries, from basic to comprehensive in scope, all with a particular controlling interest.

Even better, they all have librarians. I keep thinking of the grumpy reference man at the Biological Sciences Library at Columbia back when I studied there. I made the mistake of asking him where the men's room was. He scowled and grimaced and pointed: Leave. I found the bathroom on my own. When I came back in I saw a fellow grad student and sat beside her. I don't know why Mr. Librarian got so upset: The young woman and I were certainly talking about biological issues (and, okay, grinning and laughing and ignoring every book in the room)!

A couple of days later I was back. The guy remembered me all right. He pointedly ignored me as I slunk obsequiously to his throne behind the reference desk. But now I had a question: How do I find information on the dust glands of great blue herons? (I was writing a chapter for *Summers With Juliet* about a heron I'd spent an intimate morning's fishing with in Florida.) The librarian's eyebrows rose. His hooded eyes blinked, grew warm. All was forgiven. I wanted information and information was what he had. We marched about the library, comrades in arms, finding everything there was. He made calls for me to other libraries; he loaded my arms with books; he visited me with further information at my table, sent me three notes in subsequent weeks, helped me research further chapters. He made me an expert on herons and other things—I read what he found for me—and this new knowledge informed my book, though I used perhaps one percent of it and never mentioned the dust glands of herons.

Exercise One: The Good Old Library. Let's not make this too hard. Simply pick a subject that's come up in your writing of late. It might be as general as art or dogs or rivers or melons. It might be more specific: Michelangelo or Boston terriers or the Hudson or Catawbas.

Schedule a specific block of time, perhaps one you can manage every week (but don't steal writing time). An hour's fine, two hours will get you some depth, more won't hurt. Maybe you'll go after dinner, or around lunch (with the meal as a break), or before that Lawrence Welk Fan Club meeting downtown. Or how about scheduling library time and a movie? Library time and handball? Library time then a beer with the gang? Can you work this into your weekly schedule?

Anyway. The important thing for this exercise is to have a subject in mind and time to do it justice.

Go in with an empty notebook; come out with a full one and a stack of books to skim and explore (and sometimes fully read) in the week ahead.

You'll have gotten the important facts (for your essay about canoeing with your family when you were little): that the Hudson River is born in Lake Tear of the Clouds in the Adirondacks, that it's 315 miles long, named after Henry Hudson, 1440 feet wide at its widest, named the North River down by Manhattan, and so forth (quite endlessly—later you'll choose what to use). But you'll also have a pertinent quote from Washington Irving and know who the mayor of Newburgh was the year your grandfather lived there and that (surprise, surprise) your grandfather was mentioned by that mayor in a speech banning dogs from trolleys.

And perhaps your essay will take a turn.

THE INTERNET

Okay, cyberpunks, it would be hard *not* to know more about the research possibilities of the Internet than I. But one of the terrific things about the Internet is that you don't need to know a whole lot to get started using it for various forms of research. I know little of the terminology, none of the finer points; I just fire up my search engine, type in my subject, point, and click. Kind of fun. (The computer craze, I'm starting to think, might actually last longer than the CB radio craze of an earlier decade.)

Just like anyplace people congregate, there are piles of junk everywhere on the Internet. Unattributed sources, misinformation, outright lies, commercial hype. If you're just getting started, it might be fun to poke around a couple of hours (some people go in and never come back), always keeping an awareness that there is more caught in the World Wide Web (the initials WWW take longer to say than the actual words!) than recipes and naked people and rants by right-wing kooks meeting left-wing kooks at six on the clockface of politics.

As it happens, *Attache Magazine*, the in-flight magazine of U.S. Airways, has just asked if I want to write about upscale bull breeding. The assignment wouldn't have caught my interest except that I used to work on a Nebraska cattle ranch—which I'll get to talk about in my piece—and I have a real interest in the subject.

My first move in deciding whether to do the bull assignment will be to go to the Internet. This is not in lieu of the library—not at all; in fact, that's where I'll go for the science and background and history (with books, at least, I have a little assurance that the information I'll uncover has been vetted by people who know bullshit when they see it). At the library I'll make myself an expert. By contrast, on the Internet I'll play consumer: look for what's happening right now, find the names and numbers of players in the cattle breeding game.

I'll report back about what I find.

Exercise Two: The Internet. Chances are, you're way ahead of me on this one. If not, I'll give you the simplest instructions: Get yourself online, or find access at a university or coffee shop or friend's house, someplace where there will be a person smarter than I to help you. Get ready to bump up against yet another learning curve, but don't be too afraid (if a little kid can surf the Internet, you can at least put your toes in the foam after the waves break).

Start up Netscape or another browser, point and click on *search*, type your subject in the search box (a phrase is best), and get ready to wade through a lot of seaweed and gull feathers. Quickly, though, you'll learn to find the real information sources among the sales pitches.

Your assignment, beginner or expert, is to find one useful fact or quote or bit of information and to write it into an existing paragraph on your subject.

Since we're talking about memoir and autobiography here, try punching in your own name. Don't be surprised with what turns up. Try punching in the names of your real-life characters—your people—to see if any surprises lurk. Certainly punch in the names of pertinent towns and companies and colleges. You'll be amazed, very likely overwhelmed.

CATTLE REPORT

Well. The first listing that came up in an Infoseek search: Cattle Breeding in Estonia. Seems to be part of a tourism/business-opportunity information package. Other listings (dozens of them) were commercial, as well, many offering bull semen for sale. Also bovine embryos. I took down the names and phones of a couple of companies thinking that a few phone calls might help me toward the kind of information I'm actually looking for. Who knows the world of bull semen better than people in the business?

Twenty-one "hits" later I find a possible score: The Cattle Breeder's Association, a home page complete with addresses and names and phone numbers. I list them all down, print a page of addresses, and I'm on my way.

PUBLIC RECORDS

Let's say you want to write about your great-grandfather's crazy life. Let's say it was so unconventional that no one talked about him much. Let's say that all those who remember the old bird are dead and gone, too. How might you track him down?

All kinds of records are carefully kept and carefully stored (and sometimes carefully concealed) by government, big and small. I'm indebted to investigative reporter Cheryl Reed Stricharchuk for some of the following ideas:

• *Property records* at a county recording office might tell you which houses Grandpa owned, when he moved, and will give dollar values, as well.

• *Court records* may turn up divorces, marriages, name changes, deaths, civil suits, criminal trials.

• *Probate records* will show deaths and inheritances, the latter sometimes in fascinating detail.

• *Police records* (available at county clerks' offices and at police department records divisions) will give voluminous information on convictions, arrests, even detailed reports from detectives' investigations.

Grandpa!

And there are myriad other public records: corporation and incorporation records at the Secretary of State's office, annual Securities and Exchange Commission reports, not-for-profit corporation reports, campaign contributions, loan records, minutes of meetings, transcripts of speeches, health inspections, driving records, on and on.

Some of my more intrepid students have used the Freedom of Information Act to get incredible material about activist parents, for example, or public figures. One student got hold of his own FBI file from the 1960s after prolonged and deathly dull and daunting interchanges with bureaucrats. The file had startlingly minute and private information, all he needed to complete his memoir of his noble and quiet work against the Vietnam War. His research led to his new project: a book about the FBI and privacy.

Several of my students over the years have looked into public records to investigate adoption—their own. One young woman, a marvelous writer named Beth Lindsmith, received via fax in her office a yearbook photo of her newly discovered birth mother (Beth wrote the slow appearance of the photo as a kind of birth—nice). She'd spent a year looking for *any* image. An interested school librarian had gone to the trouble for her. Beth's essay in the end was about her decision not to contact her birth mother.

Part of the research, when it comes to public records, is finding out which agency or library or bureau or office holds the paper or microfilm you want to get your hands on. Phone calls and visits to town and state offices do wonders. Often, the most daunting task turns out to be simple, and the simple-seeming turns out to be nearly impossible.

The point is that the information is out there for those willing to look. And sometimes the search becomes the story.

Exercise Three: Getting Started With Public Records. Which of your many subjects could use light from a little public information? Perhaps it will be something as simple as the exact address of your childhood home. Perhaps something as complicated as the number of farms in your home county the year of your birth. Perhaps hidden family information could be brought to light (one student's mother said she had never married the student's father; the father said he had indeed). Where to look for the truth?

The first step is to recognize the need for the information. This recognition is more complex than it may seem. A story may be quite good *without* any extra searching. But remember what I said at the beginning of this chapter: *Often the difference between quite good and publishable is the very stuff that research will produce, stuff you did not and could not predict finding, stuff you didn't know you needed.* It's not hard to write your way around a missing fact, but be assured that readers will notice any vagueness, will crave the extra level of information, of revelation, that your research will bring.

The second step is to pinpoint where any search should start. What's the nature of the information you want? Where would it be kept? Whom to call? Whom to write? Whom to fax?

The third step, always the hardest, is to actually look. Make the phone call, flip through the file, befriend the librarian, harangue the clerk (whose first answer, by the way, will always be "No").

The exercise? Come up with something you really do want to know, and then go in person to the appropriate office and find the facts. Follow your nose and instincts until you get all you started out to find. But be open to surprises; be willing to go down information paths you didn't expect to find.

The idea here isn't to become a famous librarian; the idea for now is just to get a little practice and get over the natural fear of musty files and chilly bureaucrats. Challenge yourself; take the dare. And listen, it's not like I'm asking you to bungee jump off the Space Needle in Seattle. Doing that, you might get arrested, mangled, even killed. What's the worst that's going to happen in your search for information? Someone might frown at you? Failure isn't deadly in this game. It's not even permanent. But success in research, now that's as exhilarating as any number of bungee jumps.

No, really!

Okay, maybe not.

But close.

PRIVATE RECORDS

Private records are pretty obvious research tools, yet too often on research missions I overlook the obvious: photographs, journals, letters, scrapbooks, and so on, my own and those of people who are willing to cooperate. Photographs are particularly helpful, adding detail to scene, correcting memory, providing clues to personality, restoring lost faces. No specific exercise here: Just remember to get out that box of photos, and remember that most of the people in your true stories have similar boxes and are dying to show someone.

FACE-TO-FACE RESEARCH

Much has been written in journalism and creative nonfiction texts about the art of the interview. Basically, I've found that interviewing for journalism is a matter of fooling your subject into revealing herself, perhaps in ways she'll wish later she hadn't. People love to talk, especially about themselves. Note-taking, the tape recorder, the endless questions, all are flattering, hard to resist.

But for the memoirist, interviewing is a more delicate tool. Your subjects aren't politicians, for example, who are used to public life and tough questions. Your subjects aren't hapless and immediate victims of accident or disaster. Your subjects aren't experts you have approached for facts and figures. Your subjects, in fact, are very often well known to you, very often relatives, sometimes even your mother. And Mom isn't going to be flattered by any tape recorder.

Further, your story may be one no one particularly wants brought up, much less written about. In many cases, you'll prefer not to have all the advice or censure that comes flooding in when a project becomes public property. Certain kinds of people will withdraw. Other types will try to control what's said about them, sometimes in unpleasant ways.

Then again, everyone may get excited about your project and want to be part of it: Uncle John calling to tell the old sunk-canoe story one more time, Dad sending over a typist, your college roommate unloading a U-Haul of photos in your driveway.

I mean, there are a million good reasons not to go to the people of your story and ask questions. But if a couple of questions will make the story better, all those reasons must be swept aside.

Interviewing even the friendliest witness takes a lot of nerve: You will be going past the small talk. But risk is what good writing's all about, no?

Exercise Four: Interview Somebody Safe. Pick a person who appears in one of your drafts. Your sister, perhaps, or your current spouse, someone who's on your side, someone who's going to be glad to be mentioned. Make it a formal interview, with prepared questions. Use a tape recorder, but take notes, too. Transcribe the interview as quickly afterward as possible; immediately is best.

Then go to the draft and write. How does the interview fit in? What must be changed? What parts get strengthened? Can you use any quotations from the chat?

Exercise Five: Interview a Stranger. Here's where the fun begins. Again, pick the memoir or essay draft you want to work on. To whom could you go for more information to add depth and light and exactitude? If you are writing about your house, could you find the architect who designed it? The builder who built it? A former occupant? If you're writing about your time in the Navy, could you interview someone who was brass then? A historian who has written about the battle you lived through? An expert on ships?

If your story is about your alcoholic brother, could you interview a counselor, a scientist, an ex-alcoholic? (In *The Perfect Storm*, a strong work of creative nonfiction about a boat lost in a terrible storm at sea, Sebastian Junger uses a brilliant device along these lines. In order to talk about what it must have felt like to drown—six men were lost at sea—Junger interviewed a man who had *almost* drowned, and in a similar disaster.) If you're writing about the pleasures of cooking—even a personal account—could you interview the chef at a favorite restaurant? People like to talk about what they do, and the more they like what they do, the more they want to talk.

The assignment? Get out there and interview someone.

Exercise Six: Interview Yourself. When I published *Summers With Juliet*, Houghton Mifflin asked me to write a self-interview, question and answer, that they could use for publicity purposes. Weird, man. I typed it up with someone named Interviewer asking all kinds of softball questions and someone named Roorbach answering them, oh so intelligently.

The exercise is to type up an interview with yourself, the idea being to learn a few things you don't already know and to find unexpected ways to say what needs to get said. Imagine that the story of your trip to China is big news—"Inquiring minds want to know"—and ask appropriate questions.

Better yet, picture yourself across from Barbara Walters in your living room. What kinds of questions is she going to ask? How will you handle the tough questions about your divorce, say, or that skeleton in your broom closet? Where will the heartwarming moments be? Where are the shockers? What will everyone be talking about tomorrow morning?

You might use a tape recorder for this one. But transcribe, no matter how difficult the task.

Exercise Seven: Get Someone to Interview You. A variation of the self-interview is to have a friend interview you. You might do this reciprocally with a fellow writer. Tell your interviewer in advance a little about your latest essay project, and let the interview focus on that material. When the talk's over, transcribe the tape (or transcribe for your partner and exchange transcripts).

The questions your interviewer asks are important: They let you know the kinds of things your readers will be interested in, let you know what's missing from your draft.

Exercise Eight: The Impossible Interview. Some people, you just can't talk to: the bad guys in your life, someone dead, former lovers, unsympathetic family members. In these cases it can be helpful to *make up* an interview. What questions would you like to ask? Well, go ahead, and then supply the answers you think your subject would give.

Certainly, don't start to believe the interview is real. No quotations from it. But use it to examine your own projections, your own role in relationships. Use it to discover the issue at hand. Use it to develop material.

Or use it to prepare yourself for a scary interview. Ask the questions on paper first, answer them yourself. Then go to your subject. What comes off as expected? Where are the surprises? What exactly was your own role in making the interview scary?

NAMING IS KNOWING

I keep asking if you remember my old student Janet Bellweather, the irascible schoolteacher I introduced in the first pages of this book. Well, folks, I'm thinking about her again.

Janet Bellweather wrote the following sentence as part of a scene depicting a violent spanking she got as a kid: "I stood alongside some flowers and watched as Grandpa closed the gate." Now, the soft spot in that sentence is the flowers. What kind of flowers are we talking about? Tall ones? Short ones? Dead ones? She fixed things up with a few well-chosen adjectives: "I stood behind some big, blue flowers. . . ."

But I sent her on a hunt: Find the name of those flowers.

The task wasn't going to be hard for her, she announced: She remembered the flowers well enough to recognize them if she saw them. Why, if it weren't midwinter she could drive around and find some right now.

Nothing happened for awhile. Then in April, Janet went home to her folks' small town for a visit. Janet popped the question: "You know those big blue flowers?" Her mother had no interest in plants but recalled that Janet's grandfather had made something of a hobby of horticulture: Every plant in his yard was some kind of trophy.

At the little library in town, Janet went through flower books till she found it: No question, the flower was a hydrangea. Yes, a bush, once she thought about it. And now she had this sentence: "I hid amid the big, blue flowers of Grandpa's prize hydrangea and watched as he closed the gate."

Driving back to the city, Janet spied a tree nursery just off the highway. Next exit, she pulled off, a few minutes for research. The nursery was in full swing: Easter lilies, saplings, perennials in flats. She asked one of the older nurserymen about hydrangeas. He knew they liked acid soils and came in colors, one a rare blue. He knew they bloomed late, August, at the earliest. Often September.

Janet motored home and went about her life and was happy to have this sentence: "I stood behind the rare, blue flowers of Grandpa's prize hydrangea—it was September—and watched as he closed the gate."

Only later did the problem hit her: What had she been doing at Grandpa's in September? (And only later did she edit out the awkward dash phrase.) Why hadn't she been in school?

Now she had a question her mother *could* answer. A long phone call led to the revelation that after Janet's drunken father had left the family (this much she knew about), Mom had got so upset she'd been unable to care for Janet or her sister and had left them at Grandpa's for two months. That's all. But it was two months during which Janet was spanked too often and too brutally in a fenced-in yard with hydrangeas, two months Janet had misplaced and partially forgotten.

Janet's essay took a turn. And before she was finished, she (and the essay) knew a few important things about her relationships with men and the bubbling anger that plagued her days.

Exercise Nine: Naming. Look for a vague spot in one of your drafts, some little bit of generic information: "a tree" (what kind of tree?); "our old car" (what make and model and year?); "the stream" (what was it named?); "the birds that flew around the pier" (what kind of birds?).

Do what it takes to properly name a tree, a piece of hardware, a street, a town, a school, a neighbor. Naming is knowing. Use maps and encyclopedias and phone calls and catalogs and the Internet and nature guides. Get that name. Even the smallest exactitude can lead to greater revelation.

NEED AN EXCUSE FOR TRAVEL?

Travel is a spectacular research tool. You're writing about your Peace Corps stint twenty years past? Go back to Guatemala. You're working on an essay about your heritage? Go visit that little town in Russia. Your essay is about craven American culture? Go study other cultures for comparison, firsthand.

Almost any essay could benefit from a trip somewhere. And the writer benefits as well. You might travel to interview someone. You might travel to see an author's grave. You might visit an old neighborhood to see how it's changed.

Exercise Ten: Travel. This one's pretty easy to articulate: Go someplace. Plan it now. An hour, a day, a weekend, a week—what's needed for the essay at hand? Really go, and really make use of the information you find, even if it contradicts memory or messes with your argument.

TALK

Too many writers (I among them) are shy about their subjects. "Too hard to explain," I always hear myself muttering. I wish I wouldn't, because so often a conversation on my subject has given me great ideas, helped me focus my argument, helped me learn what's needed. This is different from the formal interviewing above, in that your interlocutor isn't necessarily thinking of you as a writer, and certainly not thinking of your talk as an exercise.

I don't mean for you to go out and talk about your writing project *as* writing project—many writers find that this dilutes their work—

I just want you to entertain conversations on the subject about which you mean to write. You don't have to and probably shouldn't reveal that you're writing anything. Just ask the question: "Do you think it's possible to feel joy anymore?" Or make a provocative statement: "The Internet is a joke."

In the right company, you'll get what you're looking for: new ideas, new facts, new angles, new people to talk to, antithesis for your thesis, challenges to your thinking, occasionally a pithy quote.

Exercise Eleven: Talk. That's it: Talk to someone. Preferably someone smart. Tell her about your essay or not; maybe tell her what you're thinking about your subject. Then listen. Later, take notes. (This is good practice for when the time comes to talk to editors, as well.)

Or bring up your subject at the next dinner party during one of those silences when forks clink and throats get cleared.

Or just before the cotton gets stuffed in your mouth, ask your dentist what he thinks of insurance companies, if that's what you're writing about.

The idea is to reach out a little, to talk in advance and in person to a select few of your potential readers.

READING

General reading, unattached to a project at hand, is probably the best way to provision "the well-stocked mind" Elizabeth Hardwick has said an essayist must cultivate. If you read every day, your head gets filled with good lines from great books, with snatches of information from magazine articles, with examples of *the perfect way to say it* from any number of sources: novels, letters from ex-lovers, biographies, poems, plays, translations, textbooks (science, economics, philosophy, undertaking), and, of course, essays.

Exercise Twelve: Reading as Research. This is one of those continuing exercises, for a lifetime, in three parts, with part three offering the grand challenge: (1) Read a lot; (2) take notes on your reading, and keep records; (3) organize those notes and records in a way useful to your writing.

I know you already read a lot, because you've surely taken exercise two back in chapter one to heart. And probably you already take notes on your reading in some form. I write a lot in the end papers of most books while I'm reading. I write little notes on scraps of paper and transcribe quotations. I fill up notebooks.

Then I lose track of all of it.

I want to get organized, so I'm asking *you* to get organized. What's that all about? Still, I have advice: Label a stack of folders with various subjects you intend to write about in the next couple of years—*Intelligence of Pigs*; *Aggravation*; *Chocolate as an Aphrodisiac*. And then, as you bump into the odd fact or quotation or observation, you have a place to put it.

Another system is more random: folders with categories of all kinds—*Love*, *Gardening*, *Dogs*, *Parents*, you know. The trouble is, the categories just keep going and going, and it becomes difficult to know where to put an item about, say, keeping your beloved dogs out of your parents' garden.

The great challenge of this exercise is not so much to create a system, but to keep that system alive year after year by using it.

RESEARCH NIGHT

By now you've scheduled writing time and reading time. How about scheduling a research night? Say, every Tuesday. Head down to the library with a list of needs, or hop on the World Wide Web, or call a couple of people who know things you don't, making good use of the hour or hours allotted. Over time you'll get good at (and stop being shy or lazy about) finding out what you want to know and what your essays *must* know if they are to succeed.

EIGHT

METAPHOR AND MEANING

Censorship is the mother of metaphor.
—Jorge Luis Borges, as quoted by George Steiner

"Our washing up is just like our language," Niels said. "We have dirty water and dirty washcloths, and yet we manage to get the plates and glasses clean. In language, too, we have to work with unclear concepts and a form of logic whose scope is restricted in an unknown way, and yet we use it to bring some clarity into our understanding of nature."
—Werner Heisenberg, on vacation with Niels Bohr

Poetry provides the one permissible way of saying one thing and meaning another. —Robert Frost

When I say I "can relate" to a writer of memoir or to an essayist, I'm talking about a metaphorical process. Empathy is what I'm speaking of, the comparison between my experience and the writer's, the discovery that what has moved the writer moves me or that what has amazed the writer amazes me. If the subject of a given work of nonfiction were mothers, the analogy would go something like this: *I* am to *Reba* as *writer* is to *Eleanor*, with the named women being our respective mums.

Okay. That's complicated. Let me back up a ways and try to make it simpler. In fact, I'll go all the way back to a discussion I started in the introduction to this book, about the ongoing debate over the value of memoir. In that debate, one of the common (and often querulous) questions is: Who cares about Joe Blow's personal life? Or, What makes Jane Brain think I want to read about her life?

This complaint finds an echo (is presaged, really) when students tell me, oh, they started writing pretty well, got a few pages or even chapters into a true-story project, and just came up against a wall: Who's going to care about *me*?

The critics who ask, Who cares? (for instance, James Wolcott in the October 1997 *Vanity Fair*), really do have a point, up to a point. No one wants to read a dully written, self-serving, self-pitying memoir. And if that's the kind you're writing, that wall is there for a reason (and some particularly stubborn types will knock their heads against it for years). But your story isn't dull, and you aren't the self-serving or self-pitying type. Your story is important, resonates with family and friends and colleagues and acquaintances in ways you have seen or can predict. That's why you want to write it. That's why you can't abandon the project, even though repeatedly you come up against that wall of self-doubt.

Well, let the wee critic afraid of life complain his little complaints about memoir when people insist on writing their lives fearlessly. Let the bigger critic say whether a given memoir—once written—is good or bad. But let the writer (that's you) write.

Who's your favorite writer? The answer for me is such a long list that I just stare when I'm asked. But I ask it all the time of students (which proves what an insensitive beast I really am). When I asked my class last summer, one woman said, "Mary McCarthy."

I got all huffy, playing the wee critic above, said, "Why Mary McCarthy? Who cares about Mary McCarthy? Why would you want to read Mary McCarthy's life?"

My student said, "Because she's like me."

Another student, also a woman, said, "Tobias Wolff."

I said, "Why him? He's nothing like you."

"But he is," said she, growing indignant, and without commas: "I mean our experiences aren't the same and our circumstances aren't the same but he's a person like me and we have that in common and it's enough to make me endlessly interested in him."

"He's a good writer," our calm class physician said. "That's why Marilyn's interested, and that's why I, too, like Mr. Wolff."

"Tobias Wolff is good because his material is good," a young man said.

The first student said, "His material is himself. And I have a self, too. There's a comparison there."

A comparison, I will add here, that is always implicit: You and me, we're the same. And, of course, one of the most interesting forms of comparison is contrast: You and me, we're different.

The reader, in a process based on metaphorical thinking, stands in for the *I*. It's subtle, but when we read the word *I*, we think of ourselves, we see ourselves in action; we feel ourselves in someone else's shoes, someone else's *I*, as it were.

Take an example from our work lately: When you let someone read your letter assignment from chapter six, that reader feels himself addressed, feels himself standing in for the person addressed: *You* equals *me*. The reader, by a metaphorical process, has *become* the person addressed, even while (obviously enough) holding on to his selfhood.

And he's become someone else, too: the writer. Preconsciously or unconsciously (and sometimes very consciously), reader and writer of a true story share a name, always, and that name is *I*.

(Note that as I use the generic *he* above, I add a layer of metaphorical substitution for women as readers. That's why I mix *she* and *he* as my generics throughout this volume and in all my writing: Spread the substitution.)

Exercise One: I and I Vibration, Yeah (Positive).

Go to a favorite writer, someone writing nonfiction with a strong voice, a strong *I*. Terry Tempest Williams is a good example, or James Baldwin or Charles Bukowski or May Sarton.

Read aloud. Read a *lot* aloud, say, ten pages, twenty. Do this by yourself: You're not putting on a show. The exercise is to feel the *I* in the work. To yourself be that *I* for the length of the pages you read, to consciously experience what is normally unconscious, to be the writer's *I* while being your own *I*, to feel what's different, to feel what's the same.

The point of this nutty behavior is to get a feeling for the power of that little word, how it invites a comparison of nothing less, really, than souls. The point is to get a sense of what a universal set of clothes the word *I* and the concept *I* really is. The point of the exercise is to wear some other writer's *I* so as to better understand your own writerly *I*. This is the first step in understanding why someone else, some stranger, some reader out there, would want to read about *your* life.

(The cryptic title of this exercise is a line from a Bob Marley song, "Positive Vibration." In Jamaican English, "I and I" can mean "me and you" and also "me and my friends.")

No man is an islande!

METAPHOR, THE SOURCE OF ALL MEANING

Okay, so the reader makes a comparison between herself and the writer she's reading: I'm *like* this writer (or not like him). Or even, in the flush of reading: I *am* this writer, leaving out the *like*. That helps answer that awful question, Who wants to read about *me*? But metaphor plays a number of other roles in the success of a good work of nonfiction, roles you'll want to understand as you approach your own work.

Let's talk some more about metaphor in general terms before we turn to the specifics of using metaphor as a tool in the making of memoir and essays, before we turn back to gathering awareness of the power of metaphor in our own writing. Language, after all, is the basic tool of any memoirist or essayist, and metaphor, as we shall see, is the elemental condition of language. It's time to add a new layer of understanding to your use of language, a new tool to your box of writerly skills and talents. A deeper and more complex understanding of metaphor than you now enjoy will enrich your relationship with language, put you in greater control of its use.

So let's back up a little farther, all the way back to high school: English teachers forever have been saying, "A simile is a comparison using *like* or *as*, and a metaphor is a comparison not using *like* or *as*." That's simple and plain, but it's not quite right. I'll buy the old definition for a simile, but a metaphor—wow!—a metaphor is something enormously greater than allowed for by Mr. Hanrahan-Bottomlifter back in ninth grade. First of all, a simile is just a *kind* of metaphor. A symbol is a *kind* of metaphor. An analogy is a *kind* of metaphor.

Metaphor is big, and gets bigger the more you think about it. It is the source, friends and neighbors, of all meaning.

Yes, metaphor is a comparison. Ho hum. But consider this: Comparison is the basic gesture of the human mind. Closer, farther. Lighter, darker. Bigger, smaller. Safe, dangerous. Then, now. And comparison, if I may be so bold, is the basic tool of the creative writer at work.

Exercise Two: A Mind Like a Steel Trap. A steel trap is one of those devices used in cartoons to capture Elmer Fudd and in life to capture fur-bearing animals. A steel trap is a pair of tempered-steel crescents joined by a powerful spring triggered by a round plate of steel. When an animal steps on this plate—wham—his leg is caught, often broken. The trap is staked to the ground at the end of a stout chain so a captured animal can't wander off.

Okay. A mind like a steel trap. What's the metaphor here? Let's see. You're so smart you hold on to an idea while it thrashes around and finally chews its leg off to escape, leaving you with only the leg of an idea and a bloody legacy of brutality? Or, as the comedian Steven Wright says, "I've got a mind like a steel trap: rusty and illegal in thirty-seven states."

Okay, okay, the assignment: In a long paragraph, compare the workings of your mind to something—anything—else. (Anything, that is, but a steel trap.) Don't be afraid to write the obvious: In classes, everyone thinks her idea is the obvious one, but never in ten years has a single class of mine produced two metaphors the same.

To get the sentences flowing, extend the comparison—the metaphor—as far as you can, to the very absurd edges of correlation.

In the steel trap cliché above, I immediately went to the ridiculous. But I left out a couple of things. If your mind is like a steel trap, what is the spring? What is the steel plate that triggers the release mechanism? If animals are ideas and minds are traps, do minds destroy ideas? Do ideas have lives separate from minds? Do ideas roam the wilderness? What are the furs of ideas? And tell me this: Who is the trapper running the trap line? What's the chain? What's the stake?

Here's a little Wallace Stevens to get you on your way.

> I was of three minds
> Like a tree
> In which there are three blackbirds.

UNDERSTANDING METAPHOR

Let's consider some of the many forms metaphor takes before we get back to writing.

Think, for example, about those troublesome analogies on the SAT. You know, x is to y as xx is to yy.

Here, let's do one. Fill in the blank: *Train* is to *track* as *airplane* is to _____.

Most would say *sky*.

Each element of an analogy is called an analog. In the above example, *train* is the analog for *airplane*, *track* is the analog for *sky*. All are comparisons not using *like* or *as*, by the way, and certainly metaphorical. And in this example (as in most) magical. No, I mean it: magical.

Think of it: Our minds easily and completely accept the idea that dense, heavy bars of extruded steel manufactured by humans are similar to—analogous to—the sky. Which is air.

Kenneth Burke, in his challenging book *A Grammar of Motives*, says that metaphor "brings out the thisness of a that." Aristotle speaks of the way metaphor helps us understand the unknown or slightly known by comparing it to what's known.

SYMBOLS

Stop signs are metaphors in that they are symbols. Symbols stand in for something, mean something else, something greater than themselves and not inherent in themselves. We've come to agree that a red octagon (my father claims they used to be yellow) with the following white shapes on it—S, T, O, P—will mean something particular. In practical terms, it means law-abiding types will put right feet on brake pedals till the motion of their vehicles is entirely arrested. The sign is a command to make your vehicle's status an analog for a word meaning, a meaning that is itself an analog for a condition in nature—stoppedness.

The Nike swoosh is a metaphor in the same way. The swoosh isn't the company. The swoosh isn't a sneaker. The swoosh merely invites us to consider the company, to compare the swoosh to what we know of the company. Swoosh does not equal Nike; swoosh only represents Nike and this representation is a form of comparison.

And, of course, most words are symbols, most language metaphorical (or, actually, if you believe Jacques Derrida, *all* words. It would take a Ph.D. candidate in English to explain, and I happen to have one right here—Jennifer Cognard-Black from Ohio State: "Give me an instance of language that *isn't* a representation. Even articles are metaphorical—although they don't stand in for a real world thing or action, they *do* stand in for an idea or concept; *a, an, the*, and conjunctions—*and, but, for*—have no *meaning* in and of themselves").

These letters—*T R E E*—aren't a tree, though they make me think of one. And my thinking of a tree (I can see one clearly in my head, right now) isn't a tree, either. I've a conception in my mind that I compare to the great plants outside my window and both of which I compare to those four letters above and to a sound I can make with my lips. The sound isn't the plant or the letters or the conception, but a fourth element of the *tree* continuum.

ETYMOLOGY, METAPHOR, AND THE WRITER

Etymology, the study of the origin and development of words, amounts to the study of a long record of meaning shifts along metaphorical paths. To be a student of etymology is to have subtle layers of meaning at your command as you write. Probably, you've perused *The Oxford English Dictionary* from time to time. It's a fine tool for the amateur etymologist. In a standard American dictionary, definitions are listed and numbered from most used to least used, from major meaning to minor. The OED, by contrast, is a historical dictionary. Its definitions are numbered from oldest to newest, and there's a lot of fun in there, a lot of useful knowledge, the fullest meaning and nuance of every word laid out before you.

Here, by way of example, is something I just learned in the OED: The Romans used a stone sledge called a tribulum to grind and crush corn down to meal. When Christians came along, they found their torment at the hands of their Roman oppressors to be like what happened to corn under the stone. *Tribulation* is the resulting English word.

Metaphor is often hidden in this manner, hidden in the words we use every day, lost in the etymological shuffle. We still know that *discard* is something that happens in a game of gin, but at the same time we freely talk about discarding unwanted objects that aren't playing cards: a broken couch, an old dress, a page of manuscript. We even discard notions. The comparison we are making to the move in a card game is largely forgotten. A *pedagogue*, now a teacher, was once a slave—what's the etymological story behind that comparison-then-meaning-shift (and how far have we really shifted)? See the OED. A *gossip* was a godparent, the person who knew the story behind the closed gates of the neighbor's castle. Comparison extended the word meaning to anyone who knew and told secrets. Simple words, too, arrived at their present-day meanings through comparison-driven meaning shifts: *Corn*, for example, referred at first to any hard particle. To *inspire* was to breathe life into (generally God's job).

This is kind of fun, no?

The ancient Greek meaning of *metaphor* is to carry over. We carry meaning over from one object or analog to the next.

METAPHOR IN DAILY LIFE

Once you start looking, you'll see metaphor at work everywhere. Headlines, for example, are full of obvious metaphorical usage: "On the Front Lines in Battling Electronic Invader"; "War Rages On"; "Police Chief Escapes Suspension"; "The Pennsylvania U.S. Senate Race Is the Crown Jewel of Tuesday's Balloting"; "Devotees Sing Praises of the Swiss Army Knife on Its 100th Birthday."

Some of the metaphors in the examples above are *lost* metaphors or *dead* metaphors. We've used them so much we forget their sources. But still, can't you see that police chief hanging suspended under a bridge? Or a bunch of knife lovers singing in a chorus: "OH HOW WE LOVE (HOW WE LOVE) OUR SWISS ARMY KNIVES!" Or Senators Kennedy and Helms in gym shorts and sweatbands running a foot race?

And the expressions we commonly use (so commonly, in fact, that most are clichés—used so much and for so long that their luster and humor and grace are gone) are largely metaphor of the simile persuasion: strong as an ox; built like a brick shithouse; dead as a doornail (a doornail is that plate under the knocker, banged to death by visitors); rich as Croesus (he was the last king of Lydia, sixth century B.C., and rich as Bill Gates); life ain't all beer and Skittles (as my father used to say). Some unimaginative speakers compare absolutely everything to one thing: hot as hell, fat as hell, happy as hell, clean as hell. Don't do this in your writing if you want to delight readers. Spend the time it takes to come up with something new: happy as a hammer?

Lawyers make use of metaphor when they draw analogies between old cases and their cases at hand: "Your Honor, I refer you to Brimsly vs. Youngstown." Psychologists, if they aren't nuts-and-bolts cognitive-behaviorist types, find huge meaning in metaphor. What analog does that flaming sequoia in your dream have in your life? When you call your teacher a distant, uncaring soul, are you really talking to a parent?

My wife worked for a time—before turning all her attention to painting—as an art therapist. She was really good at the work, not least because of her ability to empathize (and empathy, as we have noted, is nothing if not metaphorical: I'm you; I feel what you feel). Of course there was a lot more to it than that. She had to give practical advice constantly. She had to protect her charges, who were mostly children. She had to help parents cope and help families operate better. She had to say, "Stop doing this," and "Start doing that."

But she'd use art to help her clients communicate and become aware of their struggles, especially the youngest ones, who were least articulate. A boy whose father had died some years past drew a tree with a huge black hole in the trunk, though he'd often said he didn't care much about the old man's death. A girl whose mother had beaten and starved her drew a house with no windows and no doors. A kid who'd been bullied constantly drew his class: Everyone was the same height and size but him; he was a blue speck. Jagged lines spoke of anger; obviously phallic trees and ice-cream cones spoke of too-early sexualization; fallen trees spoke of broken families. Through drawing, the kids found a way to say what could not be easily said in words, what, quite often, they'd been told not to say.

But metaphor is not all misery, especially when it comes to children. Kids are great makers of metaphor, great believers in metaphorical magic: I'm an airplane! Chili is barf! The car is a space shuttle! Adults lose a lot of that natural ability as they gain the practical view: Chili is not barf, sweetheart; sit down and eat.

But we writers can't afford to grow up, at least not as regards language, because the connections and relationships and comparisons we see in the world are the connections and relationships and comparisons that make our writing sing and jump and play, that make our work appealing to readers, who love nothing more than to remake the connections and comparisons we've made.

Exercise Three: Metaphor Watch. Spend the next few days and weeks paying attention to the overriding influence of metaphor in human consciousness and daily life. What implied comparisons live in each corner of existence? How do these comparisons turn up in your work?

Is a co-worker a *bitch*? A *prick*? Is your boss *cutting* costs? Are you on the *front lines* in the *battle* against computer *viruses*? Is your reading club turning into an *encounter group*? Is the *cold war dead*? Is there a presidential *race* in progress? Have you driven by a *mesa* lately (*mesa* is Spanish for table, of course, and a mesa a flat-topped mountain)? Is your latest project an *uphill fight*? Are you working like a head with your chicken cut off? Is love a red, red rose?

MAKING USE OF METAPHOR

All this talk of metaphor and comparison has been fairly abstract. Let's start to think about how to get metaphor into your work. On the sentence level, this will be a conscious effort to use more colorful and intense comparison to illuminate what's not known, to explain the unfamiliar, to say what's hard to say. And why do you want to make this effort? Because the conscious use of metaphor and metaphorical strategies will make your writing more colorful, more intense, more illuminating. Metaphor, skillfully applied, adds layers of meaning—subtle layers that you control and that will please readers without their always knowing why.

Here's poet Howard Nemerov.

> While I am thinking about metaphor, a flock of purple finches arrives on the lawn. Since I haven't seen these birds for some years, I am only fairly sure of their being in fact purple finches, so I get down Peterson's *Field Guide* and read his description: "Male: about size of House Sparrow, rosy-red, brightest on

head and rump." That checks quite well, but his next remark—
"a sparrow dipped in raspberry juice," is decisive: it fits. I look
out the window again, and now I know that I am seeing purple
finches.

Exercise Four: The Old Chinese Restaurant Menu Exercise.

This one comes from my days as a grad student, when I taught a
course called Logic and Rhetoric. We new teachers passed around
all our best exercises and used one another's freely (some dated from
decades past), so I'm not quite sure whom to credit for this, but be
assured: I stole it. Here goes.

Column A	Column B
Marriage	Mirror
Illness	Rain
Justice	Eruption
Literature	Battle
Politics	Healing
Art	Perfume
Love	Fire
Happiness	Football
Hatred	Mud
Separation	Can Opener

Take one item from column A, one from column B. Write a comparison—a paragraph or two—beginning with the simplest statement of your metaphor. For example: Marriage is a can opener.
Then go on to examine and elaborate the points of comparison.

After a certain number of sentences, the comparison is bound to
grown strained. At that point, start a new paragraph that examines
the inadequacies of the comparison.

A variation is to make verbs out of the words in column B. Start
your exercise, for instance, with the following high exposition:
Hatred muddies. Or how about: Politics perfumes?

The point is to get started actually using metaphorical strategies
at the sentence level. Of course you can (and should) make up your
own words for columns A and B.

ADUMBRATION

Let's think about some more sophisticated ways to get conscious control of metaphor in our writing.

Like foreshadowing, adumbration means to suggest beforehand. But adumbration signifies a vaguer kind of foreshadowing, more sketchy, more cloudy—the root word in there is *umbra*, Latin for shade (and don't forget that one meaning of shade is *ghost*). I like to use the word adumbration to talk about those instances in which meaning attaches to objects that appear in scenes (this is something like what T.S. Eliot called the objective correlative). If a character lights a cigarette after sex, the next cigarette—even if puffed in a grocery store—will remind us a little of sex. If a character shakes hands to make a sinister deal, the next handshake in that piece will carry some whiff of the sinister. The first handshake adumbrates; the second handshake delivers. If a character who is angelically good has red hair, the next head of red hair we see will carry a feeling of goodness.

I had a student years ago in New York who wrote an intensely moving memoir of her father. In the first scene of the essay, she shows us the man throwing a stove down the basement stairs. It's a horrific vision—drunken, enraged man tearing the stove from its moorings with bestial strength and throwing it down the basement stairs, right in front of his children.

In a much later scene of the unfinished essay, readers see the writer's newest boyfriend. He's leaning against the stove in her kitchen, affably drinking a beer. The presence of that stove—the word itself now carrying all the weight of scene one—makes us question the affability of the new boyfriend, makes us wonder: has the writer chosen the wrong man? The stove alone does the trick. The writer doesn't have to say more.

What interested me most about this stove image is that when I pointed it out, the writer looked at me sharply, revealed. She *was* worried about this new guy's drinking but hadn't wanted to say anything about it at all in her essay. Wanted, in fact, to hide it from the reader. But of all the dozens and scores of places her new boyfriend has leaned and sucked a beer, she picked a *stove*.

Our writer went home to revise and came back a week later with a new draft. She'd got so excited about the stove image that she now had stoves in every scene. She'd all but renamed her boyfriend Stove Ovenworth.

Restraint, writer. One repetition is enough. Maybe two. Our writer's next revision restored the delicate adumbration of the single stove repetition—beautiful. Also, she added just a few words of description to make the second vision of the stove more intense— beautiful, beautiful. And now, her essay was about her real fear of falling into the trap her mother had fallen into: alcoholic father, alcoholic husband. Beautiful, beautiful, beautiful.

In *This Boy's Life*, Tobias Wolff tells the true story of his childhood and adolescent years under the reluctant wing of a bad-news stepfather named Dwight. What follows is from one of their first encounters.

> Dwight drove in a sullen reverie. When I spoke he answered curtly, or not at all. Now and then his expression changed, and he grunted as if to claim some point of argument. He kept a Camel burning on his lower lip. Just the other side of Concrete he pulled the car hard to the left and hit a beaver that was crossing the road. Dwight said he had swerved to miss the beaver, but that wasn't true. He had gone out of his way to run over it. He stopped the car on the shoulder of the road and backed up to where the beaver lay.
>
> We got out and looked at it. I saw no blood. The beaver was on its back with its eyes open and its curved yellow teeth bared. Dwight prodded it with his foot. "Dead," he said.
>
> It was dead all right.
>
> "Pick it up," Dwight told me. He opened the trunk of the car and said, "Pick it up. We'll skin the sucker out when we get home."
>
> I wanted to do what Dwight expected me to do, but I couldn't. I stood where I was and stared at the beaver.

The beaver is not only itself—a large rodent crossing a road—it also becomes an emblem of Dwight's cruelty. And when it turns up again, festering and wasted in Dwight's attic (along with a huge basket of chestnuts that carry their own meaning), the full profligate force of that cruelty hits us with a sick thud. And the beaver needn't be mentioned after that to continue to have its power. When Dwight brings home a dog—normally a blessed event in a boy's life—we know a lot about how to read the gesture, and we understand our hero's undelight.

The truth is, anything from your days that you pick as a prop for memoir—beaver or stove or chestnut or hubcap—or anyplace you choose as a setting, may have some useful meaning hidden in it. Sometimes it takes a reader to point out the metaphorical stuff. Other times it just takes time for your own clearest vision to arrive. Sometimes, the discovery of meaning, of *metaphor*, however, is a matter of conscious reading, conscious investigation, conscious searching through the attics of your imagination, and a conscious, writerly effort to make use of all you've got.

Exercise Five: Tweaking Up the Adumbration. Here's an exercise to try as you revise any of your memoirs or essays. Look for objects or places that have taken on meanings from your most dramatic scenes, then use those objects or places again somewhere in the essay to make use of the reader's unconscious associations. It's not as hard as it sounds.

Say you've got a scene dramatizing your engagement to be married. Say the big question was popped under an enormous, spreading tree. What happens if you introduce another enormous, spreading tree, perhaps in a later scene of chaos or strife?

In many cases this exercise will make you realize that you have no enormous, spreading trees in your work at all, that in order to have objects to take on metaphorical significance, you need to have objects around in the first place.

Exercise Six: Making It New. Here's an exercise quoted directly from novelist, story writer, anthologist, and critic John Clayton.

"Anaïs Nin says, 'It is the function of art to renew our perceptions. What we are familiar with we cease to see. The writer shakes up the familiar scene, and as if by magic, we see a new meaning in it.'

"Take a familiar scene (perhaps from one of your earlier exercises), and make us see it in a new way. For example, see a liaison between a man and a woman as a military engagement; see a business deal as a dance."

TRUSTING YOUR PRECONSCIOUS MIND

The biggest metaphors, the largest meanings, the universal threads arrive most often entirely on their own. You as writer work and work to make a clear story clearer; your reader—absolutely because of the clarity you've finally achieved—sees something larger than your story, something as large as all of life. She sees meaning. She sees connections. She makes the grand comparison.

Simple examples include student stories of mountain climbing. In one memorable one, our young writer tells us about a time he decided to make the final ascent of a Utah peak when he knew a storm was coming. His bullheadedness nearly killed him, but he did make his goal. He held up his hand in class: missing fingers. He offered to take off his shoes. (We said, "Nah.") The mountain might be seen as life; the bullheadedness as a particular aspect of the human spirit. The missing fingers? The price, perhaps, of hubris. What if, the class asked, the writer went back to his draft thinking in those grand terms? He might wreck everything, the class answered, making such an image too obvious, might steer toward the hackneyed. But he might—ever so subtly—find a way to make use of the big stuff, find a way to understand his own essay, and so find a way to bring understanding to his readers.

In a much later draft, our mountain climber included a long section about his failed marriage. His actions as a climber became analogs for his actions as a husband. The mountain became a woman, the wife a mountain. The writer showed himself to be too much the conquerer, too little humble before great forces (nature, femininity). The essay showed the writer to himself, made him his own reader, taught him enough to bring a real close to the piece, to fill it with meaning, to approach universal wisdom.

Gow Farris—good old Gow—struggled and struggled to write about his brother. Now that Gow had broken into scenes, it wasn't hard to bring the dead one to life. The trouble was all the emotion. Gow couldn't read the stuff aloud, and sometimes at his keyboard he'd cry till he had to get up and do something else. Someone in our class suggested he not get up but write about something else. And so he turned back to his project of the story of his reporting career, some days working on that, some days working on the memoir of his brother.

Quickly, it became apparent that Gow's story of himself as reporter involved scene after scene with another man. Gow and his succession of bosses. Gow and President Johnson. Gow and the guy at the next desk. Gow and an undercover police officer. One of Gow's classmates said, "It's like you were always looking for a brother."

Gow grumbled at that, but within a day he was glowing: He'd found out that his two stories were one, that one informed the other. It was true: All of his relationships with men his whole adult life were failed searches for the lost brother. Gow was on his way to writing something important, not only about himself but about men, and not only about men but about the human condition.

Juxtapositions, he'd discovered, make meaning soar.

Exercise Seven: Juxtaposition. Please pick at random five or six scenes you've written over the last several months. Take them straight out of larger pieces, whether these pieces are finished or not.

Now, one at a time (one a day, perhaps), splice a scene—something like your first ski trip—into whatever you're writing now. You've been writing about the death of your great-aunt, and now—page break—there's a ski scene.

The challenge of this exercise is to make seemingly unrelated scenes work together. What has skiing to say about death? What do Aunt Lurlene's doilies have to say about skiing? Write your way out of the problem. Of course, some juxtapositions won't yield anything but silliness.

But some will bring inspiration, God's breath.

DO NOT GO GENTLE INTO THAT GOOD NIGHT

People afraid or wary of their own unconscious or preconscious minds tend also to be wary of any discussion of metaphor. Lots of my students like to shout at me the amusing old saw, "Sometimes a cigar is just a cigar!" True, true. Don't go overboard in your search for metaphorical truth.

But don't go underboard, either. When a cigar is just a cigar, there's not much for the writer in search of meaning to go on. Sometimes, dear reader, a cigar is a village in France!

NINE

SAYING IT RIGHT

I cut adjectives, adverbs, and every word which is there just for the sentence. You know, you have a beautiful sentence—cut it. Everytime I find such a thing in one of my books it is to be cut.   —Georges Simenon

Every morning I jump out of bed and step on a land mine. That land mine is me.   —Ray Bradbury

In college and in the years just after college, I sang and played keyboards in good bar bands with names like Klondike and Sky Acres and Them Apples and The Daily Planet Band and The Blues Rangers. In one of these outfits, we had a drummer I'll call Ditch who would pull up late for practice on his Harley, pull up late for gigs in his monster van, all our equipment trapped inside. He'd be at fault, but somehow it was always he who was angry. He was nearly seven feet tall but had never played basketball. He had a sharp wit and a cold eye.

Ditch was a really terrific drummer in all but one fatal way: He didn't take criticism too well. But he was very smart and studied hard, copping fills from records, learning hot licks by the dozen, borrowing tricks from every drummer he saw, inventing his own (he could throw both sticks in the air while doing a bass drum roll with his feet, catch the sticks exactly in time, crash them on huge ride cymbals to end a song). His drumming was lush and worked well on the lush songs—lots of smacks and booms, lots of cymbals, fills everyplace. He loved Emerson, Lake and Palmer—that big, big sound. So did we! He loved Cream and their cranked octopus of a drummer, Ginger Baker. So did we! He loved the Allman Brothers

Band and did everything he could to approximate the sound of their two drummers with his two long arms. We loved the Allman Brothers, too, but we weren't the Allman Brothers. We wanted a spare sound. Rhythm and blues, man.

Ditch bought a new drum or cymbal to add to his kit with the money from each gig. His hands on stage were a blur. He didn't leave a lot of room to think, filled every pause, killed the drama of every silence, flattened the dynamics. The places we wanted to get loud he couldn't come with us: You can't play so many notes and play them hard. You can't play so many notes and play them softly, either. But our music—the stuff we'd agreed we wanted to play—needed those highs and lows. We wanted Ditch to whack that snare drum sharply. We wanted gaps of silence. We wanted dynamics. Forget the flourish.

Jack, our fearless lead guitarist, brought up the subject with Ditch at every practice and before every gig. Ditch got testy. He'd spent years learning all that stuff. All the adornment was his *style*, goddamnit.

We needed a new drummer. The problem was going to be protecting any new drummer from Ditch, who had a bit of a temper. The problem was going to be protecting *ourselves* from Ditch. Jack figured it out: We break up, wait a month, take a new name, and reform with a new guy in Ditch's place.

Maybe two weeks before this uncourageous plan was to be implemented, Ditch did something unheard of: He showed up early. For a gig. Frat house at Cornell. Early, yes, but in some kind of fulminating rage. He slammed his kit together at the back of the makeshift stage, smacked each of his forty drums in his signature roll (thirty seconds of subtle din), then had a kind of fit, kicking cymbals out of his way, knocking one of his base drums into a stairwell, breaking the heads of two of his snare drums with the base of his seat, breaking his hi-hats, crushing his tom-toms, flinging all of them around the room, scaring us *shitless* (but delighting the frat boys, who were already drunk).

Turned out Ditch's much-tattooed girlfriend had run off with someone from the Wharf Rats, a motorcycle club. Fearless Jack the guitar man led old Ditch outside and there in the middle of the sweeping frat house driveway they had a talk, and whatever it was

Jack said, it got Ditch back in the room for the start of the first set, just as the busload of young women from Wells College arrived, giggling.

Ditch, darkly sulking, set up one bass drum, one snare, one hi-hat, one ride cymbal (all those other drums and cymbals represented the excesses of love somehow, and in any case he'd damaged them beyond immediate usefulness), and without them his usual lushness of play got boiled down to single hits on single drums. He was pissed and he played hard—those single, spare hits let him do so. He was pissed and Marlene wasn't there and some other biker was caressing her tattoos right now and Ditch wasn't about to play those luxuriant fills if she didn't care enough to listen!

He'd never played so well and the band was electrified by his focus and we'd never played so well and the frat boys had never heard anything like it in their broken mansion and the Wells College women danced and stripped out of layers of fancy sweaty clothes and we played hours extra, roaring into the night.

From then on, Jack made sure he pissed Ditch off before every gig. Pissing Ditch off wasn't hard. You just told him you'd seen Marlene on the back of some guy's bike.

By the time Ditch got over her, by the time his heart was mended, he was a new drummer.

Exercise One: Forget About Style. In this exercise you are to throw a fit—perhaps you're furious because of the latest round of rejection slips—throw a fit and kick the pieces of your style kit around the frat house while the drunken brothers yell. Break the bass drum of your punctuation with the pedal of your adjectives. Ram your stout verb sticks through your adverbial tom-toms. Nix prolixity. Fling cymbals out the windows; listen to the crash.

The best kit is the essential kit.

Hit it hard when you're hitting, but don't be afraid of silence.

As for style: Just get mad and stay that way.

THE NEXT STEP

Writing is all about language, and writing in English is all about the English language. Mastery of its many nuances and subtleties and, yes, rules, is a lifetime proposition. Words and sentences and paragraphs are endlessly adaptable, always plastic. It's up to writers—

you and me—to discover strategies that produce clarity, motion, density, rhythm, precision, texture, urgency, all the things that in the end can add up to beauty.

Now, most of us have come to writing because of a facility with words. This facility was noticed by our teachers early on, and we've been told for years by various authorities—from parents to teachers to bosses to friends—that we are good writers. Some of us have even had editors give the thumbs up. Okay, we're good. We've got a way with words. But we want to be, well, *great*. What's next?

I'm not going to dwell here on the rudiments: All that's been well covered in other places, in books that are accessible to you already, probably right on the shelf above your desk.

Instead, let me pull some fairly abstract words out of a sentence you read above: *clarity, motion, density, rhythm, precision, texture, urgency.*

Fair warning: These are difficult topics to grasp, and they certainly interweave, each fading into the provinces of the next. They are also difficult topics for me to write about. But let me try it. Let me try saying the unsayable. I want to help you further plumb the differences between merely competent writing and writing that knocks people out.

CLARITY

If writing isn't clear, it's nothing. If readers have to guess at your meaning, only some will guess right. Leave nothing to chance, writer. In your control of the language lies your authority.

Under the heading of clarity come most of the rules of grammar. Those commas you're not quite sure how to use have been given jobs by agreement of good writers over many years. Learn how to put them to work. Those semicolons and colons you avoid so assiduously—and those dashes—divide your thought into discrete and functional blocks of meaning. Mechanics, man: You got to know the basics (for example, how does one punctuate around parentheses?). Usage? Good usage is a matter of knowing the difference between *that* and *which, further* and *farther, principle* and *principal, except* and *accept,* and knowing—never guessing—about pronoun cases: *he* and *him, who* and *whom, me* and *mine* (". . . between you and I . . . ," says Donald Trump, in a full-page ad decrying today's educational standards). And word choice. Word choice is everything. If you say perspicacious when you mean perspicuous, you lose your reader every time.

Do you know how modifiers work? Apostrophes? Do you understand predication? Subordination? Can you recognize an independent clause? (If not, you'll have a hell of a time with commas.) Most of us, even with our fine facility of language, answer the questions above with sheepish negatives. Most of us do our grammar by ear. All of us need to do the work of checking our intuitions against the conventions of grammar, punctuation, and mechanics—the rules.

But don't beat yourself up about this stuff: One learns the ropes slowly, and even the best writers make strange errors; even the best editors let howlers through. And don't be a slave master: This language is alive, and writers have every right to fling aside rules of all kinds to help it breathe. But bucking the system is different from being ignorant of it.

The only rule, really, is clarity. If you can be clear using fragments, use fragments. If you can be clear with no quotation marks in your dialogue, cool. If you can be clear using not one mark of punctuation, go for it. But if I'm your editor, get ready to argue with me. Sometimes you'll win, especially if you know what you're talking about. (Though I'll never accept *its* for *it's*, never accept an unnecessary comma, never accept the wrong word in the right place.)

I used the word *conventions* above. Yes, the rules of our game are merely conventions. Groups of smart people have convened and agreed on them. That's all. There's no natural law that says one way or the other is correct. But if we can all agree what an ellipsis should do, we'll have an easier time getting our ideas across clearly. Why fight it? If you're going to be unconventional, why not in your content rather than in your grammar and mechanics?

Spelling? Good spelling tells your reader (and prospective editors) you know what you're doing, that you care about your material, even in early drafts. But don't forget that it's only been a hundred years or so that spelling has been standardized at all (Samuel Johnson did an awfully fine job of writing clearly, spelling words this way, then that). A few typos? So what? And don't get all superior when your workshop rival spells chocolate wrong: Spelling can be fixed. (But don't trust your computer's spell-checker to do the job alone.)

Did I say that the language is alive? Always growing? Always sneaking through the legs of the language police?

Exercise Two: Time to Become an Expert. For this exercise, you buy books, then read them. I own, like, twenty-two grammar handbooks, because I teach and edit (and, okay, because I get them in the mail constantly for free). You only need one, really, though owning more than one helps you see that even the experts aren't always in agreement in matters of style, usage, grammar, and mechanics. If you're on a budget, college-town bookstores generally have a great supply of used handbooks.

Buy two, so you can compare authorities. Put one in your bathroom. Handbooks are perfect toilet reading: small sections you can read quickly. You'll find your most cherished ideas about commas, say, are not entirely correct. You'll learn how to use a word you've had wrong since you were fourteen. Also, you'll be affirmed in all the stuff you do know how to do, and you'll learn the names of the things you do so well intuitively: Here as everywhere, naming is knowing. Next time you see an error in the newspaper, name it, using your handbook.

Along with the grammar handbook, buy a dictionary. And not one of those dollar college editions from the street. Get a fat one that provides etymologies. And use it. Read it for fun, find magnificent words, learn their histories, use them in conversation (my mother used to tell me what her mother told her: "Use a word ten times and it's yours." And look up words as you do your daily reading. Of course you'll want to look up the words you don't know, but listen: Look up the words you do know, too. Be honest with yourself. Do you really know what a solecism is, for example, or just sort of?

And how about H.W. Fowler's *Modern English Usage*? It's old and antiquated in many charming ways, but Fowler is a blast: He's funny and interesting, collects a dozen examples for every point he makes, quoting authors when they're right and when they're wrong, praising them or making fun. He's got, like, eight pages on *that* and *which*. (Note that most handbooks have at least a small usage section, with advice on commonly misused words and expressions.)

A thesaurus? I don't know. Very useful for getting that word off the tip of your mind. Very dangerous for a certain class of lazier student writers, who will often use it to dress up their prose with the wrong synonym: "I marched on Washington to bring a message to Congress" becomes "The self paraded on the first president so as to transport a bulletin to intercourse."

Handbooks, dictionaries, usage manuals—these aren't books to sit down and read in an afternoon. But they are not books to use only as needed, either. They're books to peruse, a little every day, as part of our work.

And that perusal, gentle writer, is your assignment.

CLAIRE AND ME

In the interest of clarity, let's look at an example of student work (this one I'll make anonymous).

> Jane and Claire and me stood to our feet, drunkly. She went straight to the car to get the box of books. It was parked outside under a tree at college, the berries had stained the windshield like bruises. They were important to us. She came back with them and Jane said "Now is the time to read the mystery quote". Falling open to our certain page, we read it out loud.

Let's get out our handbooks out and name the problems above.

Jane and Claire and me. The writer is subject of this sentence, along with her college friends. The problem is pronoun case. The proper case is *I*, of course (though there're plenty of times when voice demands just such an error).

Stood to our feet. What else can you stand to? Perhaps *struggled* for *stood*, or some other verb that gets it exactly right—*tottered*? Apparently the protagonists here are *drunkly*. Where would you send this writer to check her adverbs?

She went straight. Which she? This is a pronoun reference problem (often these are much more subtle than we have here: check your pronouns carefully). *Went* isn't much of a verb to describe an intoxicated young woman rushing outdoors (is she stumbling down some stairs? Into snow? What exactly?). *To the car.* What car? Whose? What kind? How much might a writer slip in here?

It was parked. What was parked? The box of books? That's the first referent the reader comes up with before switching to the correct referent. *It* is a pronoun of particularly pesky vagueness. I'd check every *it* you ever use for clear reference, and I'd check to see how often you use that little word. I've seen *it* five, six, seven times in a single paragraph, with references flying every which way.

Under a tree at college. Wouldn't hurt to name the tree, especially given the berries (what berries?) that follow. Mulberry tree, is my guess. College? What college? Are we at college? Was that a dorm room we were in? Name the school, and you solve all kinds of problems: location, setting, class and success level of protagonists, and so forth.

Stained the windshield like bruises. Our writer is reaching for a nice metaphor here, but it's a faulty analogy: The wording here says that bruises cause stains. That's not it. And did you find the comma splice?

They were important to us. Again, pronoun reference. Does *they* refer to bruises? To boxes? To books? To what? The reader, of course, can figure it out, but to do so she's got to leave her dream. And most readers will resent even momentary confusion.

Is our writer in control of quotation? Where do final periods and commas go when you have quotation marks? (In American usage, always inside.) How about question marks? Colons? The rules are clear and easy to find: Read up in your handbook, and carefully examine dialogue by good writers. (Parentheses have their own conventional punctuation with a logic different from that of quotation marks: Read up!)

Falling open to our certain page, we read it out loud. Faulty predication, for one thing: This says that *we* fell open, not a book (and by the way, what book is it?) Notice the vague *it* here.

I could say more about this passage, lots more, but suffice it to say: It's not clear. And despite a pretty interesting story lurking back there behind the fuzz, as reader, I'm about to give up, move on to something clearer.

MOTION

The notion of motion is mighty metaphorical, but let's give it a shake.

Motion is about verbs, of course, and it's about voice (eschew the passive!). It's about transitions between sentences and paragraphs and sections, but it's about something else, too, something less concrete. Say you're on a ship: Always you feel its connection with the living ocean. Prose without motion is like a ship in drydock: no connection with the great sea that is our language.

Prose is like a shark: If it quits moving, it's dead. Prose is like a relationship: If it quits growing, it becomes stifling. Prose is like sex: It's better if you move.

Prose should be made of movement the way a symphony is: allegro, andante, cantabile. Prose should change before our eyes, like Proteus, from this form to that.

Let's examine for motion the opening paragraphs of "Giving Good Weight," the title essay from the collection *Giving Good Weight*, by John McPhee.

> You people come into the market—the Greenmarket, in the open air under the downpouring sun—and you slit the tomatoes with your fingernails. With your thumbs, you excavate the cheese. You choose your stringbeans one at a time. You pulp the nectarines and rape the sweet corn. You are something wonderful, you are—people of the city—and we, who are almost without exception strangers here, are as absorbed with you as you seem to be with the numbers on our hanging scales.
>
> "Does every sink grow on your farm?"
>
> "Yes, Ma'am."
>
> "It's marvelous. Absolutely every sink?"
>
> "Some things we get from neighbors up the road."
>
> "You don't have no avocados, do you?"
>
> "Avocados don't grow in New York State."
>
> "Butter beans?"
>
> "They're a Southern crop."
>
> "Who baked this bread?"
>
> "My mother. A dollar twenty-five for the cinnamon. Ninety-five cents for the rye."
>
> "I can't eat rye bread anymore. I like it very much, but it gives me a headache."
>
> Short, born abroad, and with dark hair and quick eyes, the woman who likes rye bread comes regularly to the Brooklyn Greenmarket, at Flatbush and Atlantic. I have seen her as well

at the Fifty-ninth Street Greenmarket, in Manhattan. There is abundant evidence that she likes to eat. She must have endured some spectacular hangovers from all that rye.

Look at all the movement here. We start in the voice of a kind of everyman market person observing the hordes of city folk, move through quickly shifting voices of the market to an authorial voice—the voice of McPhee, who has seen the rye-bread woman around. We slip from city to country and back again, taking both points of view. We slit and excavate and pulp and rape. And we move to surprising places—women allergic to rye bread (she's from *abroad*, too), for example. We leap from Brooklyn to Manhattan. The flow of information in this short opening is prodigious—already we know stuff we didn't know before, already our preconceptions are challenged.

Movement is the sense of going somewhere as we read. It's easy to say, "Use better verbs." I say it to students all the time. But what I'm saying now is, "Make it *all* a verb." ("God is a verb," Reverend Mullendore said once in church—I puzzled over that one for years as a teen.)

The motion of your stuff puts the reader in motion, too: Maybe that's what we mean when we say a story *moved* us.

Exercise Three: Get Moving. Picture a schematic chart of a great river. On it there will be the flow to the sea, of course, rather a big arrow, but in addition there will be hundreds of smaller arrows indicating eddies and currents and boils and inversions. Always part of the water is flowing upstream, part is flowing to the river bottom, part is flowing right, part is flowing left.

The exercise is to chart the movement of a more-or-less finished piece of your work, an essay or memoir or other true story.

On a large piece of paper, draw the sea. Label this with some appropriate word or phrase. This will be harder than it sounds. To what ocean is your essay flowing, anyway? The grandest terms will do: Reader Satisfaction. Truth. Also, the most prosaic: The Story of My First Job.

Now for your sentences: Where does each fit in the flow toward your sea? Do any of your eddies threaten to become whirlpools?

The point is to help you recognize what's flat in your writing, to isolate the stuff that only moves one way: downhill. And sometimes you'll find that a piece isn't moving at all; it's caught behind a dam (usually of personality—yours) and growing stagnant.

DENSITY

Sentences are a little like purses: They come in various sizes and can hold a little or a lot. Meaning is a bit like money: The more the better, in most cases. And if your purse can only hold so many bills, you might as well make them large-denomination bills, right?

Here's a first sentence from a student essay.

> My mother walked to the kitchen table and placed the scissors normally kept in her sewing basket on the table.

Let us try to add some density to this perfectly acceptable opening sentence, get it doing all the work it can do—characterization, scene building, setting, poetry, and so forth—without making it any longer. Right now, it's twenty words.

First, I'd like to get rid of the double use of the word *table*. This will free up some space for further meaning. But which *table* will I cut? That will depend on other changes, as follow: I want to get rid of the passive "normally kept in her sewing basket." I want to do something about the bland verbs: *walked, placed* (*kept* will go when we fix the passive construction). As reader, I want to finish reading this first sentence having some clues about Mom's character, her age in the present of the sentence—the daughter's age, too.

Let me take some liberties here and add meanings and attributes wholly fictional for the sake of example (only the sentence's writer could do the real work here).

> Momsy blundered into the kitchen, slammed the sewing-basket scissors into my place mat.

Not great, but an improvement. Best of all, it's only thirteen words. We've got seven words to play with as we get the thing back up to twenty.

> Momsy blundered in, stabbed my place mat with her sewing-basket scissors; they quivered (as I did) in the trailer's new silence.

Okay, it's twenty-one words, but now we have a name for mom, a sense of her character, a sense of her life. We've lost nothing in the way of meaning. We managed to get rid of both *tables*—where else would a place mat be? We dropped the explanation about the sewing basket, without losing its image, and kept the sense that the kid's in trouble for using Momsy's scissors. We've mentioned the trailer, and with it managed to give the socioeconomic condition here. We've given the reader a picture of the child, too: She's quivering.

How much can you get into a sentence? How much can you get into *every* sentence?

This is what density is all about.

Exercise Four: Density. For this exercise I want you to consider the first sentence of one of your "finished" works of creative non-fiction. Take a half hour or more (really—set a timer if necessary—you're working out, after all; be a tough trainer) and play with getting as much as possible into that sentence, but keeping it at the same or near-same word count as the original. When that's done, go to the next sentence. What must change? And keep going, all the way to the last sentence of your piece.

A variation is to try boiling your first paragraph down to one sentence.

And keep in mind it's possible to boil things down too far: once I made maple syrup so thick it wouldn't pour. And I've made sentences massive as lead ingots. Neither was much good.

RHYTHM

A drum beating one note continuously, regularly, becomes quickly either unbearably irritating, or recedes into background noise. Even a complex beat, endlessly repeated, recedes.

Rhythm in prose is a matter not so much of prosodic mathematics (iambs, tetrameter, syllabic feet)—though naming is knowing—but a matter of ear. And the question is, Do you have an ear? A sense of rhythm is a cultural sense, a sense of tradition. Do your sentences pick up the cadences of childhood rhymes? Of marching bands? Of biblical phrasing? Of television scripts? Of the squad room? Of a preacher's repetition? Or are writing rhythms always and only variations on the beating of a human heart (perhaps the one we listened to so comfortably in the womb)?

Variety, as in all things, is key. Too many new writers rely on a single rhythmic strategy, or none at all, letting the words fall where they may, so long as things are grammatical. Rhythm, of course, is one of the components of voice. Rhythm assumes a spoken discourse, sentences designed to be heard, and not just seen. I'll reproduce three passages from three fine writers. Try reading each out loud, listening for the music here, listening for the ways the writers control the beat.

Listen as Truman Capote makes use of a variety of rhythms in his opening to "Handcarved Coffins: A Nonfiction Account of an American Crime," from his collection *Music for Chameleons.*

> March, 1975.
>
> A town in a small Western state. A focus for the many large farms and cattle-raising ranches surrounding it, the town, with a population of less than ten thousand, supports twelve churches and two restaurants. A movie house, though it has not shown a movie in ten years, still stands stark and cheerless on Main Street. There once was a hotel, too; but that has also been closed, and nowadays the only place a traveler can find shelter is the Prairie Motel.

The opening phrases here are blunt. The sentence fragments cut the rhythm short—shorter, that is, than our ears expect. This chopping isolates the fragments' beats from the beats of the full sentences that follow. But Capote doesn't allow those longer sentences to flow, either. He breaks them with commas, a semicolon, with subordination, interruption, and apposition. This is the vocal rhythm of someone with bad news to tell: hesitant, throat-clearing, yet resolute. And note that each of the last words in these sentences ends with a tongue-stopping (and beat-stopping) "t," except the last sentence, with its *motel*, whose "t" echoes the earlier stops, but trails into the "el" enough to carry the music forward into a new paragraph. Capote wants the delivery halting, but not so halting that the reader stops and turns elsewhere. Note that you can't read this paragraph in a joyful rush.

The next passage is from Doris Lessing's memoir "Impertinent Daughters."

> Modern-minded John William McVeagh, proud of his clever daughter, was thinking of university for her, but was confronted with a rebellious girl who said she wanted to be a nurse. He was horrified, utterly overthrown. Middle-class girls did not become nurses, and he didn't want to hear anything about Florence Nightingale. Any Skivvy could be a nurse, and if you become one, do not darken my door! Very well, said Emily Maude, and went off to the old Royal Free Hospital to begin her training. It was hard: conditions were bad, the pay was low, but she did well, and when she brilliantly passed her finals, her father was prepared to forgive her. She had done it all on her own, without him.

This one you could sing. Note the alliteration that opens the paragraph: "Modern-minded . . . McVeagh." Note the long opening sentence, its singsong rush. Note, too, how hard the sentence lands on the word *nurse*, which turns out to be the critical word of the passage (an instance of rhythm providing meaning). Note the tongue pleasure of the phrase "utterly overthrown." I want to say it again and again. And why does Lessing use Emily's middle name ("Very well, said Emily Maude, and went off . . .") when she hasn't used it earlier and doesn't use it later? Why else but rhythm? And listen to the rhythm of this series: "conditions were bad, the pay was low, but she did well." The repetitions in structure here give the sentence the sound of a folk tale, very nearly a folk song.

In the next passage, Annie Dillard quite purposefully plays with biblical rhythm, even conflates it with the rhythms of childhood song. The passage, in which she gives a child's misinterpretation of what goes on in Sunday school, is from her memoir of intellectual awakening, *An American Childhood*.

> James and John, the sons of Zebedee, he made them fishers of men. And he came to the Lake of Gennesaret, and he came to Capernaum. And he withdrew in a boat. And a certain man went down from Jerusalem to Jericho. See it here on the map? Down. He went down, and fell among thieves.
>
> And the swine jumped over the cliff.

And the voice cried, Samuel, Samuel. And the wakened boy Samuel answered, Here am I. And at last he said, Speak.

Hear O Israel, the Lord is one.

And Peter said, I know him not; I know him not; I know him not. And the rich young ruler said, What must I do? And the woman wiped his feet with her hair. And he said, Who touched me?

And he said, Verily, verily, verily, verily; life is not a dream. Let this cup pass from me. If it be thy will, of course, only if it be thy will.

There's plenty to say about this passage, of course, but I'd better stick to rhythm. Along with the doggerel rhythms of childhood songs, note the use of rhyme and repetition to create rhythm. Normally, of course, good writers avoid repetition hoping to make full use of the richness of English, avoid obvious rhyme to avoid sounding childish, but here Dillard makes it plain that repetition and rhyme can make music of our words. A name repeated, *he-said*, *she-said* tag lines repeated, whole phrases repeated, all are rhythmic techniques. Dillard makes a joke of repetition in the end, but there are lessons here. Dillard crafts a joyful rush, indeed. How different in every way from Capote's dirgelike opening, both appropriate to their subjects and intentions.

Rhythm should be attended to in each sentence we write, of course, and each paragraph, but there is a rhythm of paragraphs, as well, a rhythm of sections in an essay, a rhythm of chapters in a book, and all of it ought to be in your control as you write.

Exercise Five: Tap Your Feet. Pull out the work of a favorite writer, and read it listening and feeling for rhythm and rhythms. Tap your feet as you read out loud. Look for repeated words or phrases that set up a beat. Listen for sentences that rise, for sentences that fall. Where does the prose stop? What kinds of words create pauses? What kinds flow? How do paragraph lengths fit into the music of the work? Is there a visual rhythm? Can you sing any lines?

Then pull out another author, and do it again. What accounts for the changes you hear in rhythm?

Finally, pull out your own draft, and read the same way. Are you satisfied? Can you get more music in there? More of a beat? More aural surprises? More variety?

I'll make your charge more concrete: Do you start most sentences with the subject? Do you always subordinate in the same way? Do you avoid alliteration, repetition? Does every paragraph end on a rising note, or falling? Does every sentence have about the same number of beats, every paragraph the same number of sentences?

Shake it up, baby!

PRECISION

Precision is a matter of getting everything right, from names to weights to dates to ages to sizes to hues. Precision is also a matter of excellent grammar and usage, which we've discussed. But, as always, there's more to it.

Precision is a form of honesty. Precision will not allow self-deceit (and not the writer's deception of others). Precision means filling in the blanks, staring down our defenses, checking every fact, even when it's easier not to. Precision means knowing what our essays are *about*. Precision means that, like a good surgeon, we know where and when to cut, and when to only sew. Precision admits to limitations: We can't know everything, and we say so.

When vision is precise, clarity results, and thence beauty.

Let's go to the page.

> We met in the winter months, not surprisingly in a bar. Brenda was beautiful and tall and I knew right away we'd be good for each other. I asked her home or she asked me, I can't remember, but home we went, talking all the way, and then we made love the first time, not knowing, of course, that almost fifty years later we'd have been married, divorced, reunited twice, broken up twice, but talking on the phone again.

Not bad writing. Grammatical, clean, romantic. Still, I asked the writer—Gow Farris—to do some work: precision. Leave nothing vague, said I. Gow said he meant it to sound nostalgic, not exact. It's just an exercise, said I. (I tell you, that guy was like pulling teeth.) Anyway, here's what he came back with, an hour later, no research.

Brenda Leavenworth (this is not her real name, professor) and I met February 8th, 1950, during a record cold wave. Minus 38 degrees that night and just the two of us and Frankie (the bartender) at the Pine Tavern on the lake road. Brenda was freezing at home and so came out wearing four sweaters and a raccoon coat owned by her boyfriend, an acquaintance of mine named Tom Dell. You couldn't see any woman under all that clothing but I'd seen her before and knew she wasn't only tall. Her eyes were brown and her hair blond with roots showing and she was twenty-two years old. Frank let her sit at the bar and the three of us drank heavily (not exact enough for you? Okay:) Three of us drank shots of bar whiskey and bottles of beer (I don't know what kind of beer, professor, so give me an F). At 12:47 A.M. she aimed her eyes at me and said: I ain't walking home. I said she could come to my place, but I wasn't driving up Tom Dell's driveway or anywhere near it. At my house we drank more and kissed on the couch with all the lights off till the sun came up. At that point I had maybe twelve layers of clothes off her, leaving one or two more to go. And this is as much as I'm likely to tell anybody. Exactly 48 years, five months, and three days later, I called her on the phone. Two nights ago, to be exact.

I always loved Gow's parenthetical commentary. He *hated* learning. You should have seen his reaction when I asked him to shorten the revision back to the length of the original paragraph!

Exercise Six: Vagueness Patrol. Once again, I'm going to ask you to examine a "finished" draft. Starting right at the beginning, look for vague constructions: *about* seven years, *a* grocery store, a *good-looking* man, a *good-size* dog, *late* at night. And so on. Do everything you can and whatever it takes to bring precision to your constructions.

Gow, above, also brings precision to his observations: Brenda wasn't beautiful, exactly, but appealed to him. They "made love" that night in the old sense, certainly—flirting, making out—but not in the new sense: no actual sexual intercourse. "I knew right away we'd be good for each other." Really? Gow dumps that as too imprecise to even fix. And he confesses that he's getting embarrassed, rather than hiding behind vagueness.

The point of the exercise is to teach yourself to see as your reader sees: What's clear in your memory is opaque to your reader unless the language is direct, the details exact, the truth out there in front, including the truth of reticence or other shyness. And every "finished" draft can benefit from a reading for precision.

TEXTURE

I don't mind cross-country skiing across a frozen lake; in fact, I love the speed and squeak of snow on deep ice. You can get a real rhythm going, zoom smoothly along, as the hills ahead grow larger and the hills behind retreat. Hours can pass as you cover the miles; your mind is free to wander.

But I much prefer terrain: peaks and dales, bumps and flats, a grand and natural mix to give the pleasures of variety—chances to rest, chances to puff, hard skiing, easy skiing, views, canyons, sounds, a hundred kinds of trees, lots of smells, emotions unavailable on the lake (is that a moose?), a hill to go flailing down, a patch of ice, my big dog Wally standing right in my way around a blind corner as I roar downhill—oomph.

Texture in writing is like terrain in cross-country skiing. Texture in prose is, well, the *surprises* you give your reader, the constant shifts of speed, the layers of meaning, the vivid images, the unexpected feelings, the startling choices of words, the separate moods each section evokes.

Certainly, writing can get overtextured (Annie Dillard sometimes gets accused of just that)—too steep, too icy, too many rocks in the path—the reader isn't up to the challenge and falls down, gives up. Overtexture is a trap for some new writers. But the writing of most new writers goes the other way: one note, one direction, one layer, one mood. It's like skiing on that frozen lake—not entirely without its pleasures, but monotonous, the destination always clearly in view, the colors uniform, the trip rewarding only in terms of distance covered, with the distance not of much interest in itself.

Tim Rushford, primarily a fiction writer, decided to try something different and took my memoir course in Vermont. He wrote about his twin younger brothers, pests who used to wake him when he wanted to sleep-in. Here's his line, which comes smack in the middle of a pretty straightforward paragraph.

> And then the twins marched in and pissed in the soup of my sleep.

Oh, man, we workshoppers argued about that line. Everyone in the group had marked it. Some thought it was terrific. Some wanted it cut right now: horrid! Tim himself said he had cut it and restored it and cut it and restored it probably twenty times, deciding in the end to hear what we—his readers—had to say. We said a lot, and never agreed. I had hated the line at first, but my feeling after the discussion was: keep it. If it gets that much attention from good readers—keep it. And keep writing lines like that till you start making lines just as outrageous that *no one wants to cut*. Practice, practice, as always.

Exercise Seven: Micturating in the Soup of Your Sleepy Prose. Again, get out a "finished" draft. In each paragraph, add a line that feels wild to you, one you'd never in a million years put in that place. The wildness can come in content or punctuation or mood or language or what have you. Just let 'er rip. Be a different writer, just for that moment. Use second person suddenly, or an absurd metaphor. Use a ten-syllable word, then use it again. Admit to a craving for horseradish even as you write. Be gross, if gross is not your norm (or be polite if it is). Or throw in a description of the Grand Canyon for no reason. Anything, whatever, go for it. Don't examine the fit, not yet.

Don't edit the lines away, but print out a draft with all of them in place. Find a reader, or wait a couple of weeks and read it yourself. What can you use? What new directions are suggested, both for your essay and for you as a writer?

Texture arrives with practice, with confidence, with the acquisition of a voice. The idea of this exercise is to speed up the process, even if just a little.

URGENCY
If it doesn't matter, why write it? If it doesn't matter deeply, and right now, why read it?

The best prose gives off a sense of inevitability: This had to be written, and this had to be written this way. There's nothing extra— even the ramblings seem vital—there's something at stake. The idea is important, the event was momentous, the love was alive. I'm not saying only write about car crashes and presidential impeachments, just that when you write about the migratory paths of snails you make bloody sure your prose is alive and breathing—as you are— that when you write about images of lizards in Coleridge you never relax, never repeat yourself, never sound like a tour bus driver on the ten-thousandth run.

Exercise Eight: You Could Start This Thing Anywhere. If you're at all like me, you put a lot of time into your first paragraphs. You want to launch your memoir or essay with a bang, you want to catch your reader, you want to inspire yourself. That first paragraph, you write it over and over, this way and that; you juggle words, you rebuild sentences, you get that thing just right.

The exercise is to flip through a "finished" draft of a memoir or essay to a random place—pick a paragraph, and start to read as if this were the start of your true story or essay. How would the paragraph you choose have to change to be a first paragraph?

Go ahead and make the changes.

And do the same for every paragraph: urgency.

Exercise Nine: A Poem of Your Prose. Pull out yet another "finished" draft of an essay. Select a block of it—a page, a section— and make a free-verse poem out of that section. This you can do even if you have no experience with poetry (although if you don't know what free verse is, you might want to look into it before you start).

To get your work into lines, to have line breaks that make sense, to put stanzas together, you have to think of the shapes of the words and their relationships, and not just meanings. You might have to pare away a great deal to get rhythm; you might have to add things to get clarity, shuffle words to get texture, interlayer phrases to get density, alter structure to get urgency, invent verbs to get motion.

When you're satisfied (or fully frustrated) with your poem, wait a couple of weeks, then convert the poem back into prose—without consulting the original text of your essay.

There.

Exercise Ten: The Village Voice Prize. When I first moved to New York City for my ten years there, I was amazed by everything. I was especially amazed by *The Village Voice*, the weekly newspaper of culture and behind-the-scenes news. I was so amazed that I actually decided to enter their short-short science fiction contest. The rules: exactly 250 words of science fiction, not one word more or less.

I worked with feverish hope until my story was exactly 250 words. It was about an annoying scientist on a distant planet whose pet plant pushes him into an otherworldly pond where he's eaten by another plant.

Anyway. Getting the original draft of 1,000 words down to exactly 250 words was an exercise in narrative necessity: Cut, cut, cut; yow, yow, yow. But it worked.

The exercise: Tell a true story in exactly 250 words. Not one word more or less, please. You may use an earlier try and simply cut it down to size. Pay attention to the kinds of words and sentences (and even paragraphs) that can go, the kind that can stay.

I didn't win the prize, by the way, but I won something more valuable still: this exercise, ladies and gentlemen, which I share with you.

Yes, I'm kidding.

LEARNING TO FINISH

Slowly, I've come to see that when I'm finished with a piece, I've really just begun. It's a hard lesson, one that comes with long experience and practice. It's a matter of trudging the extra steps—no oxygen mask, toes frozen—to get to the top of the mountain. It's the tough stuff, and it's the place where real writers leave the hobbyists behind.

You've got a polished draft. You've figured out what you're going to say. You've made your scenes. Your characters are doing their jobs. You know exactly where your true story, your essay, is going to go, because it's there already. Your structure is in place. The arc of your narrative is so firm it could stand beside the Mississippi River in St. Louis. Your ideas are out front. Your images are clear as ice sculptures.

Time to go back in. Time to read more closely than ever. Time to fearlessly open up paragraphs already sealed, time to knock sentences over their heads, time to get the language just exactly right so there's no question you've got the basics of beauty alive in every corner of your essay: clarity, motion, density, rhythm, precision, texture, urgency.

The wolves are howling!

TEN

BUILDING A BUILDING

I don't believe the writer should know too much where he's going. If he does, he runs into old man blueprint.

—James Thurber

The artist is the one who never gets it right.

—Mose Allison

When I think of structure in academic writing, I see a row of identical townhouses in Anytown, U.S.A.—nice, solid-brick construction, fashionable neighborhood, smugly correct lines, conventions observed (though perhaps the doors have been painted different colors—nothing too garish).

When I think of structure in formal journalism, I see Levittown, Long Island, when it was first built: thousands of precisely identical houses lined up forever on former potato fields—liveable, serviceable, functional, three models to choose from.

When I think of structure in creative nonfiction, I see an enormous old farm in Maine, 1972. I'm there with my friends Bob Meyer and Michael Levine, trying to get ideas for Mike's cabin, miles away. A group of hippies (that's what they call themselves), part of the back-to-the-land movement (they don't actually know this), have bought this spectacular five-hundred-acre spread for next to nothing. In the course of the previous six years, individual members of the community have built themselves private houses, twenty of them by now. We get the grand tour. Variety: a geodesic dome straight from a Bucky Fuller kit; an enormous yurt, sod and timber; a Cape Cod saltbox, built from seventeenth-century drawings and home-sawn boards; two really wild tree houses, one with walkways through the canopy of the climax hardwood forest at the fringes of the farm; a plain rectangular box (its owner eschewing adornment for spiritual reasons); a three-story tower, its first floor octagonal, second floor hexagonal, third floor round; a house made of stones from the farm's creek; a house made of free slabwood from the local mill; a house made of wine bottles set in mortar. It's a goofy scene, but thrilling: all these well-planned but eccentric places, all whimsical but suited to living through tough winters, not one remotely like the next, all but a few seeming inevitable as boulders.

There are no formulas in creative nonfiction. Each successful work in our genre creates its own rules about structure, offers its own vision of what a memoir or essay or article can be. This new vision, certainly, may spring from models, may modify common forms or mix elements of several subgenres, but in the end, the right form for your material should be as individual as you, as quirky or straight, as unpredictable or inevitable, as mysterious or matter-of-fact.

FINDING YOUR FORM

It's time to start thinking about completing a true story, or an essay, or an article, or a piece, or a chapter, or a section (any of those labels will do—you choose).

Back in chapter two, I used the analogy of a stone wall: You've been piling up rocks with nice shapes and heft, various sizes, various shades of color, some rough, some smooth, some nearly round, some more blocky—all the fragments and exercises and tries and odd paragraphs and even full drafts you've been writing. How many pages have you got? I hope a great many. (If you've been skimming along in this book, doing an exercise here and an exercise there, that's fine, but probably now it's time to go back and really make some writing.) My theory is that it's best to have your materials before you start to build.

How to fashion the stone wall? And what kind will it be? How high? What shape? What length? Will it be primarily decorative? Will it serve a function? Is it part of a castle or only a cairn?

Exercise One: Arbitrary Structure. We'll get to more elaborate approaches shortly, but now—especially if you haven't already got an essay in mind—I'd like you to try one of the most productive drafting techniques I know. Let's call it arbitrary structure.

Take your response to the map exercise (way back in chapter two), attach it with a page break to your response to the "On . . ." exercise of chapter four. To these attach your letter exercise from chapter six (without salutation and sign-off, and *sans* small talk). To these add three or four more fragments—characters, places, ideas—that somehow feel right to you. Keep mixing and matching until you have ten or fifteen pages arbitrarily tacked together.

Don't labor over the selection much; if you've been working steadily in this book or on your own for a week or a month or a year, it's you yourself—your consciousness, your concerns, your consistency of interest—that will supply the needed connections and common threads.

Oh, and some hard work: The exercise at hand is to form the once-random pieces of your effort into a personal essay. As you battle to make the connections necessary and perhaps as you write new material to fill gaps, what you are doing is coming up with an original structure in a genre that isn't big on conformity.

SOME DEFINITIONS

You'll find, I think, that a large part of getting your story or idea down on paper is finding the shape it wants to take. The beauty of the essay—well, one of the beauties, at any rate—is its ever-elastic form. Structure arises as an organizing response to specific material. What works for one subject—same writer—may not work for the next subject. And what works for one writer may not work for another.

Some definitions of familiar forms (or form categories, i.e., sub-genres), in no particular order:

• *Memoir* is a rendering of lived life as filtered through memory and the wider net of the needs of narrative. Pure memoir just tells the story, doesn't pause for analysis or nostalgia—no explicit thesis here. But pureness is only a virtue in soap, so memoir often pauses to think. And of course, sections, even sentences, of memoir are becoming an increasingly important aspect of all these other forms.

• *A personal essay* is a conversation with the reader, an informed mixture of personality, wisdom, facts, and storytelling—of memoir and autobiography. In a personal essay, writers look for the universal in individual experience, explore the power of metaphor and memory, and employ a handful (or a bushelful) of the many magnificent morsels of experience, knowledge, book learning, and personal history that fill their well-stocked minds. Note the lack of form in this form: It's as open as free verse, and as difficult. Many full-length books are extended personal essays. Examples? *Great Plains*, by Ian Frazier, or *The Silent Woman*, by Janet Malcolm, or *U and I*, by Nicholson Baker.

• *A formal essay* has a thesis, explores a single idea or closely related plural ideas, begins with an introduction, ends with a conclusion. No narrative allowed. No goofing around or wandering. The *I* may appear, but only sober.

• *New journalism* is a big and varied category, but to earn the name creative nonfiction, an article must make elegant use of the tools of the novelist: scene, characters, drama, dialogue, plot. Very often, an *I* is present explicitly. Sometimes, as in *The Right Stuff*, by Tom Wolfe, the *I* is implicit in the language and approach. Sometimes, as in *Into the Wild*, by Jon Krakauer, the *I* emerges as the re-creating imagination. In the best work, the writer immerses herself in the story, living with her subjects, getting to know them well, observing and even sharing in their lives, and, if she's anything like me, feeling bad later about exploiting them.

• *A mosaic* is an essay constructed entirely of discrete blocks of text, usually short and self-contained, that are ordered and juxtaposed without any particular attempt at transition one from the next. Mark Rudman's "Mosaic on Walking" takes this form: sixty-four blocks of text (some call these crots; my colleague Sebastian Knowles points out that *tesserae* would be more accurate) divided by page breaks. The whole of the piece is about thirty manuscript pages. Some sections are one sentence. Some are several sentences. Some are two paragraphs. The longest are roughly 250 words, about one typed page.

• *A journal* is just that: a collection of dated entries that gather force by accretion of experience, always chronological. Many journals are meant from the start as public works (May Sarton's *At Seventy*, Sue Hubbell's *A Country Year*, Rick Bass' *Oil Notes*). Others are actual journals published posthumously (John Cheever's

Journals, Paul Gauguin's *Noa Noa*, George Dennison's *Temple*).

• *Nature writing* is as American as Emerson, and generally places an observing and appreciative consciousness out among the beauties and powers of the world. Nature writing is the personal essay with one foot in the woods. Or the formal essay with an environmental thesis.

• *Travel writing* is as British as gin, though Americans have done some terrific work in the form. Go to the Amazon in search of a lost tribe and exotic drugs, like Redmond O'Hanlon ("Amazon Adventure"), or attempt a circle trip around the entire shore of the Mediterranean, like Paul Theroux (*The Pillars of Hercules*). Tamer trips get immortalized, too: walks, drives, train rides, vacations in France. The structure is generally chronological, the shape of the essay or book the shape of the original trip, with the stoical traveler at the center of a ceaseless flow of minor characters, unexpected discomfort, carefully rendered scenery, and adventures and discoveries minor or major.

• *Crossed genres* actually account for most creative nonfiction. Memoir is often one of the parents of the handsome mutt that results: memoir and history, memoir and journalism, memoir and scholarly writing, memoir and book review, memoir and profile, memoir and polemic, memoir and instruction manual. Other crosses produce unusual volumes, hard to classify, fun to read: biography mixed with novel, cookbook mixed with personal essay, nature writing mixed with gardening manual, free verse mixed with formal essay, shopping list mixed with diatribe, literary criticism mixed with character assassination. The combinations are endless, usually multiple. Film and video hold distinct possibilities here. Most often, the cross isn't particularly apparent to the author, who's just being herself.

• *Experimental nonfiction* may stem from genre crossing, though often entirely new genres of writing (or not-writing) are invented. John Berger makes an essay entirely of photos, no text. Sidney Lea makes essays like extended prose poems, going more for sound and mood and emotion and image than idea or narrative. Deborah Sobeloff asks a couple dozen people to tell her what their fathers cooked for them and simply transcribes the answers, no context. Editors and teachers often look on this stuff with interest, but can't help themselves and ask for revisions: "Make this more like what I know!"

• *Hack writing* isn't a form but a trap. A lot of possible writing jobs fall into this category, though, so I think I'll include it here both as warning and definition. Hack writing, simply put, is writing for money in the way that contract killing is killing for money, or prostitution is sex for money. You know you're hacking if you don't care about your subject, you obsess over word count, your paycheck never feels like enough, you violate all your standards of language and seriousness, you say things in print that you don't believe, you know that if you were to drop dead no one would miss you—there's always someone who could do the job as well and in the same way. Speech writing and ad writing often fall under this category, but fancier stuff can, too.

Then again, any writing for publication is good practice, and it's nice to be able to afford shoes.

Exercise Two: Try a Mosaic. I want you to try all the forms above at some point (including hacking, I guess; as Voltaire says: "Once is science; twice is perversion"). Sometimes just doing it is the best way to discover one's strengths as a writer. And weaknesses.

But the exercise here is to try a mosaic. You've already got ample building blocks—I guess we'll call them tiles for this exercise—try stringing a series together around a single subject. Food, say. Just quick, discrete blocks of text. No transitions allowed.

The idea is to experience no-form as form.

WHAT ABOUT OUTLINES?

I have finally figured out a way to use all the outlining skills I learned back in junior high school: Do the outline last. Or almost last.

I'm not saying that outlining in advance can't work: In some cases it saves a lot of time and a lot of spelunking in blind tunnels and caverns. Journalist friends of mine (and I, when I'm playing the journalist role) will draw up outlines before writing (but certainly not before reporting, if they are honest at all; the reporting constitutes drafting, really, a stage of finding out what you want to say, finding out the truth).

Then again, I've found some amazing gems in blind tunnels and caverns—caverns and tunnels that outlines tend to keep me out of. Unlike traditional reporters, writers of memoir and other creative nonfiction (this includes the new journalists) seldom know exactly what a piece of writing is going to be about before the writing starts. Even the most formal writers, outlines in hand, are often surprised by the direction a true story or essay ends up taking. The experienced among them are not afraid to throw the outline away, or make a new one.

Exercise Three: The Good Old-Fashioned Outline. Yes, an outline. But rather than trying to organize thoughts you don't yet have, try outlining a piece that's done, or nearly so.

Remember how to do it?

Start with the Roman numeral *I.* That's section one of whatever you've written. Then break your section one into subsections (all with titles), and break the subsections down into sub-subsections, numbered (and lettered) as follows: *A, 1, a, i.* That gives you five levels of meaning.

To outline a piece of work already in existence is to see its form, its structure, whole. Often you'll see blank places where more is needed, or find sections you can't seem to find a label for. Oftener, you'll see the way a certain section wanders into subcategories rarer and rarer, farther and farther from the trunk of the tree that is the essay.

Remember for this exercise that we're using the outline as a tool of form rather than a tool of preparation, an event of organization that takes place after, not before, the drafting. *After.*

Exercise Four: Diagramming. Diagramming can have the same effect as late-draft outlining, without imposing the tree shape of a formal outline.

Here's the exercise: Analyze the structure of several of your finished (or "finished") works. Pick an essay that works well, and pick one that you consider a failure. Can you diagram both? Which is easier to get a shape for?

Let me make a try with this book. Okay. I've just closed my eyes for a few seconds and seen a staircase. Definitely a cliché, but useful:

step-by-step instruction, with a steep incline. And seeing the book that way, if only for the moment, gives me a tool to go back and evaluate my success chapter by chapter. Is the incline really there? Are there any gaps in the stairs for readers to fall through? Is there a rope around I can throw to them, or should I call 911?

MAKING USE OF OLD FORMS

What about structure in a book project, especially a book that's so much an extended personal essay that it is unclassifiable? I know intimately how the structure of at least one such work arrived: my own book, *Summers With Juliet*. I hope you'll indulge me the following self-analysis.

Summers With Juliet started as an idea for a personal essay, one of my first ever (before that I'd only written formal essays and fiction), nothing more than this: My not-yet wife and I had seen an enormous fish in Menemsha Pond, Martha's Vineyard, a sea sunfish, *Mola Mola*. One January day I started to write that story, and by late March, I finished it. After a year of revising and enriching the thing (while writing other stuff, of course), I sent the essay off in the mail. *The Iowa Review* published it, and "Mola Mola" eventually got an honorable mention in *The Best American Essays, 1991*.

Well, hey. I decided I was on to something, and wrote another piece—I considered what I was doing nature writing—about a great blue heron. Then another, about some blue crabs. I had friends read these new essays and several said the same thing: They liked the way Juliet (she wasn't yet my wife) turned up in all of them.

And that gave me the idea for a book: a collection of nature essays in which Juliet played a role. Somewhere in there I hooked up with a brilliant agent, and she sold the idea of the collection to a smart editor. Well, hey. Again.

When I'd finished the seventeen essays that made the first draft of the book, everyone said to tie them together. And gradually, that's how the structure of *Summers With Juliet* emerged. That structure is self-consciously classical: three acts—situation, development, denouement (this last is from the French, as you know, for *untying*).

Act one comprises six scenes (I should say "scenes," since each is a chapter in itself, and some freestanding essays): "Hot Tin Roof," "Berkshire Turkeys," "Cross Canada," "Volcano," "Bluefishing,"

"Turtles." The situation: a callow young man (myself) in love with a young woman not impressed. A romance develops despite obstacles, mostly of the young man's making. The last scene ("Turtles") ends with his realization that his own growth is required, and the arc of the narrative rises to act two.

In act two, which is comprised of "Out of the Frying Pan," "Hummingbirds," "Callinectes Sapidus," "Mola Mola," "Fishing With Bobby," and "Canyonlands," the situation (the romance) is developed in a series of tableaux, each built around a carefully nested central metaphor, each metaphor growing nearly absurd (especially when said directly, as will follow): Juliet is a wild trout in an unfished stream; Juliet is a bossy bird; Juliet is an elegant crab; Juliet is an ungainly and rare fish of enormous proportions; Juliet is a gawky heron; Juliet is dangerous as a snake and as big as the canyons of Utah. Or perhaps the word *love* should replace the name Juliet above: Act two has grand pretensions. Ends with our boy's resolve to marry.

Now, while I was about knitting my various essays together into a book (we'll get to act three in a minute), I realized that *Summers With Juliet* was doing something subversive: standing up to the boys from the cult of the expert and messing up the central mode of a traditional form—Nature Writing (yes, so self-important is the form that it must be capitalized). Which central mode is that a man goes alone into the wilderness and finds transcendence, glory, absolution, expertise, and so forth. As the central figure in his own autobiography, he finds his way to nothing less than him-ness (or Him-ness, if he gets to God). It's a male figure made countlessly by male practitioners over centuries, a particularly American figure: I faced the wilderness alone, made peace with it, and in that way conquered.

All I really had to do to subvert was to introduce a woman. And make her and her feminine contempt for the rites of the male my foil and my catalyst (because they were in life). To end the book with a wedding was to complete the subversion: Male autobiographies have not, historically, ended with weddings.

Act three, our conclusion: "Water," "Visitors," "River of Promise," "Bachelor Party," "A Wedding on the Water." The situation having been developed to an almost ecstatic height, our narrative arc begins its fall. The young man, now well feathered, bathes his beloved in an act of devotion, struggles with fear (again the trope is at work, everything to be read as an examination of love with its subtext of mortality), climbs a mountain to ask for her hand, goes fishing with his best man in Central Park (a reprise, a look back, a caesura), then is wed.

Exercise Five: Looking for Mr. Classical Structure.

Classical structure in its simplest guise is this: rising action, climax, falling action. Notice that even its definition forms an arc. (Some scholars have compared the form to male sexual experience, a point to ponder, and well taken; is the ideal structure for a female writer something different? More enveloping? Less penetrative?)

Let's go in search of classical structure. Start by examining stories other than your own: TV shows, movies, the stories told at the watercooler ("Mr. Grumbly saw me eating at my desk. He said, 'What do you think you're doing?' I said, 'Saving time?' He said, 'You're fired!' I guess it's time to look for a job"). That arc is everyplace.

Now—and this is the exercise—look for it in your own work. If it's not already there in obvious ways, see if you can start to put it there.

Exercise Six: Plot the Points of Your Arc.

Draw an arc, preferably an enormous one, perhaps on a blackboard. Easy enough. Now place a finished essay of your own or of a favorite writer on that arc.

Say what?

Relax. For a narrative piece this is fairly straightforward. Your beginning goes at the left-hand side, your ending at the right. Your rising action occupies the left half of the curve, your climax comes toward the right.

But exposition can fall along an arc as well. And so can, say, mood. And idea. And so can all the many layers of your essay, including meaning.

Plot the points of your arc for as many layers of your work as you can identify. How much of any one category falls all to one side? How many items of structure find a start at the left but never make it to the right? How many characters fall only on one side of the arc? How can you get every layer to move from right to left, rising, then falling?

Exercise Seven: Another Way to See It. I used to use index cards to write my English papers in high school. Mrs. Potts insisted. I got very elaborate, with color coding and numbering systems, and very neat—saving quotations, cataloguing facts and figures.

I use cards a different way now, as yet another way to make the abstract structure of an emerging essay (or book) more concrete. I don't use the cards exactly the same way twice: Sometimes each section of an essay gets a color and a caption; sometimes each scene within a section gets its own card.

Again, I start with the cards after I've done some drafting. I don't want to get too organized too fast, want to leave room for surprises. But when the time comes, there's nothing I love better than to see the shape of my essay laid out across the living room rug.

IN CONCLUSION

Now, to give this chapter a false arc, a forced structure, I might go back to the old farm in Maine where I saw the fabulous and individual houses of back-to-the-land hippies. I might tell you the story of the cabin Bob and Mike and I built on Mike's land after that, and about the trouble we had with our girlfriends there—they didn't share our thrill at sleeping under the stars and cooking in the rain and living without money.

I could tell you about how when I moved back to Maine as a new college professor (nearly twenty years later), one of my first thoughts was to go find that place. I perused maps till I found a town name I remembered, then inspected the blue shapes that represented water until I found our pond (kind of a W shape)—the pond we'd swum in, bathed in, drunk from.

I drove alone two hours to the town dreaming of the glorious castle we'd built, the hand-chinked logs, the hand-dug and free-poured cement pylons, the windows salvaged from a barn, the well we'd dug, the garden we'd grown, the fun we'd had, the trouble, too: pervert neighbor man, chopping accidents, too much drinking, a rumble with locals in a mill-town bar, the breakup of first Mike and his girl, then Bobby and his, then me and mine, the big snake

I'd inadvertently slept on all the night of my twentieth birthday and found crushed flat beneath my sleeping bag next morning. We finished the cabin, slept in it maybe two nights, then headed back to college, hell of a summer.

None of us had ever returned, not yet.

Oh, Professor Roorbach took a number of wrong turns on back roads, but then there was the familiar pond (was it really so small?), there was the dirt road (so steep?), there was the stone wall. I hiked in along our overgrown right-of-way, slower and slower steps, suddenly confronted with sorrow: lost youth, lost days, lost friends, lost idealism. The cabin was there, pitched by frost off two of its pilings, leaning dangerously, full of beer cans and painted with faux-Satanist graffiti, all the glass smashed, all the doors stove in, the roof gaping. The chimney at least was still glorious and gloriously eccentric. It was made from an assortment of groovy rocks we'd found on hikes—a chunk of quartz, a long shape of feldspar, a good and genuine fossil. We'd used thick mortar and still impressed in it— just where the chimney narrowed—was my girl Annie's handprint.

Really, I should never have gone back.

ELEVEN

REACHING READERS

Writing prose is a full-time job and all the best of it is done in your subconscious and when that is full of business, reviews, opinions, etc., you don't get a damn thing done.

—Ernest Hemingway

I like to just make the film, not read the reviews, not follow the box office, put it away and make another film. And then make another film. I find that if you don't like the actual making of the film, you're lost, because that's all there is. The rest of it is too mercurial, and you don't get the pleasure you think you're going to get from the success.

—Woody Allen

After many seasons of study and contemplation (sitting lotus on my mountain of rejection slips), after years of talking to and dealing with scores of editors (and after being an editor myself), I have discovered something momentous—nothing less, ladies and gentlemen, than the secret to getting published.

Are you ready?

Here it is: *Write something good.*

That's it. Simple as that. Good writing. That's all an editor wants. And the fact that every editor is going to define that simple phrase in a different way is not a problem, not really. If you're making good writing—fresh, important, well-made, compelling, top-of-the-line stuff—someone out there is going to want to publish it.

As for the next question (and the really important one)—how to *make* good writing—the answer is practice. A good start would be back in chapter one, though I don't blame you if you turned to this chapter first.

Listen to me: Publication in, say, *The New Yorker*, is the equivalent of singing with the Metropolitan Opera. And the Met's singers—even the ones in the chorus—got there because of years of practice, years of voice exercises, years of rejection and invisibility, years of the well-intentioned doubts of friends and family, years of making luck happen, years of what adds up to something noble and underappreciated in our culture: apprenticeship.

So many of my adult students come to my workshops wanting to know how it's done; unfortunately, by *it* they mean publication, not writing. They want to publish, and they want to publish now. And new writers say the darndest things! "If *The Atlantic Monthly* doesn't take this essay, I'm going to burn it."

Get the matches out!

"I've rewritten this thing twice, and I'm getting sick and tired of it!"

Twice? Wow! Here's your Pulitzer!

"People just don't understand my work."

Ah, poor thing, but isn't it a writer's job to make herself understood? As my mother used to say: "I feel for you but I can't quite reach you."

APPRENTICESHIP

Good writing is, among many other things, an illusion. The primary illusion is of ease. We read a beautifully constructed book with pleasure and admiration, forgetting that the writer had to sit down day after day for a year or two years or more (often many more) to do the job. We forget—because it's the writer's job to make us forget—all the drafting, all the false starts, all the seamlessly incorporated suggestions and corrections of editors and other readers, all the self-doubt, all the projects started and never finished, all the manuscripts in drawers, all the learning, all the patience, all the writerly reading, all the study, all the practice (here it comes again): the apprenticeship. So we read the book and feel cowed: How'd she *do* this? And worse, we get the idea that we ought to be able to sit down and write a beauty first try—*should be easy: Ten pages a day for thirty days is a book*!

Good writing occurs not in bursts of inspiration (although inspiration can't hurt) but in time so slow it feels like geologic time: Ten thousand years is nothing, a moment. A million years is but a day (that some good writers write terrific drafts fast is a function of experience, of many years' hard work in preparation, and rarely of raw talent, though there's that, too).

It's easy to get devotedly stuck to a single essay—I've had students in my summer workshops tell me the essay at hand has been work-shopped fifteen times. I see student drafts that were written twenty years past. In these cases, learning has stopped. In these cases, *writing* has stopped. Instead of seeing that dead essay as a step toward the next and the next and the next (perhaps all on the same subject, the subject, at least, being very much alive), the dead essay becomes the end point, propped up on a morgue slab with unhelpful tubes still in its nose, reluctant writing teachers leaning over it like priests and morticians.

If you're that devoted to a single piece of writing, it will be very hard to hear criticism. I have been known to spend hours on a critique for a student. And nothing's more depressing than this response (which I've heard many times more than once): "Oh, that's just what my other teachers said!"

New writers like this aren't listening. They are not honoring their own apprenticeships. They're shopping around for a teacher who'll say the work is good. And when that doesn't happen, they leave workshops furious: Those people are just as stupid as the last bunch. And go on to blast the editors and magazines who reject their work: "*The Paris Review* publishes *crap*. It's just their friends they publish!"

"It's all connections," people like to say.

Well, connections are nice, but connections only help if the work is there: Okay, you've gone to every writers conference in the universe, you know every writer in creation and they love you and want to help you. Now make your move: Write something good.

Luck is a fine thing for a writer, too, but take note: Good writing creates luck. Good writing is the ultimate connection.

Exercise One: Write Something Good. This is fairly straightforward; the exercise is the same as its title. Here it comes.

Write something good.

Preferably *really* good. As Donald Hall says, take all the time you wish. Ten years would not be unusual. Twenty is fine. If you're already eighty years old, don't worry, your life experience will surely speed things up. But the assignment is the same: Write something good. When you've done so, bring your draft back and we'll talk about it.

HOMECOMING

Ah! You're back. Wow, we missed you. But you look great. Not a spare pound after all those years! And what have you done with your hair? Love the long white beard!

And what's this? A draft of something *good*. And man, it really *is* good. Let's go public with it—but not to editors, not quite yet.

Exercise Two: Going Public. The Latin root of publish is *publicare*, which means to make public. In that light, of course, it's possible for anyone to publish. The Internet is full of embarrassing stuff people want to make public. So are bathroom walls. One of the beauties of magazines and books (and okay—grumble, grumble—Web sites, too) is that they define a particular public, a particular group of readers the editors feel they know the taste and interests of.

For this exercise, please make ten copies of your finished draft. Pass these out to people you suspect are readers. Your boss. Your neighbor. Your bartender. Your tennis coach. Your pastor. That guy at the gas station who's always talking about books. Your dentist.

Your writing group doesn't count for this exercise, by the way. They're accustomed to taking an editorial role, or perhaps a pedagogical role. What we're looking for here is plain old readers.

There. You've published yourself.

Phase two is to try to engage each of your readers in a conversation about your work. This might be difficult. Not everyone will even read what you give him. Many people will be mystified. But if you've picked your readers with a little care—people who read other stuff, people who have literary points of reference—you'll get at least some response.

"Oh, pretty good," they'll say.

You boldly answer: "What did you like?"

"I liked the subject," they'll say.

You: "What did you end up thinking it was about?"

"I didn't get it," they'll say.

You: "Well, how much *did* you understand?"

"I just can't put my finger on it," they'll say.

You: "Let me tell you what I was trying to do."

And so forth, till you've got some information you can use. Of course, the interrogation above will take a lot of guts, depending on your reader, but some version of it—very conversational—will help you understand how you're being read and misread, where you are connecting, where you aren't.

Phase three is to go back to the work at hand and make it answer to your readers. Sometimes a small change or two clarifies some point of meaning and fixes everything. Sometimes, on the other hand, your lawn-mowing guy will have made you see a major flaw. And he'll have saved you from squandering your big chance with that editor you met at Bread Loaf.

AGAINST POLISHING

I hate the idea of polishing when it comes to writing. You know? I always get the image of some poor slob (actually, myself) buffing and buffing his twelve-dollar shoes. When he's finished those shoes will shine, all right, but they will still be twelve-dollar shoes.

Polish is insidious. You polish up your essay—put a finish on it—and the surface gets so bright you can't (and don't want to) delve beneath that surface. Your prose becomes reflective, a mirror. You see yourself in it. You actually begin to confuse the writing with yourself. And now there's no way to cut into that writing, no way to smash that veneer, no way to see clearly beneath it. Revision becomes a form of suicide, absurdly, and polishers avoid real revision as if it were death itself.

Polishing is a form of tinkering, and tinkering for too many new writers is what revision amounts to. You can spend days adjusting sentences in a first paragraph that ought to be cut altogether. You can spend months moving paragraphs around in a piece that ought to be shelved forever—honorably, of course—perhaps seen as a study for work to come.

Real revision—it's right there in the word—is re-seeing.

Exercise Three: Seeing It Again. I'd start this one by taking a good, finished piece, and placing it in a drawer, or in a computer file directory labeled "resting" or "pause." Work on other things for two weeks, a month, or more.

Then, without referring to the finished (or, as always, let's use the quotation marks: "finished") piece, go to work on it. Try a new opening. Try a radically different voice. Try retelling the big central scene from memory. Yes, it's a lot of work. But that's the difference between writing that gets published and writing that doesn't: a lot of work.

When you've got a new pile of pages on the old theme, pull out the original draft. What can you use from your re-seeing?

GET OUT THE PRUNING HOOK

Cutting a manuscript is about the most painful thing you can do. Painful, that is, until you do it. Once a chunk of unneeded prose is gone, it's beautiful how fast you forget it. The trick is recognizing what's unneeded. Nothing's more annoying than the first time an editor chops a chunk out of your manuscript. Often, of course, it's the chunk you love most that goes, the sentence that everyone in your workshop praised, the paragraph that brings your mom to tears every time, the passage that contains your title. Working with an editor, though, however annoying, will help you begin to develop an editor's eye: an eye for the extra, the unneeded, the gratuitous, the filigree, the frosting.

An editor at a certain literary magazine once offered to accept an essay I'd submitted. One condition: They only had room for 5,000 words in the next number, and the piece I'd submitted was 10,000 words long.

What would you do?

At first I was pretty whiny. That was half my essay! And the problem wasn't that the editor and his board didn't like it, just that they didn't have room.

I said no.

Middle of the night I woke up and reconsidered: That essay needed a home, badly. In fact, that essay was a wild child—it was going to be hard to place in the best of circumstances.

But they wanted me to cut it in half!

I did the deed.

The brutal chopping required quite a bit of rewriting, of reimagining, but in the end the essay did its job—the same job it had done when longer—with startling economy. And it didn't end up seeming thin, not at all. In fact, while its body was smaller, somehow its soul was bigger. While I cut, I kept thinking I'd restore the original one day for a collection. But now a couple of years have passed and I find I love the cut version, find I can't even remember the original: Rather than an assault on a finished product, the cut turned out to be the final step of drafting, and that step of drafting made the essay.

Later I found out that the magazine had had all the space in the world—that editor knew he needed to concoct something to get me to finish my essay.

Well, his damn lies worked.

Exercise Four: Let's Just Suppose . . . Pick your favorite completed draft. Now, pretend the phone is ringing. It's the editor of your favorite magazine. "Love your piece," says she. "Want to publish it," says she. She lets you bubble and enthuse for a few embarrassing minutes, then: "Too long," says she. "We can't publish it unless you cut it in *half."*

And that's the exercise: Cut your draft in half.

Remember, the original is always there for you to return to—no danger of its disappearing. Do the exercise in the spirit of experimentation. But don't be surprised if the results make you proud.

Exercise Five: Clear-Cutting. This is a variation on exercise four, above. Again, I'll ask you pull out a "finished" draft. But this time take it by the ear to a literate friend, perhaps another writer with whom you can exchange the following favor: a severe cut.

This is an especially good exercise if you weren't able to get yourself to do the exercise above. I certainly understand if you couldn't: Your own work can start to seem inviolable. And this exercise isn't foolproof: Even literate friends can be squirrely about cutting sentences that have been labored over, paragraphs with neat turns of phrase. So be tough. Be arbitrary. Tell your friend that he must cut *half* the word count for you. Yes, fully half. For the cutter, it's a fun exercise, a kind of puzzle: What can go without changing the argument, the meaning, the story?

When you have your cut manuscript back, type it up new, just the way your editor asked. Fair warning: You're not going to like it at first, not at all. But type it up as suggested. Next, without looking at your original (no cheating—if you can't remember the old way in the face of the new, that's a good sign that you're on to something), go to work on a revision.

Even if you do end up going back to all or part of your original version, you'll find lessons and suggestions in the cut. Also, you'll have worked with an editor, and that's good practice, too.

PING-PONG

Okay. Now you've got a manuscript. You've examined the language of it, you've tried it on literate friends, you've cut everything that can be cut. Finally, it's time to start thinking about publication. Where to start?

Probably you've already got your *Writer's Market,* so you know how to prepare your submission: simple cover letter ("Please consider the enclosed memoir"); self-addressed, stamped envelope; manuscript clearly typed or printed out—no fancy fonts, no tiny fonts, no faint print, Name and address on the manuscript. And that's it. Nothing else. No photographs, no long explanations, no so-so manuscripts (you know when your writing's not very good; people you trust—teachers, friends, classmates, and often you yourself—have told you so), no dumb jokes, no resumes, no large-denomination bills, no bullshit.

And don't go into the submissions game thinking you're going to make tons of money. In fact, don't go in thinking about money at all. This is art we're talking about, not a job. Your payoff will be an audience. If a check eventually turns up—small or large—well, that's just gravy.

Most new writers, understandably, decide to start at the top. And why not? One or two out of a billion manuscripts are probably placed this way. *The Atlantic Monthly, The New Yorker, Harper's*— magazines like these get thousands of submissions a week, tens of thousands a year; manila envelopes fill their hallways. But try. It's nice to have a high-class stack of rejection slips to get you started.

No really, I'm serious: Collect rejection slips. This will toughen you up. Learn that a rejection from one of the great magazines of the world (or from any magazine) is not an indictment of your work, not a message that you should hang your head and quit writing. It's just not. It's only a rejection. Your envelope may well have been opened by a college student interning for a summer and seen by no one else.

Here's what's important. You know your work is good. Teachers, friends, classmates, occasional quick notes from editors, and you yourself have said so. Listen: By the time most good writers start to publish work regularly, they've amassed many hundreds of rejection slips, in all shapes and sizes. Good manuscripts have been known to rack up dozens of rejections before finding a home. Good manuscripts have been known to never find a home (but I doubt many).

Ping-Pong, my writer friend Bob Kimber once called it. You shoot a manuscript out, they shoot it back; you whack it back out there, it comes back. As long as you have done the honest work and know that what you're offering is good stuff, you have every reason to play the game. Pip. Pop. Pip. Pop. Pip. Pop. Don't get discouraged. Pip. Pop. Keep writing. Pip. Pop. Keep writing more and better. Pip. Pop. Retire any manuscript that time and experience begins to show you is inferior, but keep in the game a manuscript you know is good. Pop. Pip. Pip-Pop.

Exercise Six: Another Library Mission. Once again, I'm sending you to the library. But by now you've scheduled a regular library night, so this will be easy.

Take a break from other research one night and use the time to peruse literary magazines (the bigger the library, generally, the bigger the collection). You've already tried the appropriate big, commercial magazines with your manuscript. Now it's time to get real.

The exercise is to find ten literary or trade magazines that for whatever reason—layout, authors, apparent philosophy, genre balance, literary quality, gut instinct—you like. Make this an ongoing investigation, and over months and years you'll start to have a real knowledge of what's out there, and who's publishing what. More important, you'll start to know where the kind of stuff you like is appearing. And if a magazine is publishing the kind of stuff you like, there's that much more chance its editors will like the stuff you write.

Make a tidy chart. Or a sloppy one, if that's your style. List editors' names. List addresses. Consider subscriptions to a few favorite publications. Put together a long catalog of magazines you like, with notes about the kinds of work each magazine seems to publish, with notes about which magazines seem right for specific manuscripts of your own.

Exercise Seven: Submit. Consider one of your "show" manuscripts (it's tight, it's right, it's ready to show). Which of the magazines you've been investigating can you honestly see it in? Make a Ping-Pong list of about ten realistic choices, in a hierarchical order. Mail to number one, using the editor's name. To soften the blow when the rejection inevitably comes, get the envelope for number two ready in advance. (If you begin to see the submission process as a matter of collecting rejection slips, getting rejection slips will be, well, a kind of success.) Give the editors six weeks or so (a fast turnaround for most little magazines, granted, but a hell of a long time to freeze a manuscript from other consideration). If they haven't answered in that time, send to the next magazine on your list, and send a polite note to the first editors saying you've done so. (As for simultaneous submissions—it's kind of like elbows on the table: punishable by death in some households, perfectly acceptable in others. I've found that as long as you are clear and honest about your submissions, not many editors care much one way or the other. Personally, I like an orderly flow, and when you send to twenty-one editors in a batch, beware: If the postage doesn't kill you, the twenty-one rejections all coming at once surely will.)

Pip. Pop. Start a file of rejection slips. Have a sense of humor about it.

Pop. Pip. If you get any personal letters back, start a file of those: good bets for the future.

If you get an acceptance, wow! Have a party. Then back to table tennis. Pip.

PUBLISHING YOUR BOOK

Yes, when it comes to book publishing, you need an agent. And yes, agents are as hard to get as publishers, or harder. Again, there has been plenty written on the subject, and I'll assume you've read quite a bit of it. If you haven't and want to, hie thee to a bookstore or library: You'll have no trouble finding titles.

Nonfiction can often be sold on the basis of sample chapters. Sometimes, it can even be sold on the basis of an outline. Sometimes, on the basis of a conversation. If you know where the missing eighteen minutes of Nixon's White House tape are, you've got a book deal. If you were held captive by terrorists and your image was on TV for two months straight, knife to your throat, you've got a book deal. If you've slept with six presidents and have proof: deal, deal, deal. More prosaic stories will be harder to sell.

Dull writing about prosaic stories will be impossible to sell.

But once you've got something good going, I'd suggest a letter-writing campaign. Again, you don't want to waste time with editors and agents who aren't going to have any interest in the kind of thing you're doing. One strategy is to find out who edited and who represented the books you like best, the books most like the book you intend to write, or have written. Probably, since you're a reader, you can name ten favorite books right off the top of your head. Well, not just favorite books, but favorite contemporary books. And not just contemporary, come to think of it, but recent books. Very recent is best. If you can't name ten recent titles that knocked you out or that in some way bear on your project, you'll need to do a little research. In a big library, there will be millions of titles covering a couple of centuries. The editor of *Walden* isn't going to be able to help you much, even if *Walden* is your favorite book.

But you know the kinds of writers you like. And if you list them to most librarians these days, you'll get a longer (and more informed) list back. Spend your library night with a stack of books around you—you're looking for authors new to you, titles new to you, and in some cases, publishers new to you. You are looking for literary soul mates.

Exercise Eight: Finding Ten Names. This one's fun. You get to use the phone.

Okay. I've got you at the library. Narrow down a list of books to ten titles that have real affinity in scope, style, subject, ambition (and so forth) to your book or book idea. Don't limit the search in any other way (one of my students with a good book—it did eventually find a prestigious Southern home—at first wouldn't contact any publisher not located in New York City). Only two criteria: one, you like the book; two, it has some definite point of connection to *your* book.

Now comes the detective work: Who's the editor? Occasionally you'll find him or her named by the author in the acknowledgments. More often, there'll be no clue. Next question: Who's the agent?

To find out, just call the publisher. You'll get a receptionist. Ask: Who is the editor of such and such book? In a smaller place, the receptionist will know. In a bigger place, you'll be connected to layers of secretaries and assistants and mumbly apparatchiks, perhaps some publicity people, perhaps the guy from permissions, but eventually you'll find out. Next questions: Does that editor still work there? What's the address there? And finally: Who's that author's agent?

Do not call the editor. Do not call the agent. That is, don't call unless you have a great phone style and a genuinely hot topic that you can explain in four seconds.

Exercise Nine: Letter Campaign. Now you've got the editors' names and the agents' names for ten terrific books, ten books all of which have some bearing on your own project. (And your own project is good. Of this, you are confident. If the project is a proposal for a book not yet written, you are confident that you have the ability to carry the project out and that you have the credentials to prove you can carry it out.)

Write up a description of the project. Get it in one paragraph, one smashing, fascinating, elegant, urgent, startling, fresh paragraph that not only presents the idea but shows what a terrific writer you are. Try this paragraph on a bunch of friends. Do they understand your project? Or do they end up with lots of off-the-mark questions? Keep writing until anyone who reads your letter looks up at you and says, "Wow! Eek! Gasp! Where can I read this book?"

Only then, make neat and businesslike letters containing your paragraph and the briefest introduction of yourself ("I'm a dentist with four kids. I write at night"). Do not lie. Do not stretch the truth. Do not say anything extra.

Add one more paragraph at the beginning, written with utmost sincerity and from the bottom of your heart, something like this: "I've just finished reading Acne Bonbon's *Life of a Chocolate Addict*. It's a terrific book—I can still see Acne trying to climb out of those chocolate vats in Switzerland. Your work on that book made me think you'd be interested in my book: *The Ice Cream Diaries.*"

Or something. It needs to be true and real: Don't say you loved a book you didn't. Editors are extensively trained in the detection of crap.

End your letter by offering to send along sample chapters, should the editor or agent wish.

Send a similar letter to as many editors and agents as you've found, as many as you want, really. Out of ten editors, three will not reply at all, three will send a form letter saying they only deal with agents, three or four will politely decline in a personal note. One might ask to see a sample chapter.

Bingo. You have been solicited.

If the first wave peters out, keep going. You can send your proposal to as many editors and agents as you wish until you get some real interest somewhere. The interest—however slight—of an editor can get you the interest of an agent. And if an editor gets interested enough to make an offer, plenty of agents out there will be glad to help you out. For 10 or 15 percent—well earned—of any cash that comes in.

And if after fifty or a hundred letters you get no interest at all, don't despair: You've learned a few things, and that's a big part of the game. Don't curse the agents. Don't question the quality of the editors. Instead, question the quality of your project or the presentation you've made of it.

And always, always, keep writing.

THE ULTIMATE ASSIGNMENT

Publication isn't, I know, the real goal of everyone reading this book. Some of you just want to get your stories down for your grandchildren to read, and for their children, a noble ambition. Documents like that are priceless in families. Some of you just want to get your story right for yourself. And that is noble, too. In the end, this is just what Janet Bellweather realized: Her writing was meant for her own edification; she didn't really need or want an audience of readers. Some of you—like Janet—are going to be content with writing as a hobby. And that's good, an important fact to know about yourselves.

For others, publication is a kind of hunger, the hunger of ambition. I hope I've helped you see that the only helpful ambition is the ambition to write something good, something that will satisfy readers unknown to you in both predictable and unpredictable ways. If your ambition is about the work, the dream of publication won't eat at you, won't make a fool of you. If your ambition is about fame and fortune, well, I wish you luck, but the odds are stacked enormously against you. Nothing worries me more than students who believe they're going to be able to write when they hate to read, or students who believe they will earn huge advances for their stories and go on Oprah's show, when really they don't write, and in truth would rather not write.

But really it's a great moment when I get a thick envelope in the mail—usually unexpected—and in it is a book, or a handsome literary magazine. I pull out the book and turn it over and over and suddenly recognize the name or the photo (or sometimes even the title); I inspect the magazine article by article till I find what I'm supposed to: a former student, now a friend, whose hard work has paid off.

Someone, in fact, has just sent me a copy of *North Woods Quarterly*. It takes me a minute to find out why, but there it is, the leadoff essay: "Krock's Store." Gow Farris is on his way. The first chapter of his book has found print. I'm glowing, man.

Let me know how *you* do.

Exercise Ten: Live as a Writer. Most writers lead double lives. While neighbors are sleeping or trimming the roses or shopping for sheets or taking a drive, we're sitting staring at computer screens or yellow pads. Why?

I'll let you answer that.

The world of nonwriters conspires to make it difficult to protect writing time, difficult to daydream, difficult to find psychological space to create in, difficult to justify ourselves (my unamusing neighbor in Maine loves to wag his finger at me and say, "Some of us have to work!").

Rejection is painful and constant. And publication when it comes turns out to be emotional and difficult—nothing like what we'd dreamed. Parents don't give us much credit for our successes, much less understand our failures. Children clamor for much-deserved attention of their own. Well-meaning friends say the stupidest things about our work, enemies scoff, colleagues diminufy.

Turns out that handling all this is a large part of what being a writer is about. A writer is someone who writes, it's true, but a writer is also someone with a large capacity for adversity. You'll want to cultivate that capacity. Stamina is a writer's first quality. But if you wake up one day and decide all the hours aren't worth it, if you wake up one day and decide never to try another essay again, if you wake up one day and realize writing for you is a hobby and not more—that's okay. No dishonor. Writing something good is very much harder than it looks. And writing makes a good hobby—especially if you have an audience of family and friends. Enjoy.

But some of you have a higher vision. Some of you are going to keep at it no matter what. And while you work, I hope you'll keep something in mind: You don't need to be jealous of other writers. You will be, but you don't need to be. You don't need to feel envy (but you will, you will). Writing isn't a race, or if it is, it's only a race against time, against yourself. And writing isn't professional baseball. You're not trying to fight your way to the one starting position at third base for the Yankees. What you're pushing toward, growing toward, working toward is a place only you can occupy. It's the place to which you're capable of getting. It's a place waiting for you, and no one can usurp it, no one else can occupy it.

Here's the final exercise, and it comes along with a fond farewell and best wishes for success:

Write.

Here is my essay "Into Woods," the short memoir I described in chapter five, appended as promised, and humbly.

"Into Woods" was first published in April of 1993 by *Harper's Magazine*. My editor there was Colin Harrison, a smart guy, now a friend, who had to that time rejected a long parade of my stories and essays, sometimes with encouraging notes, but not always. He read the original draft I'd submitted of "Into Woods" (the working title was "Woods II") and made up his mind to argue for it to his colleagues. Fortunately for me, he prevailed. He phoned, then, and said, "We're going to publish your piece."

I gasped and giggled and tried to sound cool: "Wow."

"One thing," said Colin. "You have to finish it." He gave me nothing more than that to go on, only this: a deadline, one month hence.

And I sat down with the piece I'd thought quite finished and puzzled and groaned and read and tore my hair and re-read till in the middle of a deep, tossing night, one week to go, I had an idea: My dad had just visited my new house in Maine, and we'd just rebuilt the garage. Though the material was fresh—only a couple of months past—it turned out to be what I needed to bring the story full circle.

Thanks, Colin.

INTO WOODS

In a dive near Stockbridge in the Berkshire Hills of Massachusetts, I nearly got clobbered by a big drunk who thought he'd detected an office fairy in the midst of the wild workingman's bar. He'd heard me talking to Mary Ann, the bartender, and I didn't talk right, so by way of a joke he said loudly to himself and to a pal and to the bar in general, "Who's this little fox? From Tanglewood or something?"

I, too, was drunk and said, "I am a plumber, more or less."

I was thirty years old, was neither little nor a fox, had just come to work on the restoration of an inn, and was the foreman of the crew. But that seemed like the wrong answer, and too long in any case.

He snorted and said to everyone, "A more or less plumber," then appraised me further: "I say a hairdresser."

"I say a bank teller," his pal said.

I didn't mind being called a hairdresser, but a bank teller! Oh, I was drunk and so continued the conversation, smiling just enough to take the edge off: "Ah, fuck off."

"Cursing!" my tormentor cried, making fun of me. "Do they let you say swears at the girls' school?"

"Headmaster," someone said, nodding.

"French teacher," someone else.

"*Guys* . . . ," Mary Ann said, smelling a rumble.

"Plumber," I said.

"More or less," someone added.

"How'd you get your hands so clean?" my tormentor said.

"Lily water," someone said, coining a phrase.

My hands? They hadn't looked at my hands! I was very drunk, come to think of it, and so took it all good-naturedly, just riding the wave of conversation, knowing I wouldn't get punched out if I played it right, friendly and sardonic and nasty all at once. "My hands?"

My chief interlocutor showed me his palms, right in my face. "Work," he said, meaning that's where all the calluses and blackened creases and bent fingers and scars and scabs and cracks and general blackness and grime had come from.

I flipped my palms up too. He took my hands like a palm reader might, like your date in seventh grade might, almost tenderly, and looked closely: calluses and scabs and scars and darkened creases and an uncleanable blackness and grime. Nothing to rival his, but real.

"Hey," he said. "Buy you a beer?"

My dad worked for Mobil Oil, took the train into New York every day early-early, before we five kids were up, got home at six-thirty every evening. We had dinner with him, then maybe some roughhousing before he went to bed at eight-thirty. Most Saturdays, and most Sundays after church, he worked around the house, and I mean he worked.

And the way to be with him if you wanted to be with him at all was to work beside him. He would put on a flannel shirt and old pants, and we'd paint the house or clean the gutters or mow the lawn or build a new walk or cut trees or turn the garden under or rake the leaves or construct a cold frame or make shelves or shovel snow or wash the driveway (*we washed the fucking driveway!*) or make a new bedroom or build a stone wall or install dimmers for the den lights or move the oil tank for no good reason or wire a 220 plug for the new dryer or put a sink in the basement for Mom or make picture frames or . . . Jesus, you name it.

And my playtime was an imitation of that work. I loved tree forts, had about six around our two acres in Connecticut, one of them a major one, a two-story eyesore on the hill behind the house, built in three trees, triangular in all aspects. (When all her kids were long gone, spread all over the country, my mother had a chainsaw guy cut the whole mess down, trees and all.) I built cities in the sandbox, beautiful cities with sewers and churches and schools and houses and citizens and soldiers and *war*! And *floods*! And attacks by *giants*! I had a toolbox, too, a little red thing with kid-sized tools.

And in one of the eight or nine toolboxes I now affect there is a stubby green screwdriver that I remember clearly as being from that first red toolbox. And a miniature hacksaw (extremely handy) with "Billy" scratched on the handle, something I'd forgotten until one of my helpers on the Berkshires restoration pointed it out one day, having borrowed the little thing to reach into an impossible space in one of the eaves. Billy. Lily.

My father called me Willy when we worked, and at no other time. His hands were big and rough and wide, blue with bulgy veins. He could have been a workman easy if he wanted, and I knew it and told my friends so.

In my rich suburban high school in Connecticut we were nearly all of us college track, which meant you could take only two shop classes in your career there. First half of freshman year you could elect Industrial Arts, which was an overview: a month of Woods, a month of Metals, a month of Technical Drawing. Second semester, if you still wanted more, you went into Woods I, Metals I, etc.

I loved Woods. I loved hanging out with some of the rougher Italian kids, Tony DiCrescenzo and Bobby LaMotta and Tony Famigliani, all of them proud and pleased to be tracked away from college. I wanted to hang out with Tommy Lincoln and Vernon Porter and Roland Fish, the three black kids in my class, all of them quietly (maybe even secretly) tracked away from college. Wood shop was first period, and it was a wild class. Mr. Schtenck, our little alcoholic teacher, made no effort to control us and often left the shop for the entire period to sit in his car.

The rough kids used the finishing room to smoke pot, the storage room to snort coke. We all made bookshelves and workbenches and record racks and knickknack shelves and lamps and tables and guitar stands and frames for photos of our girls. The year was 1968, so we also made elaborate bongs and stash boxes and chillums and hollowed-out canes and chests with secret drawers. Wood shop (and along with it the very act of working with my hands) took on a countercultural glow, the warm aura of sedition, rebellion, independence, grace.

Sophomore year I signed up for Woods II, which was the advanced course. My guidance counselor, Miss Sanderson (a nice enough lady, very well-meaning, very empathetic—you could make her cry over your troubles every time if you played your cards right), thought I'd made an error on the electives form. "Only one elective a semester, William. Surely you'd like a writing course! Journalism! Or how about Occult Literature?"

"Woods II," I said, flipping my hair. I had to get parental permission to take Woods again and thought a little note with my mother's neat signature would be easy to snag, but it was not. "Why do you have to reinvent the wheel?" Mom said, one of her phrases, something of a non sequitur in this case, her meaning being *someone else will build the furniture.* Her next question was, "What kind of kids are in that class?"

Dumb kids, Mom. Mostly Italian kids and blacks and, of course, Alvin Dubronski (the class moron) and Jack Johnsen (the plumber's kid!) and me.

My dad thought it was fine, especially with the alternative being literature courses where who knew what kind of left-wing occult hippie doubletalk Mrs. Morrisey would tell you!

So into the wood shop again, every day first period (if I wasn't late for school; by that time I was hitchhiking to avoid the uncool school bus). I was the only college-track kid taking Woods II, maybe the only college-track kid who had *ever* taken Woods II, though the other kids got to take it semester after semester. And I got peer-pressured into smoking pot in the finishing room and occasionally even into blowing coke in the storage room, always a sweet, nerve-jangling prelude to another round of boring college-track classes.

One day when I was in the storage room with my high-pressure peers (and the two smartest kids in Woods II, maybe in school, both destined by their blackness for bad times in Vietnam) Roland and Tommy, fat Tony Famigliani stuck his head in the door: "The Stench is coming!" But Schtenck was already there, standing in the door. I saw my college-track life pass before my eyes.

"What are you little fuckers doing?"

"We're tasting coke, sir," Tommy said, the idiot, total honesty, as we'd all learned in Boy Scouts.

Florid Schtenck raised his eyebrows clear off his face and said, "Jesus Christ, boys, put it away—you want to get me canned?"

He never looked in the storage room again.

And later that year he stumbled and cut his finger off on the band saw. For two weeks then we had a substitute who made us file all our plans and actually checked them, stood beside us as we drilled holes in our wood or turned bowls on the lathes. It seemed an eternity before Schtenck came back and we could finally fill all the bong and hash-pipe and stash-box orders we'd been sitting on. *Sedition.*

The next year I took Woods II again, having secured special permission from the principal to go along with my parents' special permission and the special permission from Miss

Sanderson. Senior year I signed up for the class once more—what the hell—but I don't think I ever got to school in time to attend.

Somewhere in there I stopped being a willing volunteer for my father's list of chores. Now he had to *command* me to help with his corny weekend projects. I had better things to do, things in the woods with Lauren Bee or cruising-in-the-car things with some of the guys in my various garage bands—minor-league dope runs into the Village or actual gigs in actual bars in Port Chester, where the drinking age was eighteen and we could get away with it.

At home things were quiet. Except for my long hair, you wouldn't have noticed that a teen was testing his folks. I was good at talking to my elders, and good at hooking grades without working too hard—college track—and very, very good at staying out of trouble. I was on the student council. I helped with the student newspaper. I went to the homecoming rallies and proms and parades. I memorized the headlight patterns of the town police cars (I still get nervous around those big old Plymouth Furys), could smell a cop from miles away, leagues away, light-years. I had a plan for every eventuality and an escape route from every party.

Weeknights I'd turn in early, out to my room over the garage, wait for the main house to quiet down, then slip out into the night. I was caught only once, coming home about five in the morning with a friend named Melanie. Someone had called me after I'd left, and Dad couldn't find me. He was asleep in my bed when Melanie and I walked in. I was grounded, and here was the punishment: I had to spend the next four Saturdays and Sundays helping him build a playroom in the basement—drilling holes in the concrete for hours to anchor the sills for a Sheetrock wall, running cable for a hanging light over the bumper-pool table, slamming up paneling, churlishly working side by side with my dad and his distinctive smell, Aqua Velva mixed with cigarettes and Head & Shoulders and sweat.

The college track barely got me to college. As part of my desultory rebellion I put off applying until well past all the deadlines, never lying to my folks, never lying to my guidance counselor, but showing all of them the forms ready to go, then just plain old not mailing them. My plan was to play rock and roll and maybe—if necessary—make money working as a carpenter, or maybe drilling holes in concrete, or maybe making furniture or bongs. Then Miss Sanderson got a list of our school's applicants from one of my supposed top choices, and I wasn't on it. Crisis! April already, when most kids were hearing from Colby and Yale and Michigan and the U. of Hawaii.

My trusty guidance counselor got on the phone and found some schools that would look at a late application. She was crushed for me, so crushed she spared my parents the full brunt of my dereliction. At hastily arranged late interviews, admissions counselors never failed to ask why I'd taken Woods II *six semesters straight*. Finally I was accepted by one famously lame school, to which I resigned myself; then, at the last possible minute and by great good fortune, I was put on the waiting list at Ithaca College, where, on August 21, one week before school started, I was admitted into the freshman class.

I never saw my father at work, and he never talked about his work, which I vaguely knew was Executive and had to do with Mobil Oil and was desky and involved meetings and much world travel and made us pretty rich. And because I'd never seen him at work, my natural adolescent impulse toward emulation had little to go on. What to imitate? How to surpass, destroy? What I saw of my valiant dad was his work around the house, and so, emulation gone awry, I set out to be a better home handyman than he'd ever be, the real thing, even, a tradesman.

Two dollars and fifty cents an hour was well known as great money, nearly double what I'd made stocking frozen foods at the A&P during high school. Two-fifty an hour was what truck drivers got, longshoremen, a full hundred rasbuckniks (my father's word) a week. I dropped out of Ithaca College in my junior year (just when most of my buddies were heading off for a year abroad), went back to Connecticut (not my hometown, God forbid, but one nearby), and went to work for an electrician.

Lawrence Berner was a former electrical engineer who'd thrown it all over at age sixty, a theory ace but a fairly clumsy worker, a guy who had actually tossed away everything and left the college track for good. Larry was British and Jewish and unconventional and very charming, all qualities that impressed me. Best of all, he was divorced, the first divorced person I'd ever seen up close. He was filthy of habit—decadent, disgusting (maybe not as bad as my friends at school, but Larry was *old*). He lived in his marital house, wife long gone, and had trashed the place—filled the garage with electrician junk, filled the kitchen with dirty pots and jars and cans and dishes, filled the refrigerator with his important papers (fireproof, he said), filled the bedroom with the most slathery skin magazines imaginable, filled the whole house with take-out cartons, TV-dinner tins, and his own filthy underwear. His living room seemed buried in death.

He paid me $2.50 an hour.

Working beside him (tradesmen often touch—four hands to pull the cable, four arms reaching into a small space, heads together to look into a service panel . . . *hey, hold my legs while I lean out over this here abyss*), I'd feel sometimes like I was with my dad. It was Larry's thin hair, maybe, or the Aqua Velva and cigarettes, or just regular old transference. I spent every day beside this parallel-universe effigy of my father, and I was mad at Larry almost always and desperate to impress him.

One day he said I had good hands, and that little compliment was everything—I glowed, I crowed, I told my friends, my folks. I stared at my hands late at night in bars, stared at them for hours, entranced. And my hands got callused, grotesquely calloused, were always covered in cuts and scratches and dings and scabs that I hardly felt. Your knuckles never healed. And Larry mostly worked *hot*, meaning with the power on, because it saved time. I got shocks and blew holes in screwdrivers. I hit my head on rafters and and slammed my thumb with hammers and fell off ladders and sliced my fingers (daily) and once even poked a screwdriver hard into my eye (the blade didn't penetrate the eyeball but rolled past it and into the socket so that old Larry had to pull it out . . . and we kept on working). I drove the truck sometimes, sweet-talked the customers, ate in diners, worked squinting with a Lucky Strike in my mouth. I put in panel boxes and wired 200-amp services and installed a thousand outlets and a million switches. I drilled holes for cable, sawed rafters, snaked wire through walls. I wriggled into crawl spaces, sweated in attics, dug trenches.

I got tired of it. All that *body* work. Like every college-track kid in America, I'd been taught that someone else would do the rough stuff if I'd just use my mind. I went back to Ithaca, pleasing my parents enormously. Suddenly I was a good student—all A's, excellent attendance, papers handed in on time— fully engaged in a tough fight against the possibility of being a tradesman, the possibility of taking Woods II for *life*.

But after the college track had run its course, I needed to make money. I failed tests for newspaper jobs (*twenty minutes: neatly type a 500-word story around the following facts* . . .), gagged at the thought of ad agencies, moved around the country for a long time, worked with cattle, bartended (which left your hands clean, at least), then landed in New York, where I got the bright idea to put up posters around the Village and SoHo and be a handyman. Independence! I did every sort of odd job for every sort of odd person, moving over the months and years to larger home repairs, leaving town to restore that Berkshires inn, coming back to sub myself out to contractors. I graduated finally to a specialization in kitchen remodels and new bathrooms, getting more and more deeply into it, hiring helpers, wearing suits to estimates, taking ads in fancy magazines, cracking the codes for admittance to the wholesale supply houses, getting good at all of it, twelve years in all, Woods II, until one day I woke up and realized I was about to take out a bank loan to buy a truck and some very expensive tools, about to start looking for a storefront, about to start paying my employees *on the books*. I headed straight to graduate school.

My wife and I spent lots of our free time last summer looking for a house to buy up here in rural Maine (where I teach college), our first, an old farmhouse, we hoped. I kept telling myself that I had an advantage, which was my haphazard twenty-year fund of construction knowledge and restoration experience. I looked up at the beams and poked at the foundations and lifted the vinyl siding and pulled away carpets. I wiggled toilets and pulled on feeds and pushed on all the walls and ceilings. I got in crawl spaces and pried open hatch doors, inspected wiring, eyeballed plumbing, made the real-estate folks nervous.

And sometimes, in light of this commitment, this buying a house on a wee piece of our little planet, I thought about what would happen if the legislature shut down my branch of the University of Maine, or what would happen if I didn't get tenure, or what would happen if I just couldn't take the bureaucracy anymore and quit. Education presidents come and go, but people always need a plumber or someone to fix the roof, replace rotten sills, plaster the stairway wall. I could build furniture. Or renovate inns. I could take my clean college hands and plunge them into work, open all the old scars, stop being mincy and fastidious, once more revel in goo and slime, get into it: wrestle cable, kick at shovels, stand in the mud all day, hook my leg around ladders in the wind, lay tile, lift toilets and plunge my hand down that reeking fuzzy hole to pull the clog (poor Raggedy Andy one time, usually worse).

My wife and I found a house, bought it, moved in. And immediately my dad, now retired, came up to visit, tools in hand. The two of us got up early the first morning he was here and headed out to the garage, a forlorn little outbuilding about to fall down and stuffed to the rafters with the owner-before-last's junk (mostly pieces of Volkswagens and cans of old bolts and misshapen gaskets and used spark plugs and odd shims and clips). My plan was to leave room to park a car, sure, but to build a wood shop, a work space from which to operate while my wife and I renovate the house (a neglected nineteenth-century quarter-cape with many additions, the newest of which is a porch built in 1953, my own year).

So for hours my dad and I worked. We cleared out and sorted all the junk, ripped down the cardboard that made the walls, stopped to stare, to think, came up with opposite plans, argued, convinced each other; then, having switched sides, we argued again. Finally we jacked up the north side of the garage, replaced the sill, dropped a corner post in cement, took the jack away, rebuilt the wall. Next we shored up the south side, then added wiring, finally installed a metal roof over the leaky old asphalt shingles. We hit our heads and cut our fingers and ripped our jackets. We peed in the woodpile. We argued, mostly about technique and a little about the Education President (who was about to go), but really, I guess, about who was in charge of the work in my garage. And even though Pop was helping me for free, even buying some of the materials, I fumed and fulminated, almost sulked: instant adolescence.

We rebuilt the barn-style sliding door and cut in a window. We ate companionably in the Farmington Diner with sawdust and plain dirt in our hair and new hammer holsters on our belts (the acerbic Down East waitress looked me over, said, "Hi, Professor," and I introduced her to my dad); we went to the dump; we gabbed at the lumber yard; we swung hammers, climbed ladders, cut wood; we gazed at our work a long time in the dark when we were done.

Pop said, "You saved that building," as if I'd done it on my own, and we went on in the house to wash up.

SUGGESTED READINGS IN CREATIVE NONFICTION

These are books and collections I've enjoyed and learned from over the years (or have been impressively irritated by), united simply by their places on the shelf of creative nonfiction. Remember that that shelf represents a broad continuum covering several subgenres, the subgenres themselves broadly conceived. Most of the titles here could be listed under any of a number of subgenres, but I've chosen to list each book only once.

Don't be daunted by the length of the list—just know that there are lots of good books out there that might inform whatever project you are working on. A good place to start would be in one of the anthologies listed here. (*Anthos* is the ancient Greek word for flowers; an *anthology* is a gathering of flowers, a bouquet: Enjoy). In the anthologies you'll find introductions by smart editors who announce subgenres and define forms and include shorter samples from a huge array of writers, some of whom you'll surely want to follow up on. Remember this: Reading is writing, and writers read.

MEMOIR

Achebe, Chinua	*No Longer at Ease*
Adams, Henry	*The Education of Henry Adams*
Allison, Dorothy	*Two or Three Things I Know for Sure*
Angelou, Maya	*I Know Why the Caged Bird Sings*
Asher, Don	*Notes From a Battered Grand: A Memoir*
Austin, Mary	*Earth Horizon: Autobiography*
	The Land of Little Rain
Baker, Russell	*Growing Up*
Baldwin, James	*Notes of a Native Son*
Barber, Phyllis	*How I Got Cultured: A Nevada Memoir*
Bateson, Mary Catherine	*With a Daughter's Eye: A Memoir of Margaret Mead and Gregory Bateson*
Bernhard, Thomas	*Gathering Evidence: A Memoir*

Bogan, Louise	*Journey Around My Room: The Autobiography of Louise Bogan*
Bourke-White, Margaret	*Portrait of Myself*
Broyard, Anatole	*Kafka Was the Rage: A Greenwich Village Memoir*
Buechner, Frederick	*The Sacred Journey: A Memoir of the Early Days* *Now and Then*
Burn, June	*Living High: An Unconventional Autobiography*
Cantwell, Mary	*American Girl: Scenes From a Small-Town Girlhood*
Chesnut, Mary	*A Diary From Dixie*
Cisneros, Sandra	*The House on Mango Street*
Cohen, Leah Hager	*Train Go Sorry: Inside a Deaf World*
Colebrook, Joan	*A House of Trees*
Conrad, Joseph	*The Mirror of the Sea*
Conroy, Frank	*Stop-Time*
Conway, Jill Ker	*The Road From Coorain*
Cooper, Bernard	*Truth Serum: Memoirs* *Maps to Anywhere*
Crews, Harry	*A Childhood: The Biography of a Place*
Dahlberg, Edward	*Because I Was Flesh*
Dana, Richard Henry	*Two Years Before the Mast*
Davison, Peter	*Half Remembered: A Personal History*
Day, Clarence	*Life With Father*
Day, Dorothy	*The Long Loneliness: An Autobiography*
De Beauvoir, Simone	*Memoirs of a Dutiful Daughter*
Debuys, William, and Alex Harris	*River of Traps: A Village Life*
Delaney, Sarah and Elizabeth	*Having Our Say: The Delany Sisters' First 100 Years*
Delbanco, Nicholas	*Running in Place: Scenes From the South of France*
Digges, Deborah	*Fugitive Spring: A Memoir*
Dillard, Annie	*An American Childhood*
Dinesen, Isak	*Out of Africa*
Doig, Ivan	*This House of Sky: Landscapes of a Western Mind* *Heart Earth*

Doty, Mark	*Heaven's Coast: A Memoir*
Douglass, Frederick	*Narrative of the Life of Frederick Douglass*
Dubus, Andre	*Broken Vessels: Essays*
Dunham, Katherine	*A Touch of Innocence: Memoirs of Childhood*
Durrell, Lawrence	*Bitter Lemons*
Eastman, Charles Alexander	*Indian Boyhood*
Eighner, Lars	*Travels With Lizbeth*
Eiseley, Loren	*All the Strange Hours: The Excavation of a Life*
Ernaux, Annie	*A Man's Place*
	A Woman's Story
Facey, A.B.	*A Fortunate Life*
Fairey, Wendy W.	*One of the Family*
Fishman, Steve	*A Bomb in the Brain: A Heroic Tale of Science, Surgery, and Survival*
Fitzgerald, Robert	*The Third Kind of Knowledge: Memoirs and Selected Writings*
Ford, Ford Madox	*Your Mirror to My Times: The Selected Autobiographies and Impressions of Ford Madox Ford*
Fox, Suzanne	*Home Life: A Journey Through Rooms and Recollections*
Franklin, Benjamin	*Autobiography*
Garland, Hamlin	*A Son of the Middle Border*
Ghosh, Amitav	*Dancing in Cambodia*
Gilmore, Mikal	*Shot in the Heart*
Glasgow, Ellen	*The Woman Within*
Goldbarth, Albert	*A Sympathy of Souls: Essays*
Golden, Marita	*Migrations of the Heart*
Gonzalez, Ray	*Memory Fever: A Journey Beyond El Paso Del Norte*
Gordon, Mary	*The Shadow Man*
Gorky, Maxim	*My Childhood*
	My Apprenticeship
	My Universities
Gornick, Vivian	*Fierce Attachments: A Memoir*
Grant, Ulysses S.	*Personal Memoirs of U.S. Grant*

Graves, John	*Goodbye to a River*
Graves, Robert	*Good-Bye to All That*
Gray, Spalding	*Sex and Death to the Age 14*
Grealy, Lucy	*Autobiography of a Face*
Green, Henry, and Sebastian Yorke	*Pack My Bag: A Self-Portrait*
Greene, Graham	*A Sort of Life*
	Ways of Escape
Grumbach, Doris	*Coming Into the End Zone: A Memoir*
	Extra Innings: A Memoir
Guinness, Alec	*Blessings in Disguise*
Hall, Donald	*String Too Short to Be Saved*
	Life Work
Hall, Edward T.	*An Anthropology of Everyday Life*
Hampl, Patricia	*A Romantic Education*
	Virgin Time
Harnack, Curtis	*We Have All Gone Away*
	The Attic: A Memoir
Harrison, Kathryn	*The Kiss*
Hart, Moss	*Act One: An Autobiography*
Hecht, Ben	*A Child of the Century*
Heilman, Samuel	*The Gate Behind the Wall: A Pilgrimage to Jerusalem*
Hellman, Lillian	*Pentimento*
	Scoundrel Time
	An Unfinished Woman
Hemingway, Ernest	*A Moveable Feast*
	Green Hills of Africa
Herr, Michael	*Dispatches*
Hongo, Garrett	*Volcano: A Memoir of Hawai'i*
Horgan, Paul	*Tracings: A Book of Partial Portraits*
Howard, Maureen	*Facts of Life*
Hudson, W.H.	*Far Away and Long Ago: A History of My Early Life*
	The Purple Land
Hughes, Langston	*The Big Sea: An Autobiography*
Hull, John M.	*Touching the Rock: An Experience of Blindness*
Hurston, Zora Neale	*Dust Tracks on a Road*
	Mules and Men

Huxley, Elspeth	*The Flame Trees of Thika: Memories of an African Childhood*
Jacobs, Harriet	*Incidents in the Life of a Slave Girl*
James, Henry	*Autobiography*
Johnson, Fenton	*Geography of the Heart: A Memoir*
Johnson, James Weldon	*Along This Way: The Autobiography of James Weldon Johnson*
Johnson, Joyce	*Minor Characters*
Jordan, Teresa	*Riding the White Horse Home: A Western Family Album*
Kaplan, Alice	*French Lessons: A Memoir*
Karr, Mary	*The Liars' Club: A Memoir*
Kaysen, Susanna	*Girl, Interrupted*
Kazantzakis, Nikos	*Report to Greco*
Kazin, Alfred	*Walker in the City*
Keillor, Garrison	*Lake Wobegon Days*
Keller, Helen	*The Story of My Life*
Kilgo, James	*Deep Enough for Ivorybills*
Kincaid, Jamaica	*A Small Place*
Kingston, Maxine Hong	*The Woman Warrior: Memoirs of a Girlhood Among Ghosts*
Kittredge, William	*Hole in the Sky: A Memoir*
Kusz, Natalie	*Road Song; A Memoir*
Larson, Thomas	*River of Fathers*
Lavender, David	*One Man's West*
Lawrence, T.E.	*Seven Pillars of Wisdom*
Levi, Primo	*Survival in Auschwitz: The Nazi Assault on Humanity*
	The Reawakening
Levin, Harry	*Memories of the Moderns*
Levi-Strauss, Claude	*Tristes Tropiques*
Lewis, C.S.	*Surprised by Joy: The Shape of My Early Life*
Lorde, Audre	*Zami: A New Spelling of My Name*
Lusseyran, Jacques	*And There Was Light*
MacNeil, Robert	*Wordstruck: A Memoir*
Mason, Robert	*Chickenhawk*
Masters, Hilary	*Last Stands: Notes From Memory*

Mathabane, Mark	*Kaffir Boy: The True Story of a Black Youth's Coming of Age in Apartheid South Africa*
Maxwell, Gavin	*Ring of Bright Water*
Maxwell, William	*Ancestors: A Family History*
McCarthy, Mary	*Memories of a Catholic Girlhood*
	How I Grew
McConkey, James	*Court of Memory*
McCourt, Frank	*Angela's Ashes: A Memoir*
McKain, David	*Spellbound: Growing Up in God's Country*
McKay, Jean	*Gone to Grass*
McKenna, Rollie	*A Life in Photography*
McLaurin, Tim	*Keeper of the Moon: A Southern Boyhood*
Mead, Margaret	*Blackberry Winter*
Mehta, Ved	*Vedi*
	Face to Face
	Up at Oxford
	Daddyji
	Mamaji
Merrill, James	*A Different Person: A Memoir*
Merton, Thomas	*The Seven Storey Mountain*
Michaels, Leonard	*Sylvia: A Fictional Memoir*
Middleton, Harry	*The Earth Is Enough: Growing Up in a World of Fly Fishing, Trout, and Old Men*
Miller, Henry	*The Books in My Life*
	Big Sur and the Oranges of Hieronymous Bosch
	Remember to Remember
Mitchell, John Hanson	*Living at the End of Time*
Mitchell, Joseph	*McSorley's Wonderful Saloon*
Momaday, N. Scott	*The Way to Rainy Mountain*
	The Names: A Memoir
Monette, Paul	*Becoming a Man: Half a Life Story*
Moodie, Susanna	*Roughing It in the Bush, or, Life in Canada*
Moody, Anne	*Coming of Age in Mississippi*

Morris, Wright

Muir, Edwin
Muir, John

Munro, Eleanor
Murray, Pauli

Nabokov, Vladimir
Naipaul, V.S.

Nelson, Richard K.
Newby, Eric
Norris, Kathleen
Offutt, Chris
Olmstead, Robert
Ondaatje, Michael
Owens, William
Pemberton, Gayle
Phibbs, Brendan

Ponce, Mary Helen
Porter, Gene Stratton
Price, Reynolds

Puleston, Dennis
Rawlings, Marjorie
  Kinnan
Rhodes, Richard

Rodriguez, Richard

Rogers, Annie G.

Solo: An American Dreamer in Europe, 1933–1934
Will's Boy: A Memoir
A Cloak of Light: Writing My Life
An Autobiography
The Story of My Boyhood and Youth
My First Summer in the Sierra
Memoir of a Modernist's Daughter
Song in a Weary Throat: An American Pilgrimage
Proud Shoes: The Story of an American Family
Speak, Memory
Finding the Center: Two Narratives
The Enigma of Arrival: A Novel
The Island Within
Love and War in the Apennines
The Cloister Walk
The Same River Twice: A Memoir
Stay Here With Me: A Memoir
Running in the Family
This Stubborn Soil: A Frontier Boyhood
The Hottest Water in Chicago
The Other Side of Time: A Combat Surgeon in World War II
Hoyt Street
Moths of the Limberlost
A Whole New Life: An Illness and a Healing
Blue Water Vagabond
Cross Creek

A Hole in the World: An American Boyhood
The Hunger of Memory
Days of Obligation: An Argument With My Mexican Father
A Shining Affliction: A Story of Harm and Healing in Psychotherapy

Roorbach, Bill	*Summers With Juliet*
Roth, Phillip	*Patrimony: A True Story*
Saint-Exupery, Antoine de	*Wind, Sand and Stars*
Sandoz, Mari	*Old Jules*
Sarraute, Nathalie	*Childhood*
Sartre, Jean-Paul	*The Words*
Scott, Evelyn	*Escapade: An Autobiography*
Segal, Lore	*Other People's Houses*
Selzer, Richard	*Down From Troy: A Doctor Comes of Age*
	Raising the Dead: A Doctor's Encounter With His Own Mortality
Shammas, Anton	*Arabesques*
Sheed, Wilfrid	*Frank and Maisie: A Memoir With Parents*
	My Life As a Fan
	People Will Always Be Kind
	In Love With Daylight: A Memoir of Recovery
Shen, Congwen	*Recollections of West Hunan*
Shulman, Alix Kates	*Drinking the Rain*
Simon, Kate	*Bronx Primitive: Portraits in a Childhood*
	A Wider World: Portraits in an Adolescence
	Etchings in an Hourglass
Simpson, Eileen	*Poets in Their Youth*
Slater, Lauren	*Welcome to My Country*
Smith, Annick	*Homestead*
Smith, Lillian	*Killers of the Dream*
Smith, William Jay	*Army Brat: A Memoir*
Soyinka, Wole	*Aké: The Years of Childhood*
Spark, Muriel	*Curriculum Vitae: Autobiography*
Spiegelman, Art	*Maus*
Staples, Brent	*Parallel Time: Growing Up in Black and White*
Stegner, Wallace	*Wolf Willow: A History, a Story, and a Memory of the Last Plains Frontier*
Stein, Gertrude	*The Autobiography of Alice B. Toklas*
Styron, William	*Darkness Visible: A Memoir of Madness*
Talayesva, Don	*Sun Chief: The Autobiography of a Hopi Indian*

PERSONAL ESSAY AND BOOK-LENGTH ESSAY

Ackerman, Diane	*A Natural History of Love*
	A Natural History of the Senses
Auster, Paul	*The Art of Hunger: Essays, Prefaces, Interviews*
Baker, Nicholson	*The Size of Thoughts: Essays and Other Lumber*
	U and I: A True Story
Baudrillard, Jean	*The System of Objects*
	The Transparency of Evil: Essays on Extreme Phenomena
Berry, Wendell	*Another Turn of the Crank: Essays*
	What Are People For?: Essays
Blount, Roy, Jr.	*Crackers*
	One Fell Soup, or, I'm Just a Bug on the Windshield of Life
Burroughs, Franklin	*Billy Watson's Croker Sack: Essays*
Butler, Hubert	*Independent Spirit: Essays*
Buzzi, Aldo	*Journey to the Land of the Flies and Other Travels*
Codrescu, Andrei	*The Dog With the Chip in His Neck: Essays From NPR and Elsewhere*
Cohn, Nik	*The Heart of the World*
Cronon, William, ed.	*Uncommon Ground: Toward Reinventing Nature*
Crouch, Stanley	*Notes of a Hanging Judge: Essays and Reviews, 1979–1989*
Daniel, John	*The Trail Home: Essays*
Didion, Joan	*The White Album*
	Slouching Towards Bethlehem
Dunn, Stephen	*Walking Light: Essays and Memoirs*
Ehrlich, Gretel	*Questions of Heaven: The Chinese Journeys of an American Buddhist*
	A Match to the Heart
	The Solace of Open Spaces
Eiseley, Loren	*The Immense Journey*
	The Unexpected Universe
	The Night Country
Elkin, Stanley	*My Tuxedo and Other Meditations*

Elkins, James	*The Object Stares Back: On the Nature of Seeing*
Ellison, Ralph	*Shadow and Act*
	Going to the Territory
Epstein, Joseph	*A Line Out for a Walk: Familiar Essays*
Fitzgerald, F. Scott	*The Crack-Up*
	Afternoon of an Author: A Selection of Uncollected Stories and Essays
Frazier, Ian	*Great Plains*
	Family
Gates, Henry Louis, Jr.	*Colored People: A Memoir*
Gonzalez-Crussi, F.	*Notes of an Anatomist*
Gornick, Vivian	*Approaching Eye Level*
Gutkind, Lee	*Stuck in Time: The Tragedy of Childhood Mental Illness*
Hall, Donald	*Here at Eagle Pond*
Hearne, Vicki	*Adam's Task: Calling Animals by Name*
	Bandit: Dossier of a Dangerous Dog
Heilman, Robert Leo	*Overstory—Zero: Real Life in the Timber Country*
Hoagland, Edward	*Balancing Acts: Essays*
	Walking the Dead Diamond River
	The Tugman's Passage
Kingsolver, Barbara	*High Tide in Tucson: Essays From Now or Never*
Kittredge, William	*Owning It All: Essays*
Levi, Primo	*The Periodic Table*
Lopate, Phillip	*Against Joie De Vivre: Personal Essays*
	Bachelorhood: Tales of the Metropolis
	Portrait of My Body
Lopez, Barry	*Crossing Open Ground*
Lynch, Thomas	*The Undertaking: Life Studies From the Dismal Trade*
Mairs, Nancy	*Voice Lessons: On Becoming a (Woman) Writer*
Malcolm, Janet	*The Silent Woman: Sylvia Plath and Ted Hughes*
Montaigne, Michel de	*Essays*
Oliver, Mary	*Blue Pastures*

Ozick, Cynthia	*Art and Ardor: Essays*
	Metaphor and Memory: Essays
Pollit, Katha	*Reasonable Creatures: Essays on Women and Feminism*
Sanders, Scott Russell	*The Paradise of Bombs*
Sante, Luc	*The Factory of Facts*
Schor, Mira	*Wet: On Painting, Feminism, and Art Culture*
Schwartz, Lynne Sharon	*Ruined by Reading: A Life in Books*
Sedaris, David	*Barrel Fever: Stories and Essays*
Seneca	*Letters From a Stoic*
Shacochis, Bob	*Domesticity: A Gastronomic Interpretation of Love*
Simic, Charles	*The Unemployed Fortune-Teller: Essays and Memoirs*
Sontag, Susan	*Illness As Metaphor*
	Under the Sign of Saturn
Thomas, Elizabeth Marshall	*The Hidden Life of Dogs*
Thoreau, Henry David	*Walden*
Vidal, Gore	*Matters of Fact and of Fiction: Essays 1973–1976*
White, Bailey	*Mama Makes Up Her Mind: And Other Dangers of Southern Living*
White, E.B.	*Essays of E.B. White*
	The Second Tree From the Corner
White, Edmund	*The Burning Library: Essays*
White, Katharine S.	*Onward and Upward in the Garden*
Winterson, Jeanette	*Art Objects: Essays on Ecstasy and Effrontery*
Wolff, Geoffrey	*A Day at the Beach: Recollections*
Woolf, Virginia	*Moments of Being: Unpublished Autobiographical Writings*
	A Room of One's Own

JOURNALS AND DIARIES

Bass, Rick	*Oil Notes*
Bukowski, Charles	*Notes of a Dirty Old Man*
Cheever, John	*The Journals of John Cheever*

Dennison, George   *Temple*
Ellis, Edward Robb   *A Diary of the Century: Tales From America's Greatest Diarist*
Frank, Anne   *The Diary of a Young Girl*
Gauguin, Paul   *Noa Noa*
Hubbell, Sue   *A Country Year: Living the Questions*
Pepys, Samuel   *The Diary of Samuel Pepys*
Sarton, May   *At Seventy: A Journal*
     The House by the Sea: A Journal
     Journal of a Solitude

NATURE WRITING

Abbey, Edward   *Desert Solitaire: A Season in the Wilderness*
Barnes, Kim   *In the Wilderness: Coming of Age in Unknown Country*
Berry, Wendell   *Clearing*
     A Place on Earth
Carson, Rachel   *Under the Sea Wind*
     Silent Spring
Dillard, Annie   *Pilgrim at Tinker Creek*
     Teaching a Stone to Talk: Expeditions and Encounters
Galvin, James   *The Meadow*
Gould, Stephen Jay   *Ever Since Darwin: Reflections in Natural History*
     The Panda's Thumb: More Reflections in Natural History
     Hen's Teeth and Horse's Toes
     The Flamingo's Smile: Reflections in Natural History
     An Urchin in the Storm: Essays About Books and Ideas
Hauser, Susan Carol   *Sugartime: The Hidden Pleasures of Making Maple Syrup With a Primer for the Novice Sugarer*
Heat Moon, William Least   *PrairyErth*
Hersey, John   *Blues*

Hölldobler, Bert, and Edward O. Wilson	*Journey to the Ants: A Story of Scientific Exploration*
Hubbell, Sue	*A Book of Bees . . . and How to Keep Them*
Lea, Sydney	*Hunting the Whole Way Home*
Leopold, Aldo	*A Sand County Almanac, and Sketches Here and There*
Lopez, Barry	*Of Wolves and Men*
	Arctic Dreams: Imagination and Desire in a Northern Landscape
McPhee, John	*Coming Into the Country*
Middleton, Harry	*Rivers of Memory*
	On the Spine of Time: An Angler's Love of the Smokies
	The Bright Country: A Fisherman's Return to Trout, Wild Water, and Himself
Mowat, Farley	*The Siberians*
Norris, Kathleen	*Dakota: A Spiritual Geography*
Thomas, Lewis	*The Lives of a Cell: Notes of a Biology Watcher*
	The Medusa and the Snail: More Notes of a Biology Watcher
Thoreau, Henry David	*The Maine Woods*
	Cape Cod
Williams, Terry Tempest	*Refuge: An Unnatural History of Family and Place*

TRAVEL WRITING

Bryson, Bill	*Neither Here nor There: Travels in Europe*
Chatwin, Bruce	*In Patagonia*
Chatwin, Bruce, and Paul Theroux	*Patagonia Revisited*
Eighner, Lars	*Travels With Lizbeth*
Frazier, Ian	*Great Plains*
Gutkind, Lee	*Bike Fever*
Heat Moon, William Least	*Blue Highways: A Journey Into America*
Muir, John	*Travels in Alaska*

O'Hanlon, Redmond	*Into the Heart of Borneo*
	No Mercy: A Journey to the Heart of the Congo
	In Trouble Again: A Journey Between the Orinoco and the Amazon
Theroux, Paul	*The Pillars of Hercules: A Grand Tour of the Mediterranean*
	The Great Railway Bazaar: By Train Through Asia

NEW JOURNALISM

Capote, Truman	*In Cold Blood: A True Account of a Multiple Murder and Its Consequences*
	Music for Chameleons
Conover, Ted	*Rolling Nowhere*
	Coyotes: A Journey Through the Secret World of America's Illegal Aliens
	Whiteout: Lost in Aspen
Didion, Joan	*Salvador*
Frey, Darcy	*The Last Shot: City Streets, Basketball Dreams*
Hersey, John	*Hiroshima*
Johnson, Joyce	*What Lisa Knew: The Truths and Lies of the Steinberg Case*
Junger, Sebastian	*The Perfect Storm: A True Story of Men Against the Sea*
Kidder, Tracy	*House*
	Among Schoolchildren
Krakauer, Jon	*Into the Wild*
	Into Thin Air: A Personal Account of the Mount Everest Disaster
Mailer, Norman	*The Armies of the Night: History as a Novel, the Novel as History*
	The Executioner's Song
Malcolm, Janet	*The Journalist and the Murderer*
McPhee, John	*Alaska: Images of the Country*
	Assembling California
	Coming Into the Country
	The Control of Nature

	Encounters With the Archdruid
	Irons in the Fire
	Looking for a Ship
	Oranges
	The Pine Barrens
	Rising From the Plains
Powers, Ron	*Far From Home: Life and Loss in Two American Towns*
Wolfe, Tom	*The Right Stuff*
	From Bauhaus to Our House
X, Malcolm, and Alex Haley	*The Autobiography of Malcolm X*

ANTHOLOGIES

The Anchor Essay Annual, Phillip Lopate, editor

The Art of the Personal Essay: An Anthology From the Classical Era to the Present, Phillip Lopate, editor

The Best American Essays, annual anthology, Houghton Mifflin

Essays on the Essay: Redefining the Genre, Alexander J. Butrym, editor

The Granta Book of the Family, Bill Buford, editor

In Short: A Collection of Brief Creative Nonfiction, Judith Kitchen and Mary Paumier Jones, editors

The Literary Journalists, Norman Sims, editor

Modern American Memoirs, Annie Dillard and Cort Conley, editors

The Norton Book of Nature Writing, Robert Finch and John Elder, editors

Sisters of the Earth: Women's Prose and Poetry About Nature, Lorraine Anderson, editor

Turning Toward Home: Reflections on the Family From Harper's Magazine, Katharine Whittemore and Ilena Silverman, editors

Writing Creative Nonfiction: The Literature of Reality, Gay Talese and Barbara Lounsberry, editors

Writing Women's Lives: An Anthology of Autobiographical Narratives by Twentieth-Century American Women Writers, Susan Neunzig Cahill, editor

ABOUT THE AUTHOR

Bill Roorbach is the author of *Summers With Juliet* (Houghton Mifflin, 1992) and is at work on a novel called *Here on the Ground*. Other work, both fiction and nonfiction, has appeared in *The New York Times Magazine*, *Harper's Magazine*, *The Missouri Review*, *Granta*, *New York Magazine*, *Creative Nonfiction*, *Poets and Writers Magazine*, *Attache*, *The Iowa Review*, *Witness*, *Gulf Coast*, *Philadelphia Inquirer*, *Columbia*, *Newsday*, and many other magazines and journals. Bill holds an M.F.A. from Columbia University and has taught there and at the University of Maine at Farmington and the University of Vermont. Currently he is Associate Professor of English in the Graduate Creative Writing Program at The Ohio State University.

INDEX